D0874186

CHASING THE WIND

CHASING THE WIND

The Autobiography of Steve Fossett

Steve Fossett
with
Will Hasley

First published in Great Britain in 2006 by
Virgin Books Ltd
Thames Wharf Studios
Rainville Road
London
W6 9HA

A catalogue record for this book is available from the British
Library.

ISBN (10) 1 8522 7234 1
ISBN (13) 978 1 8522 7234 0

Typeset by TW Typesetting, Plymouth, Devon
Printed and bound in Great Britain by CPD Wales

CONTENTS

Foreword by Peggy Fossett   vii

Preface: The Ultimate Flight, February 2006: Breaking the
    Absolute Nonstop Distance Record for Aircraft   xi

Part I: Calculated Risks

1. Steps in Advancement: 1944–60   3
2. Stanford vs Berkeley: 1960–68   15
3. Vows and Options: 1969–80   26
4. New Horizons: 1980–92   41

Part II: For the Record: 1992–2005

5. Getting My Feet Wet   73
6. A T-shirt and a Bottle of Wine: My First TransAtlantic
    Balloon Flight, August 1994   83
7. Sailing *Lakota* Singlehanded in the Route du Rhum,
    November 1994   92
8. A Little on Edge: My First Solo Balloon Flight across the
    Pacific, February 1995   98
9. Shaken Up: My First Solo Round the World Balloon
    Attempt, January 1996   104
10. Overjoyed: A New Pacific Ocean Singlehanded World
    Record, August 1996   110
11. Qaddafi Changes His Mind: My Second Solo Round the
    World Balloon Attempt, January 1997   114
12. Russian Hospitality: My Third Solo Round the World Balloon
    Attempt, January 1998   121
13. Breaking Records: Sailing Singlehanded, 1998–99   129
14. Going South: My Fourth Solo Round the World Balloon
    Attempt, August 1998   131
15. Flying with Richard Branson: Round the World Balloon
    Attempt, December 1998   140

16. A Bigger and Better Boat: Learning the Ropes, 1999–2000   149
17. Missing the Jetstream: My Fifth Solo Round the World
    Balloon Attempt, August 2001   162
18. Breaking the TransAtlantic Sailing World Record, October 2001   172
19. *The Bud Light Spirit of Freedom*: First Solo Circumnavigation
    of the Globe in a Balloon, June 2001   178
20. Breaking the Round the World Speed Sailing Record,
    February–April 2004   197
21. The First Solo Nonstop Airplane Flight Round the World,
    March 2005   221
Epilogue   254
Steve Fossett Records   258
Index   260

FOREWORD

by Peggy Fossett

Steve Fossett does not believe in unconquerable obstacles; he believes that there are no barriers that can't be broken, provided that you plan carefully for every contingency and that you have the right team to support you. It is this pragmatic approach which has led to his phenomenal success and which has inspired young people all over the world to pursue their dreams. Not many have been inspired to compete in the extreme adventures in which Steve excels, but many have been encouraged to follow his example in refusing to believe that difficulties cannot be overcome, with determination, training and logic. I am extremely proud of Steve and his extraordinary achievements, an unbelievable 115 official world records, in balloons, sailboats, airships, airplanes and gliders. But unparalleled though this is, he has also succeeded in outstanding trials of endurance and skill, like mountaineering, the Iditarod, even swimming the English Channel! But it is probably the example that he has set and the encouragement he has given to others that are perhaps my greatest source of pride.

Thirty-eight years ago when Steve asked me to be his wife, I could not have imagined this life we have lived together. I had absolutely no idea that the man I was going to marry was an adventurer in the true sense of the word, a man who would pit himself against the elements and undertake some of the most dangerous feats in the world. Although, since our second date found me pressed to the back of a small, single-engine plane by centrifugal force, as Steve competed in an air show with me on board, I should perhaps have seen the signs!

Was this the start of a lifetime of shared adventure on the highest or most difficult mountain peaks on five continents and on the oceans and in the skies above them? Well no, to be honest I am a white-knuckle flyer and I am terrified of heights. I prefer the comforts of home in a beautiful location and getting together with good friends, to the trials and discomfort that Steve faces in his solo adventures.

Over the years the press have asked me for my reactions to Steve's achievements. I have always tried to keep a low profile. Journalists can be extremely pushy, that is their job of course, but it does become tedious when they ask the same inane questions over and over again: What do you think about all this? Don't you worry? Do you ever go along? For the record, I have never tried to prevent Steve from pursuing his adventures, but I am by nature risk-averse. I will always consider the dangers in any situation, even the most mundane, and take the safest route. I think it is great that he is doing exactly what he wants to do.

Do I worry? Well, of course I do, something might be seriously wrong with our marriage if I didn't! The Webster's dictionary definition of Adventure is *1. the encountering of danger and 2. a daring, hazardous undertaking.* That about sums up most of Steve's projects, whether sailing, mountaineering or flying. Some of the events he has undertaken like ballooning and gliding have nearly cost him his life and, yes, Steve's adventures involve huge dangers. He is not a reckless risk-taker and every risk is as far as possible a calculated one.

One of Steve's great talents is the ability to engage and inspire enthusiasm in others. Even though he is a relative newcomer to many of the sports and events in which he has excelled, he has always attracted the very best people in their field to join his team. But I do still worry! Maybe, though, Steve has had to take that little bit of extra care to try to allay my fears and that has kept him safer than he might have been with an equally adventurous partner!

Do I ever go along? Not a chance! That would not be practical, even if I shared his dreams in this regard, as many of his record attempts are by definition solo events. But I did get to share in the adventure of the *Virgin Atlantic GlobalFlyer* flights. I spent a great deal of time in Mission Control hanging out with the bright young aviation students from Kansas State University, and it was fascinating to see all that was going on from Mission Control.

Ultimately, I do wish he wouldn't take these risks, but I am thrilled at the results he has achieved. Steve has made his mark as one of the greatest distance balloonists of all time.

He has set more sailing records, including the most important, than anyone, ever, in the history of competitive sailing. He now holds three of the seven absolute records in airplanes, and he flew each of them solo. He has set absolute records in five sports and has shown the world that lofty goals can be achieved with determination and persistence.

I am proud to be his wife, supporter and a member of the crew.

Peggy Fossett
June 2006

PREFACE: THE ULTIMATE FLIGHT, FEBRUARY 2006: BREAKING THE ABSOLUTE NONSTOP DISTANCE RECORD FOR AIRCRAFT

The idea is both scary and thrilling—one small engine that you depend on for four days to fly further than man has ever flown before. The craft itself is beautiful and has come to represent the shape and novel approach that Burt Rutan has made so effective. Every NASA astronaut and scientist is excited when they see something so apparently simple and efficient. We hope that this flight of Virgin Atlantic GlobalFlyer will be successful and that it is just the beginning for a beautiful new craft to take to the skies from the Kennedy Space Center. Thank you for beginning your bold endeavors from the NASA Space Center as an inspiration to all who dream of flight and space travel.
            —Mike Foale, Astronaut: speech prior to take-off

S tanding behind the *Virgin Atlantic GlobalFlyer* at the first light of dawn, I took a moment to contemplate the obvious danger to my life that I would soon face. Usually the greatest dangers on my adventures come as the startling surprise of an accident or equipment failure—rarely have I confronted such serious risks knowingly. I was at the end of the Shuttle Landing Facility of NASA's Kennedy Space Center. It is a huge runway at 15,000 ft long and 300 ft wide and it is maintained in immaculate condition. But there are problems: the relatively warm Florida temperature of 48F makes it difficult for the Williams jet engine to develop its maximum thrust. Even in the optimum conditions I was going to require most of this runway length to get airborne because of the massive load of fuel required to make the longest aircraft flight of all time.

Two days earlier we rehearsed takeoff rolls in a truck while team member Jim Reed, in the Control Tower, called out minimum speeds required at each 1000-ft runway sign in order to get aloft before the end of the runway. For the actual takeoff, the callouts only continue half way down the runway because after that I would be committed to takeoff. If my acceleration was too slow to reach rotation speed before the end of the runway, I would have to make the abort decision at the 7500 ft mark or I would be unable to stop the GlobalFlyer before running off the end of the paved runway, crashing into the leading lights and careening into the swamp. The abort decision would involve immediate cutoff of the engine, deployment of both drag chutes, then gentle application of brakes after the aircraft slowed below 60 knots.

Another danger that troubled me was the antiskid grooving in the runway. Not significant for the heavy tires of the Space Shuttle, but the GlobalFlyer had small, light tires, which had most of the tread shaved off to save weight. If this extraordinarily long takeoff roll created too much tire heat, there could either be a blowout or the tires could just abrade down to core with the same result. A blowout would be catastrophic: the landing gear on that side would collapse and the GlobalFlyer would careen off the runway and explode into a huge ball of fire.

The time had come and Crew Chief Philip Grassa declared the GlobalFlyer ready for flight, 'Steve, the airplane is yours.' We had almost got to that point the previous day, but as the GlobalFlyer nose wheel was lowered off its leveling block, fuel began streaming out the left wheel well. 'This plane is not going anywhere' was the first reaction of Jim Reed. A vent line had become disconnected near the top of the boom tank. I was hugely disappointed because we had waited for over two weeks to get the necessary weather conditions: cool enough ground temperatures to develop proper jet engine thrust and a good forecast of jetstreams around the world. We were nearing the end of the season for sufficiently cool temperatures in Florida. Surprisingly but fortunately, my team fixed the leak that day. Meteorologist David Dehenauw ran the wind forecast for the following five days and we found that the very next day was the best, and perhaps only good day for launch and RTW (round the world) wind pattern. This time it was happening.

I strapped in and started the engine. It was a Hot Start! The engine temperature spiked over the redline or maximum reading, past 950°C and carried on climbing. I instantly pulled the throttle to cutoff. Philip reminded me that there was no problem: my checklist said the maximum temperature permitted was 850°C but the true limit for the Williams engine was 1000°C. After cooling, I started again. During my run up with full throttle, I expected to be able to reach redline of 105.2% but the reading was only 102.8%. It's a strange thing in aviation that the engine manufacturers don't specify what 100% represents. Philip reassured me that redline would not always be reached depending on outside temperatures. I called for my flight plan clearance and the tower gave me the routine 'Cleared to Kent, England as filed'.

I announced, 'Brake Release' and the *GlobalFlyer* was on the roll. At each speed callout, I glanced down to see my actual speed on the Chelton Flight Management System screens. I was caught by surprise: I expected that I would easily be exceeding the minimum speeds, but I was only equaling them. I wondered if there was a mistake and Jim Reed was giving me the projected rather than the minimums. Oh well, I was at least at the minimums, so I continued.

The end of the runway was rushing toward me. I started pulling back on the stick in my right hand, then as I reached rotate speed of 124 knots, I applied a full 50 lbs of back pressure on the stick—still the nose would not come up. A horrifying thought raced through my mind: perhaps the CG (center of gravity) was so far forward at this heavy weight that the wings would not generate the lift to raise the nose. I took my left hand off the throttle and shifted my body so I could push on the stick with my left hand while pulling with the right hand. I wasn't going to take this: I was determined to break the damn stick linkage cable before I would allow myself to run off the end of the runway. It worked. With little more than 1000 ft of the 15,000 ft runway left, the wings bowed up, the nose lifted and I was off the ground.

There was even more drama in that takeoff than I was aware of. Soon reports came in that a flock of large sea birds flew across the runway and I had hit two of them during the takeoff roll. Robert Scherer's Starship, which was acting as chase plane during the climbout, flew in for a close look. Fortunately there was no noticeable damage to the *GlobalFlyer*; the birds were not so fortunate. More disturbing was what was learned after my eventual landing: there was a deep diagonal cut on the right tire with a leak that allowed the tire to deflate entirely during the flight. I must have hit something on the runway. I was that close to the feared catastrophic blowout. I'm lucky to be alive!

As I approached 10,000 ft altitude, it was time to pressurize the cabin of the *GlobalFlyer*. I turned the pressurization valve and opened the engine bleed air which is the source of air in pressurized airplanes. Suddenly hot air rushed in and just kept on coming. I redirected the air away from the plastic canopy for fear that it would melt. We always get heat in the *GlobalFlyer* below 20,000 ft after pressurizing, but this was extreme. I estimate the heat in the cockpit at 130°F (54°C)—just bearable. The stick became too hot to touch, but I was able to fly on autopilot. Two of my instrument screens were LCDs and both those screens turned completely black from the heat. Anything metallic, such as the metal frames of the Chelton, reached searing temperatures. Who knows what would be damaged by this heat. I called Jon Karkow who was flying in the Starship and he theorized that the heat was due to the higher outside air temperature combined with the extraordinarily heavy airplane the engine needed to propel. Jon figured the heat would abate as the outside air temperature decreased when climbing above 20,000 ft. I was dehydrating rapidly, and had to drink plenty of water. From my prior solo sailing and ballooning, I knew that I would drink almost exactly 3 liters of water per day and that is what I had brought for this trip. If this extreme heat continued for long, I would upset my carefully calculated water supply. Eventually the heat would decrease, but that decrease did not start until over 25,000 ft and it was still over 110°F in the cockpit at the end of two hours. My instrument screens slowly started to reveal digits behind the dark gray and the airplane systems did not seem to have been permanently damaged. Another risk to the success of the Ultimate Flight was passing behind me.

I truly enjoy flying. If carefully organized, the pilot workload is not excessive and I'm totally relaxed. I really don't see very much of the surface because I'm usually flying above the jetstream cloud band. Sometimes though, the scenery is spectacular. Flying over Libya at night reveals the oil field activity with gas flares and brightly lit towns supporting this extraction business. At sunrise the shadows on the high and endless sand dunes in western Egypt create a remarkable sight. Mostly I enjoy the sense of travel: it is an extraordinary feeling to be crossing oceans and continents at my inexorable pace. What an opportunity I've had to circle the globe, over and over again. Sometimes I think I'm the Ultimate Tourist.

I never sleep on the first and the last nights of a solo endurance trip whether it is by balloon, sailboat or airplane, but I was looking forward to getting a series of power naps on my second night. The key to being able to sleep is for my Mission Control team to handle all position reporting to the respective Air Traffic Control Centers. Leaving the Persian Gulf, Pakistan insisted that I make all position reports the traditional way: by VHF radio. India imposed the same requirement and the Indian controllers were too friendly—so many questions to clutter the radio waves. I would have to abandon hopes of sleeping during the second night.

Then things got worse. Approaching Bhopal in central India, turbulence reports were being called in by all the airliners. Soon I was in it. Richard Branson called on the Blue Sky satellite phone for his thrice-daily updates and to encourage me on. I quickly told Richard I can't talk now. I put on my parachute because I knew I was in trouble. I set up my oxygen mask for the possibility of bail out at my current altitude of 45,000 ft.

The *GlobalFlyer* was built as light as possible to complete its mission in good conditions. It is only supposed to sustain 2 Gs of centrifugal force, which means it can sustain no more than light turbulence. As the turbulence built, the *GlobalFlyer* was pitching and rolling and unable to maintain altitude or course. Turbulence had crossed the level of Moderate and was now turning Severe. Fearfully I anticipated that the main wing spar might break at any moment. I didn't give myself much chance if that happened because the plane would immediately go into a spiral. I would have to depressurize the cabin, pull the 'green apple' to activate my bailout oxygen bottle, remove the hatch, and dive out. Then I would need to pull the black ball to deploy my drogue chute to stabilize my fall from high altitude. The automatic parachute opener would fire at 14,000 ft altitude, then I would have to make a safe landing in the pitch dark of night. This is not an ideal scenario for survival, but of course I would fight like crazy to survive anyhow. In 15 minutes the turbulence abated and I kept my parachute on for the next two hours in case there was a resumption of the turbulence, but there was not. During all this air traffic control continued to ask for position reports. I didn't want to give any—I had other things to contend with. Like pitching up and down 1000 ft at a time. At least I now knew the plane could take the turbulence but it probably would have broken up if it carried the weight of full fuel.

The day after landing in England, my team pointed out that the securing point of the center hinge of the left aileron had broken. They asked if someone had pushed on the wing after landing, but I had made sure no one did. I believe this carbon attachment was broken in the severe turbulence over India. At first look, it would be presumed that the aileron would rip off in flight without this support point. A more careful look revealed good stability so long as there was not any large deflection of the aileron or high-speed flight where 'flutter' would be initiated. If I had not flown conservatively for the rest of the flight, the aileron would have ripped completely off. I wonder what it would have been like trying to fly *GlobalFlyer* down from 45,000 ft and land with the left aileron missing!

Smooth-talking Kevin Stass got the Chinese to accept reporting from Mission Control. After such a hard time over India, I was desperate for sleep and I was relieved that I could rest over China and not be tied to the VHF radio. In the morning I was proceeding northeast along the coast of Japan. Suddenly Fujiyama popped into view through my side window. This was not a new sight to me because I had flown this route before on my First Solo Pacific Balloon Flight, on the ICO Global Balloon attempt with Richard Branson and Per Lindstrand, on my Citation RTW Speed Record, and on the previous year's First Solo Nonstop RTW. Nevertheless, it is an inspiring sight and a kind of welcome to the long Pacific crossing. Soon I was leaving sight of land and trucking across the western Pacific in the best jetstream in the world.

Fuel was the issue for completing this flight. I was stretching the distance and duration limits of the *GlobalFlyer*. That was the idea: I wanted to fly this airplane to its full capability before it is retired to the Smithsonian's National Air & Space Museum. I had chosen to attempt a distance, which was at the limit of what could be achieved—and that means that if anything went wrong, I would not be able to complete the flight. In the First Solo Nonstop RTW in 2005, I had lost 3100 lbs of fuel out the fuel vents during the climb to altitude. The fuel vent system was subsequently revised and then tested at moderated fuel loads but never at full fuel. This flight would be the final test of the fuel vent system. With a vent shutoff valve I would operate in the cockpit during the climb, it was hoped the fuel loss would be stopped. It was not a 100% success: I lost 750 lbs of fuel during the climb of this flight. We would need to apply every form of fuel conservation to make it to the finish. For nearly three days I would live with the uncertainty of whether I would have enough fuel to continue across the Atlantic a second time. Western Ireland was where I had to get to break the Absolute Distance Record and also to have a dry landing. For this reason I pre-declared Shannon, Ireland as my official finish line even though I hoped that I would have enough fuel to continue to Kent International on the English Channel for landing.

For record purposes, I only get credit for the distance between the start, six intermediate waypoints, and the declared finish. The waypoints must be at least an average of 5000 km apart for this record. The actual route is set by air traffic standards and follows high altitude airways. This results in a lot of wasted mileage— distance that does not count toward the record distance. Kevin Stass and his team of Pat Rinearson and Nancy Milleret, both of Kansas State University, attacked this wasted mileage problem. After I left China where the routing does not have mandatory waypoints to cross, they sought 'Directs' from each air traffic control zone. The results were outstanding. Virtually all standard airway crossing points were eliminated and I was able to fly the minimum distance between my mandatory record waypoints.

Meanwhile our Performance Engineer, Clint Nichols, constantly ground the numbers through his computer models to find the optimum speed and altitude to fly. Just like automobiles, slower speeds consume less fuel for the distance covered. Clint would assign optimum Indicated Airspeeds and convey those to me. Usually I couldn't fly quite that slow because incipient stall would cause the *GlobalFlyer* to 'Dutch Roll', which is a slow vacillation from left to right. Altitude strategy was very important. Worldwide the average maximum speed of jetstreams is at about 40,000 ft. However, jet engines are more fuel-efficient the higher you fly. For me 45,000 ft is a good compromise between best tailwinds and fuel efficiency. For the final leg across the Atlantic to the British Isles, the jetstreams were rather weak. The strategy would be to fly as high as possible. After crossing the United States to St Petersburg, Florida I climbed to 51,000 ft and flew mostly at that altitude until reaching Ireland. There is no company up there—the airliners are flying mostly between 33,000 and 41,000 ft altitude. At 51,000 ft the curvature of the earth is clearly visible and the air is so thin that the airplane must be flown very carefully. Sudden control inputs could cause a stall at these speeds. Quick change of throttle setting could cause a flameout of the engine. The fuel strategy was a huge success. By the time I reached Florida, I knew I could make it to Ireland. Even if I ran out of fuel at the end of the Atlantic, with the

32:1 glide ratio of *GlobalFlyer* and a flight altitude of 51,000 ft, I could glide the final 270 miles to land at the Shannon, Ireland airport.

By the time I reached Ireland, I could see that I had just enough fuel to continue to Kent with a satisfactory reserve. Richard Branson got in my Citation X at Kent and flew out to greet me, 'Steve, Congratulations—you've now flown farther than any man or woman has ever flown before. And you've done it solo. What an achievement. We look forward to seeing you on the ground. Remember you have to be alive 48 hours to get credit for the record!' To this I gave a good laugh and 'See you on the ground in an hour.' Then the problems started.

A red light on the panel came on and the warning horn sounded. It was the Low Volts light indicating a generator problem. I made a quick check that circuit breakers were all in, then reset the generator switch—no help. I decided this was serious. Normally I would pull out my checklist and start working through the problem as is the normal procedure in airplanes. This time I decided to get all the help that was readily available. I dialed the Mission Control number, which had been moved from Gatwick to the Kent Control Tower in anticipation of my arrival. Jon Karkow answered and without any greeting, I blurted, 'Jon, Low Volts light.' We retried the generator switch, which didn't help. The generator had failed and there is no backup generator on this experimental airplane where we conserved every pound in design and construction. The generator runs off the engine and recharges the battery continuously. Without charging, the battery will go dead in approximately 25 minutes and everything will be dark in the cockpit.

I told Air Traffic Control I wanted to land as soon as possible. He suggested Cardiff, Wales. That was northwest of my position and jetstream had been forming from the northwest. This ran against my glider pilot instincts and I asked the controller for another choice which was downwind. He then suggested Bournemouth, England. Great, I knew this airport because I used to fly my Citation X there when we were making sailing record attempts out of nearby Southampton. Jon and Clint meanwhile had spread the wiring diagrams and checklists out on the floor of the Control Tower of Kent. We proceeded with 'load shed' procedures to slow the drain on the battery. Jon gave me which circuit breakers to pull and which non-essential instruments to turn off.

I really didn't like this situation: I'm low on fuel, the inside of my canopy is obscured with a thick accumulation of ice from the long flight, and I'm going to lose all electrical power soon. And I'm not too fresh myself! All I could think is that the worst accidents in aviation occur when there are multiple emergencies and the pilots cannot deal with them all without major errors. I decided to call the Controller, 'Virgin 101 declares an emergency.' 'We figured that,' was his relaxed answer.

Next I lowered the gear in order to increase the drag for a quicker descent. Nose gear came down and locked. The two main gear came down but would not lock in place. Another problem! Finally they locked and I had three greens on the gear indication lights. I was already high over Bournemouth, but had made no progress on getting enough heat on the canopy to clear the ice. I didn't want to land blind! I got vectors out into the English Channel, then back to the north of Bournemouth as I continued my descent. Finally as I was crossing the field for the third time and now at 3000 ft, the ice loosened and I was able to push it off the inside of the canopy. I immediately entered the downwind leg of the pattern and deployed one drag chute so I could descend quickly enough to land on this circuit without going around. On final approach I pulled out the second drag chute to be sure that I would not glide beyond the runway on my steep approach.

The drama was not over. As I touched down, the left tire blew out. The wheel brakes apparently were seized and the tire wore through immediately. Perhaps they were frozen from the cold of high altitude and did not have a chance to thaw with my emergency descent. The right tire was already flat before landing. As described earlier, it had a leak from a cut during the takeoff. With no tires, I sure didn't need much runway to stop! Fearing fuel leak and fire, I immediately shutdown the engine, turned off the master switch, removed the side hatch door, and was ready to jump and run within 5 seconds of the *GlobalFlyer* stopping on the runway.

I never imagined so much might go wrong on this flight. The *Virgin Atlantic GlobalFlyer* had been proven with the successful First Solo the previous year. This was a difficult flight by any measure, but it was a huge success. I had just flown the Absolute Distance Without Landing Record, which is one of only seven Absolute records for airplanes. My official distance was 41,467 km (25,766 miles), which broke the extraordinary record of Dick Rutan and Jeanna Yeager in the Voyager in 1986 by 1,255 km (780 miles). I also exceeded by 651 km (404 miles) the balloon distance record by Bertrand Piccard and Brian Jones from their successful RTW in 1999. This gives me the Guinness Record and bragging rights for the Longest Aircraft Flight, that is, for any kind of aircraft. I had fulfilled another important goal: I had set out to fly the *Virgin Atlantic GlobalFlyer* to its full capability. The First Solo the previous year was a magnificent flight but we had learned that, with a solution to the fuel venting problem, the *GlobalFlyer* was capable of flying farther than any aircraft ever has. It was important for my self esteem as a pilot that I attempt this flight, and now I have succeeded. It is the destiny of the Virgin Atlantic *GlobalFlyer* to be put on display in the Hazy Center of the Smithsonian's National Air & Space Museum. I, and my entire team, will be proud for everyone to see this remarkable airplane and to recall what we have done.

After all the time and money that went into designing and building this state-of-the-art plane, I wasn't surprised that the wind would play a decisive factor in the outcome of this endeavor. Throughout my career as an extreme sports-adventurer, I have come to understand the literal meaning of the phrase 'the winds of fate.' Indeed, the wind is not something you can buy. Rich or poor, healthy or ailing, wise or dim-witted, the wind remains impartial. Millions of dollars can be spent on developing the latest record-breaking technology and the wind is going to do exactly what it wants when it wants. It can act like your dearest friend carrying you to the heights of record-breaking victory or it can be your foe. No wind in sailing literally translates as 'no go,' while gale-force winds that I have encountered while ballooning have plummeted me to the edge of death.

To partner with the wind successfully, one must be willing to study it, watch it—catch it. Competitive aviation, sailing as well as ballooning, all involve chasing the wind. It has not been uncommon for me to fly, sail or balloon hundreds of miles out of my way in order to find a beneficent wind pattern or jetstream. In addition, I have relied upon expert weather routers to track this elusive element meticulously in an ongoing effort to determine the most favorable start times for these adventures that would allow me to have the wind on my side. In preparation for the *Virgin Atlantic GlobalFlyer* flight, thousands of others and I patiently waited a month before a 'Code Green' was finally issued which signaled the presence of an amenable weather system that would facilitate and expedite my flight. On the day of my scheduled takeoff, I nearly lost my chance because of the safety hazards of strong crosswinds that were blowing that afternoon. However, this didn't deter me. Having partnered with the wind for so many years, I was prepared for the unexpected.

This book is about chasing the wind and the people who have helped and inspired me, those who I've teamed with, the records we have broken together, the difficulties we have faced and overcome and those who have rescued me when I was literally at the mercy of the winds of fate.

Part I

CALCULATED RISKS

1. STEPS IN ADVANCEMENT: 1944–60

One of the proudest moments of my life came in the Court of Honor when I was awarded the Eagle Scout badge. I still have that badge. It is a treasured possession.

Gerald Ford—the first Eagle Scout to become Vice President
and later President of the United States of America

My father, Richard L. Fossett Jr., always had a very technical mind. He received his Bachelor's and Master's Degree in electrical engineering at MIT. As an undergraduate he was Class President for his last three years. After college, he first went to work for Bell Laboratories assisting with the development of a microwave system, which was extremely experimental back in the 1930s. He didn't stay at Bell Laboratories very long and was laid off in 1933. One couldn't be choosy about jobs in the depths of the Great Depression, so my father was pleased to accept a job far afield of his training: soap manufacturing at Proctor & Gamble in Kansas City, Missouri. Soon he would meet my mother, Charalee Mizell when he moved into a rooming house in Kansas City, Missouri, where Charalee was rooming with her sister, Faye. Having seen Charalee at the house, he formally introduced himself one afternoon when she happened to pass by while he was washing his car out in the back of this rooming house. He offered to take her out for a ride in his old Plymouth and she accepted. They started dating and within two years, in 1935, they were married in Heavener, Oklahoma—Charalee's hometown.

After their honeymoon, they went back to Kansas City where Richard was quickly promoted to a supervisor job at the Proctor & Gamble plant there. The first day as a supervisor, my father witnessed a dramatic moment that proved the almighty power of the laundry detergent Tide, a product of Proctor & Gamble. He was standing beside a control panel next to a large towering vat, which rose up 20 ft from the floor. As the Tide brewed, my father adjusted the controls that regulated the brewing process. Suddenly the temperature alarm sounded. The Tide had gotten too hot. Racing up the ladder that led to a platform at the top of the vat, Richard looked down into the sea of Tide and saw that it was starting to bubble. A thick layer of white foam had formed on the surface. The level of the liquid began to rise and fall threateningly, according to the pressure building and releasing inside. It looked like a volcano ready to explode. Frantically, my father climbed down the ladder to the control panel to adjust the temperature valve. It was too late. A stream of Tide followed him. The thick liquid began to run down the sides of the vat. In the next instant, the sea of Tide erupted sending the hot detergent gushing down the outside walls of the enormous container. On the floor, it turned into a thick river that spread to every corner of the room. When the help that my father called for arrived, he and his co-workers slipped and slid in the soapy mixture underfoot as they tried to take control of the situation. The friction of their movements generated bubbles that floated through the air. After covering the entire warehouse area, the sea of Tide moved in the only direction it could—up. It continued to rise until it escaped through open windows. Flowing out and down the front side of the building, the detergent was so powerful that it removed the paint from the façade. Outside it collected into a massive pool on the ground. Bystanders, who cautiously approached, shook their heads in amused disbelief. It had been quite a while since something so dramatic had taken place at the plant. Although it was quite a fiasco, it proved that Tide can remove stains as well as paint. Needless to say, things didn't go so well for my father that first day.

In 1938 my older brother Richard Fossett III was born. When World War II broke out, Proctor & Gamble lent out their managers to work in the war production facilities. At a very young age my father became the manager of a shell loading plant in Milan, Tennessee, which had 10,000 workers.

I was born on 22 April 1944 in nearby Jackson, Tennessee. I suppose, as a very young child, I was as precocious as any other. Although I don't remember, my family tells me that when I was three, I locked my mother out of the house and started playing her records on the phonograph. Dancing to the music, I beamed at her through the sliding glass door/window as the volume of the music drowned out her pleas to let her in. It was about this time that I taught myself to drive a car—sort of. You just get in the front seat then push the starter button on the lower left. That's all it took to get the car to lunge forward a couple of feet. I just kept repeating that process. With great persistence, I kept jerking the car along down the street. My father was aghast when he came out of the house and saw his car doing this awkward jig down the street. Running out to take possession of the vehicle, he seemed half amused and half serious when he told me in a quasi-stern tone of voice never to try this stunt again. Reflecting on this sequence of childhood events as an adult, I have to admit that it is somewhat emblematic of my personality. Usually, once I have learned a skill or mastered a certain challenge, I tend to move on to bigger and better adventures.

After the war was over, we moved to Long Beach where my father resumed his role as a soap production supervisor for Proctor & Gamble. The modest one-story house we moved into was in North Long Beach, just off the main runway of the Long Beach Airport. One of my brother's and my favorite pastimes was to watch the planes come in low over our house as they made their landing approach to the airport. They were so loud that the whole house just vibrated. One time my uncle, Archie Mizell, who had been a Navy pilot in the war and continued to serve in the Navy, flew his plane into the Long Beach airfield and we all went out to meet him. This was a real treat for me, as I had never seen a plane up close like that before. Looking up from my vantage point, the propeller appeared colossal to me. My imagination went into overdrive when my uncle explained to me that he often landed the plane on a huge boat that had a runway on it. When we got home, my brother told me that these 'boats' are called aircraft carriers as he pointed one out to me in the encyclopedia. However, I didn't have to read in a book how dangerous this maneuver could be. Within two years, Uncle Archie was killed when his plane crashed and went over the side during an aircraft carrier landing.

We moved from Long Beach to Dallas, Texas in August of 1949 when my father was transferred to management in the Dallas plant. This time, there were more of us to move. Earlier that spring, my little sister, Linda, was born on 9 April 1949. She was the last addition to our family.

Besides the significance that moving out of state entails, because that move involved flying by airplane, this memory holds special importance for me. When we arrived at Los Angeles Airport it was fogged in. The planes were grounded at LAX and our flight to Dallas had been rescheduled to depart out of Long Beach Airport, roughly 40 miles away. This detail the airline forgot to tell the passengers. Luckily, we learned it in the nick of time. Racing to catch our flight out of Long Beach with very little time to spare resulted in a wild, wild cab ride. We just barely made it and I was relieved that this big opportunity would not pass me by.

Needless to say, as we boarded the plane, I was really excited. Having imagined that I was behind the controls piloting all those planes that flew over our Long Beach house, when I got on the aircraft, I wanted to check everything out, to know what everything was. Pausing to take in the cockpit as we walked by, my brother nudged me along as I stood there motionless with my eyes transfixed on all the zillions of gadgets and instruments spread out on the control panel.

What I remember about the flight was that it was really cool, in terms of temperature. My brother informed me that it was because of the air conditioning. Later when we landed in Dallas and into a sweltering 104 degrees of heat, the weather seemed all the more intolerable after having just been in the nicely air conditioned cabin. It was upon arriving in Dallas that I got a crash course in humidity—it was actually hard to breathe! For all the time we lived in Texas, I never got used to that awful weather.

One of my favorite memories of that time was my brother teaching me how to ride a bike. The feeling of utter liberation—that I could ride this bike down the street and around the block—was intoxicating. Quick to show off my new skills to the girl next door, I took off riding at breakneck speed up her driveway with the plan to jump off in the nick of time to stop the bicycle. Careening up the sloping incline, my eyes were wide and my mouth was open as if ready to shout. I realized that I had lost control of the bike. I crashed, fell flat on my face and knocked off a big chip from my front tooth. My first experience trying to impress a girl was a humbling! Neither she nor my parents were impressed when they saw my tooth.

When my father's job brought us back to Long Beach, California, none of us complained about leaving Dallas. After we arrived in Long Beach, we stayed in a hotel on the beach while my parents looked for a house. Although it was a hassle for my parents to live in a hotel, my brother and I didn't mind so much. It was great living on the beach. Over the summer, my brother and I spent our time building elaborate sandcastles to the squeals of delight of my little sister, only to watch our masterpieces quickly disappear with the afternoon's rising tide. It was on the sands of Long Beach where I first watched an offshore sailboat race. It was a surreal vision to behold these countless, clean, white triangular shapes, which I learned were 'sails', gliding seemingly effortlessly across the water's surface. Although I had no interest in sailing at that time and had never been on a boat, the race held me spellbound to the point that I didn't resume my sand castle building project until the entire fleet had completely moved out of my line of vision.

By the time school started, we had moved from the hotel to a house that my parents rented, which was again near the airport. Although my father made a decent salary, raising three children was a constant exercise in making the most of their dollar. One thing that stands out in my mind about my mother was her resourcefulness and the extra effort she made to make our home warm and special despite the amount of money my parents had to work with. In addition to preparing wonderful and nourishing meals, my mother would light candles every night to create an intimate atmosphere as we sat down together for dinner. After dinner was over, my sister and I would argue over whose turn it was to blow out the candles.

The following summer, my parents looked into buying a home in Garden Grove, California. One of the houses they were interested in cost a little more than what they had planned on spending. After discovering that this house had a swimming pool, my brother, sister and I secretly got together and decided that this is the house they should buy. Together, we campaigned really hard to persuade them to buy this house with the swimming pool. Finally they caved in and we got our pool.

As we moved further into our adolescent years, Richard and I started to evidence marked differences in the type of people we were becoming. Taking after my father's technical side, my brother developed an interest in amateur radio, my father's hobby. I took after the side of my father that loved the great outdoors and all that it had to offer. I took after the side of my father that had been an

Eagle Scout. I think my father had the best of both worlds with us. He enjoyed the amateur or 'ham' radio with Richard and he had me to go hiking and camping with.

The minimum age to become a Boy Scout is 11 and as I turned 11 my father made a point of getting me into a Scout Troop. I loved being a Scout from the start. It was an exciting time for me as it introduced me to a whole new avenue of adventures to pursue. Without wasting any time, I wholeheartedly applied myself to meeting the requirements necessary to advance through the various ranks of this organization. Beginning with Tenderfoot, a Scout is given the opportunity to work his way up through Second Class, First Class, Star, Life, and then, finally, Eagle Scout. The higher a Scout attempts to move up in rank, the more difficult and challenging the requirements are for attaining that rank.

I eagerly went to work studying the Boy Scout Handbook, like a chef might peruse a cookbook earmarking all the recipes he would make. Reading the handbook from cover to cover, I went about following the 'recipes' or, rather, doing what I had to do in order to earn a particular badge. With an abundance of enthusiasm, I went to work on many projects at once. I started earning merit badges as fast as I could. Although my father would sometimes help me and there was an expert in that field who would be the merit badge counselor, this was really when I began to develop my own mental processes and learned to rely on figuring things out for myself.

The Boy Scouts quickly became the most significant influence and occupying recreation of my life at the time. Although my father was not the Scoutmaster, he helped out by attending most of the camping and hiking trips that my troop went on. I was 12 when my troop went on a camping trip to climb Mt San Jacinto outside of Palm Springs, California. At 10,804 ft, it was the second highest mountain in Southern California. Making it to the top was quite an achievement for me. To this day, I can still remember the enormous sense of personal satisfaction that I experienced after reaching each peak. This was my first mountain climb and the beginning of my life of adventure.

The more time I spent hiking, camping and climbing in the California Mountains, the more I enjoyed it and I was motivated to learn all the mountaineering skills. One technique I practiced at home was aid climbing directly up a rope. Our single-story home was in the shape of an 'L'. On the long side of the L, where there was a sloped roof with a high edge 14 ft over the patio, I tied the rope to the chimney, rappelled down, then climbed back up using foot loops which I slid up the rope. I used to hoist myself up the side of the house and wait for my little sister Linda or my mom to look out the window and then I'd quickly rappel down and dangle from the rope like a spider and scare my onlooker.

Although my dad and I did a lot of hiking and camping with the Scouts, we also started climbing together. I vividly remember our week of backpacking, camping and climbing in Sequoia National Park. The most difficult climb we did in that region was Mt Kaweah, which at 13,802 ft is one of the most prominent and remote peaks in the Sierra Nevada of California. Departing from the road head at Mineral King, we set off to climb over a ridge to reach the distant center of Sequoia National Park.

After several days of hiking, we were both thrilled when we reached the summit of Kaweah. After unscrewing our canteens and drinking some revitalizing water, we just sat there silently, each in our own mental space, as we stared out at the majestic view before us for a long time. My father and I didn't talk much while hiking together. However, walking in each other's footsteps on the trails that we shared, the summit views we beheld together and our mutual enjoyment of nature's elements was nevertheless a type of communion. It wasn't until the end of a long day, when my father and I would sit around relaxing in the warmth of a campfire, that we discussed what we had seen on the trails before we went over the itinerary for our next day's adventure.

It was from my father, who was a very slow hiker, that I learned the virtue of pacing myself. I realized that it made no sense to hike faster than him, nor was it effective to hike so fast that rest stops were required. I began to appreciate that by sticking to a slow and steady pace, we could cover greater distances in a day than faster hikers who lost huge amounts of time in rest stops. This slow and consistent approach would be a recurrent theme in my life.

Soon after climbing Mt Kaweah, my father and I joined the Sierra Club, the prominent conservation and outdoor organization founded by John Muir. We went on numerous climbing trips with the Sierra Club. Over the next decade my father went on to climb over a hundred peaks in Southern California that were 5000 ft or higher. For this accomplishment, the Sierra Club presented him with the Hundred Peaks Emblem. I climbed about 30 of those with him.

The big adventure that we undertook as a family was in the summer of 1956. We embarked on an extended three-week vacation. Loading up our 1955, four-door Buick to full capacity, we set off to make this long loop through several states before ending up back home. I must admit that my father's decision to stop at a given place was determined by his knowing that there were hiking trails prevalent in that area. Shortly after having reached St. George, Utah, our first stop, my father and I hit the trails while the rest of the family relaxed. For us, hiking was our way of relaxing.

We drove into Wyoming where we stayed at Yellowstone National Park. So impressive were the great hiking trails and natural wonders of the area that I could have spent the whole summer there. We continued north to Glacier National Park where we were able to take some excellent hikes up the steep canyons surrounded by the precipitous mountains. On the way south, we made a stop at the Grand Canyon's South Rim in Arizona. Looking out and as far as the eye could see, I could still not see the end to this geological wonder. No one needed to convince me why the Grand Canyon was included as one of the Seven Natural Wonders of the World. Eyeing the steep craggy walls of the 'temples' projecting from the center of the canyon, I tried to visualize a route to climb to their summits. The vacation ended way too fast for me and finally we were homeward bound. Pulling up to our Garden Grove driveway, Richard, Linda and I sleepily thanked my parents for the greatest vacation we ever had.

Over the next year, I devoted my time to qualifying for the Eagle Scout Rank, which required earning 21 merit badges after reaching the First Class rank. Some of the merit badges required special training such as Life Saving and First Aid. Others were sports oriented such as Swimming, Canoeing and Physical Fitness. Mandatory to attain Eagle Scout at that time was the Physical Fitness merit badge. While I had no problem with the running, push-ups and sit-ups, I did not know how I would ever do the required six pull-ups. At first I couldn't do any and worried whether there was some difference in the geometry of my arm muscles. After installing a pull up bar at the side gate of the house, I made the attempt twice a day and after more than a month I was finally able to do a single pull-up. In another two months I was able to do the required six pull-ups. There wasn't anything wrong with my muscles—I just had to do the necessary training. This important lesson stuck with me and was invaluable when it came time to prepare for future endurance sports events.

When I earned the 21 merit badges and met all the Eagle requirements, I was presented with my Eagle Scout badge at a Court of Honor ceremony that took place before my entire troop, family and friends in December 1957. There were three of us Scouts that became Eagles at the same time. In fact, we were the first Eagles in our troop. Dressed in our Scout uniforms, the three of us stood proudly before our audience as our Scoutmaster Albert Lucic conducted the ceremony and introduced us to the audience. He then spoke briefly about the special meaning of receiving the Eagle Badge, how only about 4% of all Boy Scouts go on to earn the Eagle Scout rank and how many Eagles go on to make distinguished marks in their career fields. With a glimmer in his eye, he paused to look at us and dared us to be the best that we could be. Then he pinned the Eagle badge on each of us as our friends and family members broke out in applause. I had become an Eagle Scout at age 13, just 2 ½ years after joining the Boy Scouts.

The confidence that becoming an Eagle Scout instilled within me began to find expression through the various opportunities of leadership that I embraced within my community and the Boy Scouts.

My family and a lot of the other scouts belonged to the Methodist Church in Garden Grove, which sponsored my Boy Scout Troop. Although my mother wasn't as keen on attending church as my father was, going to church on Sunday was nevertheless a part of our family routine. My father's enthusiasm for going to church spilled over into his involvement with this organization. As Chairman of the Building Committee, he led the fundraising and building of a new church. I liked going to service on Sundays because many of my friends attended the same church that also had a great Methodist Youth Fellowship (MYF), which I was a member of. The MYF consisted of youths who participate in a number of activities designed to serve the church and the community as well as promote Christian growth and fellowship. This was my primary social group. In my senior year of high school I was MYF President for our district, which encompassed the MYFs for most of Southern California.

The summer following my becoming an Eagle Scout I attended Philmont Scout Ranch in New Mexico for the National Junior Leadership Training program. There, I gained a lot of valuable experience in teaching Scouting skills. The next summer I put that training into practice when I became a 'ranger' or camp counselor at Rokoli, the local Boy Scout Camp. Nestled 6000 ft up in the San Bernardino Mountains, Rokoli was attended by local troops from the adjacent areas that came up there for a week at a time. As a

Ranger, each week I was assigned a new group of scouts whom I oversaw and instructed as they engaged in a variety of activities such as archery, knot tying, swimming, rowing, canoeing, and woodsman skills by which they earned their merit badges. We ended every day with a campfire at night. The highlight of the week was the Overnight Campout. I encouraged first troop to choose the toughest climb available and one I had not yet attempted: Mt San Gorgonio, which at 11,499 ft is the highest mountain in Southern California. This was especially challenging for young scouts who had never climbed a mountain before. Various troops led by their ranger would head up the trail on the same morning although they might only be going as far as Dollar Lake—which was roughly half the distance to Mt San Gorgonio—for an overnight camp. Applying the pacing technique I used with my father and going slowly enough so that rest stops were not required, I ensured that we passed all the other troops on the trail who were forced to rest as a result of hiking at a pace faster than the slowest hiker could sustain. After climbing the summit on the morning after a campout, I was proud when nearly all the scouts under my watch succeeded in getting to the top of San Gorgonio.

The next summer at age 16, I traveled to the East Coast where I was staff member at Schiff Scout Reservation, which, with Philmont, was one of the two national camps of Boy Scouts of America. My job was as Assistant Instructor in National Junior Leadership Training, a course I had taken as a student two years earlier at Philmont. My experience at Schiff was quite different in that we did little hiking that summer. The purpose of the National Junior Leader Training Course was instructional. As an instructor, I taught classes in such things as first aid, camping skills, and leadership. Along with a senior instructor, together we were in charge of about 24 scouts who had been selected by their local councils for this training. Although I enjoyed the responsibilities that were put upon me at Schiff, I must admit I longed for an extended overnight trail so I could hike and camp.

The next summer, when I was seventeen, I was a Ranger at Philmont Scout Ranch. This was right up my alley because Philmont was purely a hiking and camping type of camp. The programs were designed to give the scout more outdoor training. As a ranger, my job entailed escorting a troop on hikes from camp to camp. I was responsible for leading the scouts on their first five days of their 10-or 12-day expedition. Every day, we'd hike somewhere. At the end of the day, we stopped to set up camp, which involved pitching tents and preparing the evening meal. After five days I'd leave my troop to complete the rest of the expedition on their own and then I'd hike back to Headquarters alone, climbing a mountain along the way. By the end of the summer, I had climbed all 20 mountains on Philmont Scout Ranch.

I never had any great mentors growing up other than my father. That is not to say that I wasn't inspired by other people's adventures. I admired many of the great explorers that I read about, whose stories, in my opinion, are as good as the best fiction. It was enthralling to learn about Fridtjof Nansen, the Norwegian explorer who was first to cross the Greenland ice cap and then later attempted to reach the North Pole by drifting in the ice in his ship the *Fram*. And then there was Ernest Shackleton who very nearly succeeded in being first to reach the South Pole in 1909 but came up just 91 miles short. On a later expedition Shackleton made the epic open boat trip from Antarctica to South Georgia to organize a rescue of his ship's crew waiting in a makeshift shelter back on Antarctica.

Having redefined the possible, these great explorers inspired me to consider undertaking endeavors which were new, yet available to me. I was emboldened to take the initiative to hike and camp on my own. I began to enjoy independent adventures, where it was just me against the elements and alone with my thoughts. One of my first major adventures that I took on solo was when I hiked the popular John Muir Trail. I set off from Yosemite Valley in mid-June, 1962 immediately after high school graduation. I back-packed 14 days over 10 snow-covered mountain passes to the finish 212 miles trail at the summit of Mt Whitney. Due to the heavy snowpack, I was the first backpacker to complete the John Muir Trail that year.

I have heard it said that what challenges us in life serves to teach us what we most need to learn. I personally believe that to be true. Heading out into the wilderness by myself taught me to become accountable for my own survival and the consequences of my decisions. The most harrowing solo adventure I took on at that time was when I decided to climb Mt Lassen in Northern California during winter. Forty years ago weather forecasts were much less accurate than they are today and, like many climbers at that time, I set out without checking the weather first. That night as I camped on the slopes, a major winter storm hit. My tent was soon shredded by the winds, making sleep and keeping warm impossible. Since I wouldn't be able to sleep, I might as well climb to the summit. At

1.50 am and in a blizzard, I finally reached it—but I had underestimated the power of the storm. So severe were the conditions at the summit that I couldn't find the same route down and consequently missed my high camp. Fortunately I did find my mountaineering skis that I had stashed lower down the mountain. Aware that I had to get out of there that day since I no longer had any food or shelter, it took all my strength to maneuver my way through the four feet of powder snow drifts. Eventually the next evening I made it to the warmth and safety of my car, which sheltered me from the freezing cold and frigid winds. I would have to come back two weeks later to retrieve my equipment from the campsite.

As I moved into the latter half of my teenage years, roughing it on my own in endurance pursuits began to define me as an individual. In high school, I never took to team sports. I went out for football and broke my leg the second day of practice. When I was involved in groups, I often found myself seeking the position of the leader. During my years at Garden Grove High School, I was elected the president of an extraordinary number of clubs. It seemed I could be elected president of every club I joined from the Latin Club to the Science Explorers. I held a total of eight president positions before I had graduated from high school. Perhaps there were few who sought election to these offices; I embraced the challenges that leadership involves. Somehow I imagined that my future would be as a politician.

2. STANFORD VS BERKELEY: 1960–68

Stay off this island

A battered old sign on Alcatraz

Since childhood, I always knew that I wanted to go to college. My parents had offered to pay for my brother's, my sister's and my college educations and I was the only one to take them up on it. Both my brother and sister settled down to start families soon after graduating from high school. My brother went to work for the phone company. To put me through college, my parents refinanced their home, a gesture that made me more determined not to let them down.

Although during high school I was a good enough student to be in the top 10% of my class, that wasn't good enough to get in to my first choice of university. I wanted to go to Stanford but I wasn't accepted so I went to their archrival, the University of California Berkeley. Unwilling to accept second choice, I started scheming to transfer to Stanford. At Berkeley, I studied hard and got good grades in my freshman year and was soon in an honors program. Basically, I studied all the time. When I realized that it was possible to attend summer school at Stanford without being admitted as a full-time student, I enrolled following my freshman year. For the summer quarter I took a course load, which was literally double the normal 15 units. I hit the books hard to achieve grades that reflected my ability to keep up with the caliber of students at Stanford.

Upon returning to Berkeley in the Fall for my sophomore year, I applied for full-term admission to Stanford. At Berkeley, I was already the Vice President of the sophomore class. On the same day that I was elected to a student body office, called Men's Residence Hall Representative, I received my acceptance to Stanford and promptly resigned my newly elected position before I started it for the purpose of transferring to Stanford to major in Economics. Within that short timeframe, somehow the *San Francisco Chronicle* learned about my being elected to office at Berkeley and then defecting to Stanford and published my story on the front page. Berkeley students, who suffer some degree of inferiority complex to Stanford, let me know what they thought of my so-called traitorous actions.

Stanford is a paradoxical place. The students roam the idyllic campus enjoying a California lifestyle of sports, partying and just relaxing in the sun. But when they sit down for an exam in the classroom their brilliance shines through. At first I thought I might have gotten in over my head. I remember enrolling in Beginning Calculus. In the first few classes I sat there stunned as the professor raced through the fundamentals. Looking around the class, I was dismayed to observe that everyone seemed to know what was going on but me. It turned out that these Beginning students apparently went to high schools that offered Calculus. Since I didn't take Calculus in high school, I quickly dropped the course for fear of massacring my grade point average.

While I was able to struggle through other mathematical courses such as Logic and Statistics, I was more at home in the humanities. My favorite course at Stanford was a Western Civilization sequence, a broad study of Western Civilization including art, literature and history. I developed such an affinity for the material that I carried a minor in Honors Humanities. Frankly, the Stanford education was irrelevant to learning skills for a future career, but was very effective in developing an appreciation for arts, history, politics, and a wide range of subjects. All in all, I was very pleased with the type of education I got at Stanford because it enriched my life as a whole and stirred many future interests.

While at Stanford, I was inducted into the fold of a long, American college tradition. I joined Sigma Alpha Epsilon fraternity. Becoming an 'SAE' opened me up socially a bit. Up until then, I had spent most of my extracurricular time devoted to my studies. For the most part, SAE was a pretty tame, nice-guy fraternity. We didn't get into too much trouble. However, during the year I was elected social co-chairman of the fraternity, I, along with my co-chairman Len Klikunas, certainly organized some wild parties and did some crazy things.

Looking for a location for a party, we got the idea that maybe the Baptist church in Palo Alto would be a great party site. After talking the preacher into letting us rent his church hall for an evening, the date we set for our party just so happened to be the Saturday night before Easter. With a rock and roll band setting the mood, all my fraternity brothers and their dates were mixing things up at this church. I prepared the punch for the evening: 'Zombies' which were way too strong. This inebriating concoction, which consists of light and dark rums, apricot brandy and pineapple juice, was, ironically enough, first created in 1930 as a hangover cure.

As the night wore on and we consumed several rounds of these cocktails, we realized that they didn't call them 'Zombies' for nothing. Things got a little bit out of control in an altered state kind of way. As midnight approached, the realization that it was now officially Easter morning dawned on us, and we felt compelled to re-enact the Passion scene. For the occasion, one member dragged a huge cross across the stage. That was pretty bad. A few days later, the church members heard of our performance and indefinitely banned any more fraternity parties on the church grounds.

Stanford had a policy against the fraternities going on campouts. Only an extracurricular club, such as the Alpine Club, could do this. At the same time we wanted to organize a canoe trip, the *San Francisco Chronicle* was running an absolutely absurd front-page series of articles on 'Man Apes'. Also known as Sasquatch, these were yeti-type beasts that presumably roamed the wilderness of Northern California and the Pacific Northwest. While discussing some party ideas at the neighborhood pizza parlor over some beers late one night, one of my fraternity brothers, Bill Moore, who was also the Editor of the *Stanford Daily*, came forth with an excellent idea: we would form an ersatz 'club' for conducting our fraternity overnight canoe trip. We would call it the National Association for the Protection of Man Apes (NAPMA).

Our fraternity canoe trip was a big hit. As we set out in our canoes on the Russian River north of San Francisco, Bill Moore composed a spoof article which among other things described how this group of 30 men and 30 women college students split up into groups of, say, two and sat in the woods at night to commune with the Man Apes. The *San Francisco Chronicle* ran the article and Bill Moore got his first front page byline in a major newspaper, much to the chagrin of the Stanford administration. Bill's career has continued as the Op-Ed editor of the *Sacramento Bee*.

It was in college that my interest in adventure began to reach a new level. I became interested in distance swimming because I knew that with proper training I could swim indefinitely. That was, if I didn't get a disabling leg cramp or a shark-attracting nosebleed, both of which were common problems for me. To prevent these potential problems, I took salt pills for the leg cramps and had a doctor cauterize my nostrils with silver nitrate to stop the nosebleed episodes.

One of my swims would be the Golden Gate Bridge. Although a short distance, it was very dangerous due to the tidal currents, which funnel through the Golden Gate at speeds of up to 8 mph. I studied the San Francisco Bay tidal stream charts to determine the right time to make this swim because I would need to swim during the weakest tides to avoid being swept deep into the San Francisco Bay, or worse, carried out to sea. Of course this swim would have to be made at night under the auspices of darkness to avoid detection and apprehension by the Coast Guard, which increased the spookiness of this risky enterprise.

At around midnight on the night of the weakest tides, I drove over the Bridge to the Marin County end, parked and gingerly walked into the frigid water. Since I wasn't 100% confident of my proficiency in computing the slack period in the tidal streams, I stopped frequently in the early part of the swim to check that I was still tracking under the bridge. As I approached the center, I was on the lookout for ships to come barreling through the Gate and on one occasion swam in the opposite direction to get out of a ship's path. Finally the route was clear and I sprinted to the beach below the Presidio. As I touched the shore and climbed out of the chilly water I felt a great sense of accomplishment.

One task remained: I had to get back across the Bridge to my car. Wearing just a tank suit and carrying swimming goggles, I climbed up to the roadway and stuck out my thumb. I was not your standard hitchhiker. Fortunately someone picked me up. When asked what I was doing, I said I had just swum the Golden Gate. He gave me an incredulous look, which was followed by total silence for the rest of the ride across the Bridge.

Of all the swims I did in the San Francisco Bay area, the most outrageous and perhaps the most fun was the one that took place in my final year, before the Big Game between Stanford and UC Berkeley, nicknamed 'Cal'. When I attended Stanford, Stanford and Cal Berkeley were well into their seventh decade of intense football rivalry. The annual Big Game, as it is referred to, began in 1892, and quickly became a huge sporting event. In 1935, 94,000 people were in the city of Palo Alto, the home to Stanford University, to watch Stanford and Cal face off on the football field. That was the largest crowd ever to attend a football game in Northern California.

The Big Game is not only about football but also the music, bonfires, rallies, marching bands, college reunions, tailgate parties, lots of drinking and pranks that go with it. The pranks are thoroughly planned out and start well before game day. One tradition at Stanford is to hang a 'Beat Cal' banner in the most imaginative place possible. In previous years, a banner had been hung on the Great Wall of China, the leaning Tower of Pisa, Stonehenge, and in Moscow's Red Square. Once again over beers in the pizza parlor, we hatched a plan to hang a Beat Cal banner on Alcatraz prison. My assignment was to swim out to Alcatraz towing the banner.

Between the 1930s until the mid-1960s, Alcatraz was used as a maximum-security prison in which some of the most notorious criminals, such as Al Capone, had been incarcerated. Although the distance to Alcatraz is not far—one and one half miles—the surrounding tides make it a difficult swim. For years it was believed that swimming from Alcatraz was impossible. Of the handful of prisoners that tried to escape from the island, it is maintained that none of them made it to the shore. Federal prison officials had concluded that all prison escapees had drowned in the cold, swift tidal currents of the bay. Perhaps with too much faith in my tidal calculations, I was confident of avoiding this fate.

Using my Tidal Stream charts, I planned an arching trajectory from the foot of the Oakland Bay Bridge to Alcatraz Island. With the Big Game scheduled for late November, this swim would be a cold one. To combat the 48°F water temperature, I wore a short wetsuit that hardly protected me from the unbearable cold. We rented a fishing boat, loaded it up with fraternity brothers, a photographer from the *San Francisco Chronicle* and a keg of beer, and I set off on the swim. It took a little over an hour to reach Alcatraz. Although the prisoners had recently been removed as a part of the shutdown plan of the prison, it was still well guarded. As I clambered up onto the rocks and unveiled the Beat Cal banner, I discovered that the guards did not have a great sense of humor.

One of them quickly shoved me off the rocks and back into the water. My efforts were not in vain. Most importantly, the photographer took a picture of the sign before the guards could remove it and the picture successfully made the international newswires. I had 'broken into Alcatraz', the caption read. However, the day was not over yet. I wanted to swim back to San Francisco to prove to those uptight guards that an escaping prisoner could have made the swim from Alcatraz.

On my return trip the epic struggle began. I had timed the swim back for slack tides but once back in the water, I noticed there was something else happening with the tides. As the guards glowered from their towers, I completed my rounding of the island. Then I pounded away for over six hours against an ebb tide that was not shown on the Tidal Stream charts. When I finally came ashore near Fisherman's Wharf I was groggy from hypothermia and exhaustion after a total of nearly eight hours' swimming in remarkably cold water. The swim back was much more difficult than I imagined. However, that didn't stop me from having a fine dinner party at Alioto's restaurant on Fisherman's Wharf with my support team.

Unique to that experience was that it was the first and last stunt I undertook purely for publicity winning purposes. After that triumph, my motivation for achieving my goals in adventure pursuits would be for my own personal satisfaction. Any publicity and recognition that my adventures generated would only be a natural by-product.

In the imagination of the collective consciousness, the adventurer tends to stand out as a lone figure—the type of person who, stricken with an acute case of wanderlust, will at any time and anywhere head off solo into the world to collect their adventures as one might collect seashells on a beach. Although many of the adventures of my life lend credence to this perception, the adventurer is not alone when it comes to inspiration. It is often from learning about other adventurers preceding him, and their love for this lifestyle, that the adventurer is inspired to head off to taste and experience a given adventure for oneself. For instance, the famous adventurer of the 1920s and 1930s, Richard Halliburton, was inspired to swim the Hellespont after reading Lord Byron's account of his swim in 1810. Lord Byron was moved to undertake this swim after reading the Greek romantic tragedy featuring the mythical figure, Leander, who would swim the Hellespont every night to be with his lover Hero, a priestess of Aphrodite. One stormy winter night, the waves tossed Leander in the sea and the wind blew out Hero's light, and Leander lost his way, and was drowned. In a fit of grief, Hero threw herself from her tower and died as well. So captivated was Byron with this love story that he emulated Leander's swim exactly. Starting at Abydos and finishing at Sestos, the home of Leander's beloved, Byron sought to experience every nuance of this romantic adventure for himself.

As this sequence of events that has spanned millennia shows, stories of what others have accomplished create a chain of inspiration that connect the solitary adventurer to a greater whole. In fact, many would come under the inspirational spell of Halliburton's adventures. For, once Halliburton had accomplished a cluster of feats, he'd put pen to paper and write a book about them. Eventually, a succession of his books was published, enabling him to make a living as a serial adventurer.

It was in college that I read Halliburton's first best-selling book entitled *Royal Road to Romance*. I immediately identified with his writings. It was while Halliburton was a college student at Princeton that he developed a proclivity to wanderlust, which led him to climb the Matterhorn and swim the Hellespont and various other exploits. *Royal Road to Romance* conveyed a very romantic philosophy that fuelled my desire to undertake as many adventures as possible. In fact, I think from that point forward, my focus in my early adventuring years was to do things that many people would like to do, but never get around to doing. Although I could be mistaken, I think many people would like to climb the Matterhorn or swim the Hellespont. Because Halliburton had actually done these things, his accounts were extremely motivational for me.

In the summer between my junior and senior years at Stanford, I became a part of this chain of inspiration. I took off for Europe with the intent to swim the Hellespont, climb the Matterhorn and conquer other such exotic feats. I had planned out my trip early on but kept my plans secret. I didn't want to travel with anyone because I wanted to move fast and pursue my unique objectives. I was very happy traveling solo. In fact, to a certain extent, I've always enjoyed doing things on my own.

The first destination on my Grand Tour itinerary was Turkey and the Hellespont, which is the classical Greek name for what is now called the Dardanelles. Although the distance to cross is not long, only two miles one way, the Hellespont currents are treacherous. The water flows out from the Black Sea and then the Sea of Marmara creating a strong confluence that sweeps down the Hellespont. In order to avoid being washed out into the Aegean, like the mythical figure Leander, safely crossing the Hellespont requires getting the logistics right. From the town of Canakkale, I hiked upstream toward the classical location of Abydos. Unfortunately this is now on a Turkish military base. As I approached the security gate, I climbed the hillside to avoid detection and proceeded around to my planned starting point. I took off my clothes and plunged into the water wearing only my swimsuit. The current carried me at a diagonal, which I had planned for. Fortunately my calculations about the currents were correct and I made it safely to land before being swept past the point, which protected me from being carried into the Aegean Sea.

I sat content on the shore and considered my accomplishment. I had made it! But now I had to get back. I didn't think to bring any money so could not take the ferry—I would have to swim back. I hiked barefooted upstream past the town of Eceabat so that I could again make the diagonal downstream swim. There was a lot of shipping traffic and I remember stopping once while a Russian freighter passed closely in front of me. Treading water helped to disguise my presence; however, I think the captain spotted me anyhow. Fortunately no rescue boats were dispatched to fetch me. Toward the end I swam furiously to reach a sandbar extending out from a point. It was a good thing that I made it because if I hadn't I would have ended up at the next shoreline, the ruins of Troy, 20 miles away.

My very next adventure involved heading up to Istanbul and swimming the Bosporus. That was challenging just because of all the heavy boat and ferry traffic that congests the Bosporus area. More than once I had to dodge a ferry boat. It was less than a one-mile swim but it actually seemed more dangerous because of all the traffic that often didn't see me in the water.

I took the train to Greece and got off at the village of Litokhoron with a plan to climb Mt Olympus, the home of the Greek gods. Although Olympus was only 9570 ft, it was a long, hot approach and climb. Having made it to the summit, I was pleased to knock off one more classical feat. It was not long before I had reached Switzerland to pursue a number of mountaineering objectives. After completing a one-week course at the Rosenlaui Mountain Climbing School, which enhanced my technical climbing skills, I departed for the Eiger in the Bernese Oberland of the Alps. The Eiger (13,026 ft), which translates as 'ogre' in German, is oftentimes called the 'evil ogre' when making reference to the Eiger's north wall. Indeed, the north wall's danger and difficulty has earned it a special place in alpine climbing history. It was long deemed unclimbable. Nine climbers were killed making attempts before Heinrich Harrer and three climbing partners succeeded in 1938. My attempt would be on the relatively benign West Wall, where I learned that this is a treacherous mountain to climb from any angle.

Having finished the steeper climbing, I was approaching the summit on steep rock slabs, which were covered with a veneer of fresh wet snow. Suddenly my feet went out from under me and I was rocketing down the smooth snow-covered slab toward the precipice below. With my ice axe in hand, I immediately turned on my stomach and pressed the pick of the axe as hard as I could against the stone slab. After slipping over 100 ft I had finally stopped my slide with my feet up to my knees hanging over the edge of the cliff. At first afraid to budge and without a climbing partner to help me, I caught my breath and, oh so very carefully, managed to swing my feet back on the snow-covered slab and caught a knob. I dug my free hand into another section of the rock. Fingers bleeding from the slide, I cautiously pulled myself up to safety. Without looking back I quickly moved to safer ground. Pausing to rest, I tried to calm my nerves. That was the closest I have come to losing my life on a mountain.

After collecting my thoughts and regaining my composure, I continued to the summit. A reminder that danger lurks where it is sometimes not expected, I still carry the scars above the fingernails on my left hand where I had driven my hand into the rock during that ice axe arrest.

Next stop on my Grand Tour was Mont Blanc, the highest mountain in Western Europe at 15,771 ft. The normal way to climb Mont Blanc is to take a combination of train and cable car to Nid d'Aigle at 8100 ft, then proceed to the summit after one night in a higher hut. I decided to climb from the town of Chamonix at only 3400 ft to the Grand Mulets Hut at 9216 ft which proved to be much more strenuous. At 2 am the next morning I headed off from the hut on my solo ascent. With the summit still 6500 ft of climbing away, I had to reach it before the sun softened the snow so much that it would be nearly impassable. It was a long day—to the summit and all the way down—which was a total of 15 hours on the move. I was exhausted but content to have made it.

En route to the Matterhorn, I felt I was ready for the primary climbing objective of my summer in Europe. I was prepared to try it solo, but by good fortune I met fellow climber Jack Sturtzenberger, a medical student from Vermont, as we were hiking up to the

Hornli Hut. Neither one of us wanted to use a guide because that would somehow demean the achievement of climbing this awesome mountain. Since I had a rope and sufficient experience to lead and Jack was strong and willing, it was easy to see that our strengths complemented each other. We decided to team up for the challenge.

The next day it took us only four hours to summit the Matterhorn, but then it took us seven hours to descend. This was a clear example of how a descent is sometimes more difficult than climbing up a mountain. Only a few times on the ascent did we feel the need to set up a belay with the rope, but on the way down we used frequent belays for protection. Surly guides with their clients in tow would jostle past us while we were belaying, then clumsily dislodge rocks, all the while complaining about our slow climbing. What really irritated them was that, unlike practically everyone else on the mountain, we were not using the guide service. We replied in kind by swearing at them for their slovenly climbing habits. By the time we had finished the day we felt we had been through a war zone with the guides being the enemy. But we had succeeded in climbing one of the most prominent mountains in the world, and we had climbed it on our own terms.

For my final adventure of the summer, I traveled to Calais, France and to the banks of the English Channel. I had my sights set on swimming the 21 miles across the Channel, a premier endurance achievement if I could pull it off. There I tried to figure out the logistics of swimming the Channel from the French side but couldn't. The language barrier didn't help. Since I couldn't speak much French, all I could comprehend was that I should go to Dover, England. So I got on the ferry and looked up a representative of the Channel Swimming Association. It was true that Channel swims are organized in England and most of the attempts start from Dover. In addition to the expensive registration and observer fees I learned that the cost of an escort boat was quite substantial, which was not in my budget as a student. I was additionally put off when left without a clear understanding of how to organize and register for an attempt on the English Channel. It is just as well because I now know that I was not nearly well enough trained at that time. I resolved that the English Channel would be unfinished business for me.

I returned to Stanford that Fall of 1965 feeling like a different person. Although I didn't write articles about my exploits, it was no secret among my friends what I had done that summer and they enjoyed hearing my stories. I had gained self-confidence from knowing that I could take on major endurance feats and with preparation and perseverance I could succeed. I had certainly broken some barriers of self-limitation. Even though I'm not especially good at these sports, I learned that I could do these feats by applying myself. For instance, although I was very competent as a mountaineer, I was not a very good swimmer at all. But I found that I could swim a given duration anyhow, just with some planning and training. The summer of 1965 was a watershed period in my life and even though my continued participation in adventure activities was not immediate, I would eventually return to the pursuit of fascinating projects.

3. VOWS AND OPTIONS: 1969–80

Be Prepared

Boy Scout motto

Since I didn't make great scores on my graduate business school entrance exam, and therefore would not be going to business school of the highest rank, I explored other good private universities and settled on Washington University in St Louis. Once again, my parents generously offered their assistance to help me through school. Although I really appreciated that they paid for my undergraduate degree at Stanford, I decided to take on the financial responsibility for myself and took out a college loan to pay for my graduate school costs.

After the first semester break at Washington University, I returned from the Bahamas with a tan and a lot of self-confidence, all set to meet a woman. I went to a mixer party and spotted a girl on the other side of the room who was very attractive. I brashly asked her to dance, but she didn't like my swagger and very nearly turned me down. Fortunately she accepted and we danced and had a brilliant time. I had met Peggy Viehland.

Over the course of the evening, I learned that Peggy had graduated from Webster College with a degree in Music Education.

As a musician, she played bassoon in a community orchestra in addition to her full-time job as a piano teacher. When she told me that she had spent her junior year in Austria studying at the Vienna Academy of Music, I was impressed. I was delighted to learn that we shared an interest in foreign travel and doing exciting things.

On our first real date at the local Playboy Club, we talked about things we liked to do. She seemed to be interested in all forms of fun and exciting things. That was my cue.

Though limited to a student's budget, I was not deterred from spending money on what I thought was important such as enrolling in flying lessons at the local aero club. When the club picnic and air show was coming up, I figured Peggy would like to attend so I invited her. Although she knew that I was a member of this organization and that I was taking flying lessons, I made it sound kind of innocuous—like we'd just be going to the barbecue party from where we'd watch the show from a distance. I glossed over the fact that I would be flying in the air show.

On the appointed morning as we pulled into the parking lot at the airfield, I told her that I'd be competing in the show. She seemed unfazed with that disclosure and actually appeared interested in seeing me perform. Then, for some crazy reason, I asked her to fly with me. Without giving it much thought, she simply said 'Okay.' Making our way over to the aircraft, I helped Peggy climb into the back seat of the Cessna 172 and strap herself in before taking my place in the front seat next to my instructor who would be riding with us since I didn't have a pilot's license yet.

Participating in the air show involved flying at around 4000 ft and competing in different events. One event was to drop a small bag of flour on a target—pretty tame. Next was the Streamer Cut. The object of this was to drop a roll of toilet paper then cut it with the wing as many times as possible before it reached the ground. Now this was really fun. Pitching the toilet paper roll out the window, I swung the airplane sharply up on its wing to come around for the first cut then jerked the yoke to come around for the second cut. I continued on down without hesitation for a total of 12 cuts of the streamer—a winning performance. While totally focused, I once stole a glance at Peggy sitting in the back seat behind me. For a second we locked eyes. From the big smile on her face I could tell she was scared but totally enjoying the ride.

The competition ended with a dead stick landing. For this I cut the power to idle while still on the downwind leg, then glided around the traffic pattern and touched down as close as possible to a line halfway down the runway. I touched 6 ft short of the marker which was not good enough to win. After we taxied off the runway and the plane came to a stop, I climbed out and then helped Peggy crawl out of the back seat. She stepped down onto the tarmac where I spontaneously swung her into my arms for a big hug and a good, long laugh. Although I didn't win the overall title, I was pleased to win one of the events as a student pilot. Driving back from the air show that afternoon, the energy of the day lingered with us. Peggy and I were tired but still high from the excitement of our shared adventure which we discussed in great detail all the way home.

That summer, I asked Peggy to marry me. While working a summer job as a programmer for IBM in White Plains, New York, Peggy stopped over for a couple days to see me before continuing to Europe on a vacation with her parents. I had bought a one-carat marquis diamond engagement ring, which was a bit extravagant for a student, and made the proposal as effectively as I could. She accepted! Then I enthusiastically suggested that the wedding take place the next month when she got back from Europe. That's when I learned the hard facts about young ladies and their weddings: I would have to wait a full six months before we tied the knot.

Just a few days before our December wedding, with my fresh pilot's license and the flying club's Cessna 172, I flew to Minneapolis for a job interview. When a storm closed in the next day, I was forced to leave the plane there and return to St Louis on an airline in order to welcome friends and relatives who would be arriving for the wedding. We were married at the Little Flower Catholic church in St Louis.

Although we hadn't intentionally planned on making our honeymoon an adventure, it would nevertheless turn into that. First we had to get back to Minneapolis to retrieve the airplane that I had borrowed for my job interview. Fortunately a fellow aero club member flew Peggy and me there in his Mooney. From there Peggy and I took off for the Bahamas where we planned to do some island hopping. It was just bitter cold in Minneapolis—a wintry 20 below zero. As we taxied the Cessna 172 out to the runway, the engine died. The tower sent a truck out to tow us back to the ramp and into the hangar. When a mechanic checked the airplane out, he couldn't find anything wrong with it, which was unnerving. I would have preferred that he had found the problem. With nothing to stop us, we taxied back out, took off and made it to our first night's stop in Dubuque, Iowa. The second day we made it all the way to Atlanta and Atlanta Hartsfield airport, which seemed enormous.

There, my little single-engine aircraft was dwarfed by these huge commercial planes that taxied by us. That was a little intimidating. After a night in Atlanta, we continued on to Ft Lauderdale, Florida, where we stayed the next day before heading out over the Atlantic Ocean to the Bahamas.

However, when we left Florida and started flying out over the water, Peggy's composure changed. All of a sudden, she became really nervous. The experience of flying over the water in this small plane really spooked her. Since our destination was the Bahamas, I was concerned that this could be a real problem. Throughout the remainder of the flight, I did my best to soothe her worry. 'What a lovely day,' I appraised. I commented on the water's stunning azure hue, which one only finds in these regions. Her forced show of enthusiasm revealed that her fear painted the sea a morbid color in her mind. We finally made it to Nassau where we spent the night before going on to Georgetown on Great Exuma Island for a few days.

Next was the big jump to the Turks and Caicos Islands, a country to the east of the Bahamas and north of Haiti, which required a fuel stop at Cat Island. Approaching Cat Island, I was taken aback upon seeing a 25 mph direct crosswind on this single runway. Since we had no choice but to land, I resolved to do my best under the circumstances. On our final approach the plane was grabbed at a 45-degree angle to the runway. At the final moment before touching down I kicked the rudder to straighten the plane to accomplish a very challenging crosswind landing. As we came to a stop, I glanced at Peggy who was white as a ghost. She was developing a serious aversion to flying over water. The more we did it the less she liked it.

Because our last leg necessitated flying about 2 ½ hours over the ocean and my airplane only held just over three hours worth of fuel, Peggy put her foot down. She would not get in the plane. My dreams of Peggy sharing in my adventures came crashing down. Here we were stuck on Cat Island and I manically thought my marriage was coming to an end after only one week. I don't remember what I said, but somehow, I was finally able to get through to her, to assure her that everything was going to be all right.

As we climbed back in the plane, I was forced to admit to myself that this flight was a little risky. Flying over a couple hours of water without a whole lot of extra fuel was not the most sensible thing to do. There were no navigation aids en route and I did not even have a wind forecast. I would be left to dead reckoning with just a guess of the wind effect. After two hours' flying, the sun began to sink behind the horizon and I still could see nothing but water. Certain we'd be lost at sea, Peggy implored that we turn back; however, this was not a viable option as we didn't have enough fuel to make it back. Trying to remain calm, my blurting out, 'There it is!' when we finally spotted the island belied my relief. We landed safely on the Providenciales of the Turks and Caicos Islands. We made an easy flight to South Caicos Island the next day, which was our final destination.

After a lovely New Year's celebration and relaxing moments spent in this remote place, we started our trip home when we were confronted with the next drama that involved crossing the ADIZ (the Air Defense Identification Zone), the boundary protecting the USA from invaders. After refueling and filing my flight plan at our last stop in the Bahamas, Rock Sound, we headed back to the US. As the Florida coastline came into view so did an F-102 streaking past at only 100 ft off my left wing. 'Did you see that?' Peggy exclaimed. Well, I couldn't miss it. My heart skipped a few beats as I realized that we had almost been hit by an Air Force jet out on training. I began to revise this assumption when, a minute later, another F-102 streaked by off our right wing then did a climbing turn. When I called the Ft Lauderdale Tower to ask what was going on, the controller informed me that he didn't have a flight plan for us. My flight plan had been lost! I now realized that the Air Force had scrambled the jets in an effort to intercept us and force us to land. Surely our little eggbeater did not look like much of a threat! After a normal landing at Ft Lauderdale, the paperwork to explain this event started and would continue for months.

I graduated with an MBA from Washington University in 1968. Soon thereafter, Peggy and I moved to New York City where I had lined up a job with IBM. With the advent of the computer revolution, I no longer felt that it would be the financial and marketing executives who would rise to become Chief Executive Officers, but that the new top management would come from Information Systems. In addition to wanting to work for IBM because it was the dominant company in computer systems, I aspired to eventually become a corporate executive. My other interest was financial trading. For this reason I angled to get assigned to the Brokerage Branch Office of IBM on Wall Street. Back in 1968 there was already talk of electronic trading and that the stock exchanges would be replaced by the 'black box'—a computer which would match the buy and sell orders for instantaneous executions—and I wanted to be involved in the design of those systems. I joined IBM as a systems engineer, not as a marketing person. Although my education was not very technical and marketing was actually a better fit for me, I decided to take this opportunity to build a solid foundation of technical competence.

While in New York, Peggy also fell under the spell of Wall Street and her career path took a major turn in this direction. Since the prospect of teaching in the New York public schools was daunting, she sought a job of any kind on Wall Street and subsequently landed an entry level job as a research assistant with Francis I. DuPont, one of the major brokerage firms at that time. Proving herself to be a very hard worker, she became popular with her managers who quickly promoted her to serve as the Securities Analyst for the textiles industry.

Once having settled into our apartment on the Upper East Side, we embraced the big city life, attending plays, concerts and operas on a regular basis. Then suddenly, the reality of this lifestyle started to set in. It became apparent to us that this is a tough city for those without high incomes. We had to keep our car on a street in the Bronx because we couldn't afford to keep it garaged in Manhattan. Since I wasn't in a position to plan or undertake any exciting adventures at that time, I was reluctant to sell our car as driving to a ski resort or a beach was the closest I would come to any adventure at that time.

My training with IBM paid off. It provided me with a fantastic value in those boom times of the computer industry. After only nine months I was recruited by Touche-Ross (now Deloitte-Touche) to work in their management services division, which was headquartered in Detroit. Receiving a 75% increase in pay and an exaggerated job title of 'management consultant', I was on the fast track.

Before packing up and heading for Detroit, Peggy and I decided to take a much-needed vacation. Craving a real rugged interlude, I suggested that we go on a canoeing trip. Peggy agreed and we traveled up to a camp in Ontario, Canada, where we were outfitted with a canoe and other camping equipment for a multi-day trip. Since this was the first adventure I had had in a long time, I could hardly wait to get our trip underway. Well, I soon found out that camping wasn't exactly Peggy's style. In fact, she hadn't had any prior camping experience. This was problematic as our itinerary involved canoeing all day and setting up camp in the evening. After a tiring long day on the lake, Peggy still couldn't sleep at night. Her imagination kept her perpetually alert in anticipation of a bear that was sure to attack us. Every foreign noise made her jump. In the morning, when a squirrel darted across the top of our tent, it just totally freaked her out. Although we made it through the trip, Peggy's nerves were pretty frayed by the end, at which point she made it clear to me that she had had enough of camping for a lifetime. That was the last adventuresome vacation we would go on together.

After moving to Detroit and settling into my consulting role at Touche-Ross, I received a shock. The work wasn't in Detroit but rather anywhere in the country where the client's company happened to be! On one engagement, I flew from Detroit to Cleveland on Sunday afternoon; worked 14 hours a day all week then flew home on Saturday morning. As this was 100% travel—all work and no play, I was soon grumbling about this lifestyle.

While I was miserable with my occupation, Peggy was excelling at hers. In Detroit, she went to work for Commonwealth Bank as a securities analyst. She loved her job and was doing quite well. Her business acumen earned her the respect of her co-workers and the trust of her clients.

Back at Touche-Ross, I was alerted that they were preparing to make company layoffs. They began by laying off the unhappy employees and the poor performers. I'm not sure, but presumably I fell into the category of 'unhappy'. Nevertheless I was stunned when I was called in and terminated. Somehow I didn't believe that companies actually fire good people. In my rendition of the American Dream, I had edited out that ugly sequence. 'Where's my gold watch? I'm perfectly capable of this work! You're going to fire *me*?' my mind ticked off in my defense. Looking back at it now, getting laid off was a reality check, a great awakening for me to the true nature of the American business world.

I was off balance during that weak moment in the economy and had to take a job which was a step down from my position at Touche-Ross. Once again we packed our bags and this time moved to Chicago where I became a Systems Analyst at Marshall Field's Department Store. Peggy quickly adapted to our new location where she took a position as a Portfolio Manager in the Trust Department of the First National Bank of Chicago. She would keep this job for 18 years and in a nonchalant manner would rise to fill the position of Vice President and handle the investments of increasingly large and complex clients.

I was fascinated with my work at Marshall Field's, which was the last major retailer to computerize. When I arrived there, everything was done manually. The sales checks would be filed in customer folders, which were held in a warehouse-size room. Once a month the files would be pulled out and the customer bill would be typed from the sales checks. Unencumbered by any pre-existing computer systems, we went about designing a system the way it should be, taking it from the Dark Ages all the way to State of the Art. Feeling like an architect of these application programs, I threw myself into the work and achieved excellent results.

Dampening my enthusiasm for my job was a picture of this industry's future, which did not look so good to me. My futurist theory that the computer-literate would rise through the ranks to lead major corporations was 100% wrong. I noticed that at Marshall Field's only the merchandisers and the financial executives had a future. Regardless of performance, the pay raises were a meager 6% to 10% and a promotion could only be realized when my boss moved on. One thing became crystal clear—I had to get out of there! After two years, I quit cold turkey. One afternoon, I strode into my boss's office and announced that I was quitting, effective with a standard two weeks' notice.

On my drive home, it took me a while to notice that a fine mist had collected on my windshield. My mind was distinctly elsewhere. Even though, deep inside of me, my intuition told me that I was doing the right thing, that I should just trust and go with my instincts and that everything would work out fine, Peggy was not going to be happy with my decision. I was unemployed and had no idea what I was going to do for work or how I was going to tell her. Taking advantage of the time I had in the car, I tried constructing an elaborate excuse for my impulsive action but all I could come up with was the simple truth. Whether Peggy accepted this or not remained to be seen. I didn't begrudge the rush hour traffic that I got caught in that evening. I was in no hurry to get home.

When I walked in the door, Peggy was there. An argument quickly erupted after she gave me a quick kiss and asked me, 'How was your day?' I answered her question by telling her flat out what happened. Peggy didn't mince words, telling me that she didn't give a hoot about my intuition or what it told me. Quitting my job meant that she had just lost her 20% employee discount on Marshall Field's merchandise and she wasn't happy at all about it. She argued that getting fired was one thing, but quitting a perfectly good job was just plan foolish. She was also quick to point out that

I didn't have a contingency plan, another job lined up. Absorbing all her words, the only response I could come up with was that it was a dead end. Nevertheless, she was really upset with me for quite some time.

Figuring I could do well enough as an independent systems consultant, I quickly felt disillusioned with this prospect when I came up with virtually no clients. To fill in the spare time and keep a little money coming in, I got my hack license and became a Chicago Yellow Cab taxi driver. I've always regarded driving as a pleasure. The previous year while I was still working for Marshall Field's and was frustrated with my job, I took up race car driving for a short period of time. I rigged up a Datsun 510 with a roll bar and started out as a rally car driver. This was European style rallying and was called the 'Pro Series'.

The duration of a race was typically less than 18 hours straight through, starting in the afternoon and finishing the next day. I enjoyed this fast and very competitive style of car racing. I raced at full speed, over all kinds of roads, in all different seasons and over all kinds of terrain. It turned out to be highly therapeutic and was a lot of fun to boot. Crashing was very cathartic. In fact, crashing was common in rally racing. I can remember being in one race where two-thirds of the cars crashed.

Of all the crashes I experienced, the worst occurred during a race that began in Olean, New York. Coming down into Pennsylvania, I was speeding along at about 100 mph in my Datsun sedan. The little sedans make the best rally cars due to their outstanding durability. It was at night when, suddenly, the road changed surfaces from pavement to dirt sending us sliding uncontrollably off to the side of the road. There, a wheel caught the edge and the car rolled down a steep ravine and smashed into some trees that stopped our descent. The car came to a rest upside down. I remember looking over at my navigator who, like myself, was hanging inverted from the 4-point seatbelts. For a moment, we were speechless. It all happened so fast, without any warning. Then he flashed me a thumbs up, indicating that he was okay. We manipulated our bodies out of that awkward position and the vehicle; we were struck by the extent of the damage as we began to examine the car. Fortunately, the helmets that we wore and the roll bar had protected us pretty well. It was a miracle that we walked away from that crash.

We hitched a ride to the nearest town where we called for a tow truck to pull out the car. We checked into a cheap hotel room and waited until they brought what was left of the car around. We quickly went to work salvaging all the parts that we could, put them into boxes and hopped on a Greyhound bus back to Chicago. Sitting on the bus, I cringed at what would happen when I filed this accident with my insurance company. When I did, my insurance company did not hesitate to cancel my policy. However, I wasn't going to let that deter me. Since I began car racing, I couldn't help but notice how alive I felt. For the first time in a while, I was doing something that I wanted to do, that I thought was exciting. It was certainly more interesting to me than my job at the time.

As an outlet for my frustration, I continued to devote as much of my time as I could to car racing on the side. One year, I entered a World Championship event in the US. The spirit of the race was articulated by the name 'Press on Regardless'. Comprised of mostly European drivers, 'Press on Regardless' was a 24-hour race whose course crisscrossed over the Upper Peninsula of Michigan. I thought that it was so cool to be in a world championship and found the European drivers just awesome.

Although I loved participating in this sport, European-style rally car driving never caught on as a primary motorsport in the States. I decided to try some American-style car racing and turned toward Formula racing, which is more popular in the US. I got involved in the small-style, open-wheel racing car competitions. Thinking that it could prepare me for the major, professional-style racing like the Indianapolis 500, I started driving a Formula Ford then switched to Formula B, which in professional racing is called Formula Atlantic—a very competitive class of open-wheel racing.

I began considering an entirely new career and even forsaking my aspirations to be a business executive. My new plan was just to earn a living so I could do the things that I wanted. I studied income levels in Chicago and found that the two highest-paying occupations were Institutional Stock Broker and Commodities Broker. While the stock brokerage business was centered in New York City, the Commodities industry was based in Chicago, just where I happened to live. Feeling that there would be additional opportunities working in the central base of an industry, I decided to become a Commodities Broker. Methodically, I interviewed and took a job with Merrill Lynch because they were the largest brokerage firm in both stocks and commodities futures. Although the pay was only $1000 per month during the first six months of training, which was a big step down for me, the training was great and when it was over I would be on commission. It became clear that this career shoe fit.

Back in those days, being a $100,000 producer, that is generating $100,000 worth of commission revenue in a year, was kind of the standard measure of success for a broker. For my first 12 months in the business, I was a $100,000 producer. I worked my tail off during that time. It's the hardest I've ever worked, but I had to do it if I was going to get a good start in this career.

A large part of my success was due to my ability to procure and retain customers. At Merrill Lynch, we were given leads by which to solicit prospective clients and I found that if I called 20 of these leads on the phone in an evening, I could succeed in opening one account. Although I'm not really a salesman type, I was able to effectively communicate my thorough grounding in trading strategies. Uniquely, I had a strong interest in arbitrage, which is a more sophisticated strategy that entails taking an opposite position in similar markets to gain an edge for making a profit. My high credibility and uncommon strategies had special appeal. The industry-wide results of customers trading commodities are dismal, but I was able to provide the opportunity to make money and many of my customers had extraordinary results. They would take my advice and in effect I became their money manager in this volatile area of trading.

The irony is that I built my strong customer base by being willing to open accounts that many brokers turned down because they deemed them to be too small. I opened them because I knew a certain percentage of those small accounts would one day become big customers. Many of my customers succeeded in making a return on their investment even when starting off with only a $2000 account. From there, some worked up to a $200,000 account, which, in turn, generated high commissions.

After two years at Merrill Lynch, I switched firms to Drexel Burnham because they offered me a bigger percentage of payout on commissions generated. At Merrill Lynch it had worked out to be 25% whereas at Drexel Burnham I'd receive 40%.

Soon after arriving at Drexel Burnham, I got the chance to land a really big account. A man named Randall Kreiling walked in and told the manager that he had an interest in opening an account. He claimed to be the brother-in-law of the biggest traders in the commodities industry: Texas oil billionaire brothers Bunker and Herbert Hunt. My manager, Fred Uhlmann, was skeptical but referred him to me. Being a careful reader of the financial press, I knew who Randy Kreiling was and that he had substantial influence on how the Hunt brothers traded. Recognizing the importance of this prospect, every day for two months I prepared a very careful synopsis of a trading strategy about the commodity they asked me to follow, which was silver. They liked my strategy recommendations enough to one day call and say 'We're going to send you a million bucks to open an account.'

It wasn't long before we were executing grand strategies in the market. One critical day, after much study, I concluded that it was the right time to buy silver—lots of it. All the big traders were in the pit and the silver charts were ripe for this play. I recommended, 'If you buy silver now between $16 and $19 per ounce, you will be able to buy a huge quantity and while the price will go up, it will not come back down when you stop buying.' They liked that recommendation and we proceeded to roil the markets by buying thousands of contracts representing untold millions of ounces of silver. In another grandiose operation, on my recommendation they bought sugar contracts on the London Sugar Exchange to cover their short position on the New York Sugar Exchange, which was the largest ever known. With this and my other accounts, by my third year in business, I ended up being a $1,000,000 commission producer. My commissions doubled again and by my fourth year in the business, I was probably one of the top seven commodities brokers in the world at that time.

As I have a soft spot for adventure, I took a leap and made a transition from being solely a customer's man to being a trader myself. Aware that there was a lot of action on the floor, I wanted to be a part of it. Drexel Burnham bought me a membership on the Chicago Board of Trade. While still calling my customers from the floor of the Chicago Board of Trade, I also started trading soybeans for my own account. I loved the action, the energy, the excitement. The adrenaline rush was incredible. It felt comparable to what I used to get on my adventures.

On the same day that I became a member of the Chicago Board of Trade, so did Joe Ritchie. Once again our paths had crossed. The first time was at Marshall Field's when I identified him as a brilliant programmer and logician working for the consulting firm Arthur Anderson. I recruited him to become a programmer at Marshall Field's and he did, but he resigned after he quickly figured out there wasn't much future there. A couple years later after I had become a commodities broker, I counseled him to accept a position as a researcher for the commodities arbitrage firm A-Mark Financial. When we met up again he was going out on his own. Working in the same job milieu, Joe and I established an enduring friendship that would become rewarding in so many ways throughout the years to come. After becoming a member of the Chicago Board of Trade, he quickly built a huge arbitrage firm operating on virtually all US exchanges and many foreign exchanges. His firm, Chicago Research and Trading, became the dominant force in exchange floor arbitrage. In the early 1990s, he sold his firm to Nations Bank (now Bank of America) for $500 million. Inconspicuously, he may have been the most successful operator in floor trading until that time.

Even though trading occupied a large amount of my time, I decided to hold onto my customers. My daily routine began with going on the trading floor when it opened and then contacting my customers after it closed. I really had to learn to juggle my schedule when I became a member of the Chicago Board Options Exchange, called 'CBOE'. I continued trading there after the Board of Trade closed at 1.15. Because the CBOE was stock market related, it stayed open until 3.15. Now, my day began with calling customers early in the morning and then in the late morning and early afternoon I was on the floor of the Board of Trade before going to the CBOE. After that closed I called more customers and strategized about the markets. Suddenly I was making money three ways. Although I was putting in 10 to 12 hour days, the workload was enjoyable for the simple reason that I loved what I was doing.

I finally decided to concentrate just on stock options on the CBOE when I realized that that's what I liked best. I found it interesting because it was rather scientific and probabilities could be put in one's favor. What also made it interesting for me was that Joe Ritchie provided me with a key trading system. Joe had programmed the primary mathematical model for stock options, the Black-Scholes Model, on a handheld Texas Instruments computer. Fischer Black at MIT and Myron Scholes at University of Chicago determined how to value stock options and not many traders at that time understood how to use this model. Joe was a revolutionary in that he was the first person to program that into a hand-held computer that could be used on the floor. I give all the credit to Joe for coming up with that ingenious program and am eternally grateful for him sharing it with me. He explained that the reason he was inclined to show this to me was because he really appreciated how supportive I had been toward him when I coached him to get into the commodities arbitrage business where he was hugely successful.

With this program I prepared tables of theoretical values for the full range of stock option exercise prices and expiration dates. By today's standards this was rudimentary but at the time it gave me a substantial edge over the other traders on the floor of the CBOE. This would be the foundation of my trading style for my remaining years on the CBOE floor.

The whole idea of trading is to get a statistical edge just like casinos do in Las Vegas. A casino has odds in their favor, the players have odds against them, which dictates that if the player played enough, they lost and the casino won. Therefore, because the odds are that the casino would eventually win, it's a matter of how many times one plays. Now, some people made money as players in a casino, but their chances of making money overall diminished the more they played. As our business consisted of trading on the floor of the Exchange, we were the house and the public customers were the players. So we bought a stock option lower than what it was supposed to be trading at, and then sold it later when it was trading for more than it was supposed to be trading. In this way, we earned a statistical advantage. Now what went wrong with this strategy is that while we were waiting to sell it for a better price, the stock may have moved, and I may have made or lost a whole lot of money. However, hedging was a method of protecting against stock movement by establishing an opposite position, such as selling short the stock against a long options purchase. When hedged, a trader can wait for the options to return to the proper theoretical price relative to the underlying stock. If I bought options and sold short the stock, I had a neutral position. I was hedged, so that it didn't matter whether the stock went up or down. When I was trading on the floor, I traded with a theoretical edge. After considering difficulties in timely hedging, my edge was razor thin. But I took full advantage of it by trading higher volume than any other market maker in the same stock options. That translated into a handsome income.

By 1977, when I was 33, I had made my first million dollars. Since Peggy believed that we now had enough money on which to live comfortably for the rest of our lives, she urged me to retire and get out of the business while I was ahead. Peggy is very conservative and feared the unpredictable nature of the stock market. I explained to her that my involvement in trading the Exchange was about more than just making money. After enduring the frustrating times of working a dead end job, I had finally found one that I loved, that I thrived in, and excelled at. This satisfaction was something that money can't buy. Leaving the trading business was just not in my game plan.

That year, after having convinced myself that I could make money in any of the three businesses I was in (commodities broker, commodities floor trader, and options market maker), I decided to concentrate on the one I liked best which was market maker on the CBOE. I resigned my book of customers at Drexel Burnham, returned the Chicago Board of Trade membership to them and bought a membership on the CBOE. I became a one-man trading business on the CBOE.

At first my trading was disciplined and consistent. Then I started getting very bullish about the stock market, and rather than being perfectly hedged, my positions became more dependent on the market going up. I experienced some real ups and downs. In a waterfall crash of October 1978, I took quite a bath to the degree that I lost most of what I had made. It was a major blow, not only to me, but to so many market makers on the floor of the CBOE.

Realizing that I had been much too bullish, I went back to hedging my trading and I was able to recover most of my money. After recouping my losses, I once again became overconfident and took another shellacking in the market break of October 1979. This time I was left with virtually no working capital, although I had various assets which could be financed to recapitalize my trading account. Peggy was dismayed that I could swing from such financial success to a distressed condition. She would never again be confident that the money I made was permanent. This was when I realized that making money wasn't as easy as I thought. I really reflected and thought about what I had done when I gave up a very secure position at Drexel and the rather large customer business I had cultivated there. Perhaps I should have stayed put. However, because I'm not one to look back or harbor regrets, I knew that I had to move ahead and rethink what I was doing. With all the income opportunity available by using proper hedging, it was unnecessary to be as speculative as I had been. On 1 January 1980 I deposited a mere $10,000 in my trading account and resolved never again to lose my discipline. It was straight up from there.

4. NEW HORIZONS: 1980–92

I think that traders are able to assume a certain amount of risk. The trick to surviving, on the trading floor or floating above the Australian desert, is managing that risk.

Pat Arbor, former Chairman, Chicago Board of Trade
and longtime friend

T he years of my life spanning 1980–92 were marked by new adventures in both business and endurance events. But 1980 was my breakout year. After a severe drubbing in the down market of October 1979, I took a hard look at the excessively bullish strategy I was using and decided I had better change my style. On 1 January, I deposited $10,000 in a market maker account and proceeded with a trading style that did not depend on a bull market. I was quick, bold and aggressive but still used sound trading methodology. By adhering to this strategy I surprised myself by logging 25 consecutive profit months. More surprising was the income: I averaged over $5 million a year and even that doubled in the mid-1980s. I never imagined that income was available just by applying myself and grinding out the trades. In retrospect, market making on the floor of an exchange is the only thing I have ever done where I seemed to have the inherent abilities to be most successful. My competitive nature, combined with the methodical use of statistical probabilities, added up to a winning formula.

After making this financial comeback in 1980, I figured, 'Well, this really looks good. I know how to make money. All I have to do is show other people how to do the same: hire some people and train them.' At Christmas in 1980, I sat down at the dining room table in my parents' house and designed an employment contract for floor traders. I specified that my company would provide the trading capital in a separate account to an employee who would be trading as a member of the Chicago Board Options Exchange. There would be a small salary but the most rewarding aspect was a bonus plan to pay 45% of trading profits without any upside limit. The trader's performance dictated his compensation without risking his own assets. In exchange for teaching them my trading strategy, the traders would sign a three-year commitment, after which they would be free to go into business for themselves. Or they could renew for additional years at a higher percentage of profit, like 55%. It was a golden opportunity. In those days, most of the people who ended up trading on the floor of the Exchange worked their way up from being runners and other lower level positions and by happenstance got an opportunity to get into trading. Now I was able to offer an employee an entrée into the trading floor straight out of school, which was very appealing as a first-time job.

Since I would be training them, I decided that experience was not important and that the brightest and most professional would be most likely to succeed. Therefore, I turned to the best employment pool for this venture—graduating MBAs. With the unlimited income opportunity, I attracted applicants from the top Graduate Schools of Business. By the mid-1980s there were between 50 and 60 traders working for me and I was still trading on the floor myself. Although I was not successful in training anybody to trade just like me, there were many success stories and the business was highly profitable until I sold it in 2000. I take particular pride in the fact that, over the years, I brought 168 people into this business as exchange members on nine different exchanges.

Having my own business meant I could make my own decisions on how much to work and how much time to take off. I worked hard. But I was also determined to dedicate about six weeks a year to do some of the most interesting things I could think of.

In 1978 and 1979, I participated in the World Loppet League, which organizes national distance cross-country ski races in nine countries. These races ranged from 42 to 90 km (26 to 56 miles). I sought to be the first person to complete all nine races. A number of other skiers had the same idea so that in February 1979 a total of nine of us completed the sweep of the World Loppet League races on the same date. In the years since, it is interesting that over 1000 skiers have completed this challenge. I also took up cycling for exercise and endurance training. In September 1983 I entered the Paris–Brest–Paris cycling race. I didn't plan on winning. My goal was simply to finish the 762-mile race, which I did. I was dead tired after crossing the finish line. In hindsight, I could have really used a few more months of serious training. The more extreme adventures I pursued during those years lured me to the remotest corners of the world. In addition to doing marathons, cross-country ski races, and triathlons, I took on the Seven Summits mountaineering project and swimming the English Channel.

SWIMMING THE CHANNEL

My first major project was to swim the English Channel. Although I'm not a flashy swimmer and in fact didn't even make the varsity swim team in high school, I thought that, with my prior distance swims during my college years, I could do it. To develop my endurance for this challenge, I trained by swimming a mile a day after work in the Chicago Union League Club pool. On weekends I would head out on longer swims of three to five miles in Lake Michigan. On one particular Sunday, after I had already made two attempts at swimming the English Channel, I was swimming the inside perimeter of the breakwater outside of Navy Pier when a police boat pulled up and informed me that I had to get out of the water.

'Why? What's wrong?' I asked them.

'You're not allowed to swim here,' they replied.

Apparently, this was actually a law; one that I had not been aware of. They ordered me into the boat, but I refused at first as this didn't make any sense to me. As I was treading water, I explained what I was doing, that it was part of my training program, but they wouldn't listen. I didn't put up a struggle when they practically pulled me out of the water. When they brought me to shore, I looked around for my clothes that I had left on the beach but soon discovered that my shirt and pants had been stolen. I was able to find my tennis shoes and put them on just before they escorted me to the police car and hauled me off to the station. I was being arrested! I was charged with the city ordinance of 'endangering my life and the lives of others'. I was fingerprinted and put in a cell next to three just arrested transvestites who found my predicament hilarious. I was still in my swimsuit and my tennis shoes were clumsily, half falling off my feet. As a standard practice to prevent self-hangings, the officer confiscated the shoelaces from my shoes. Having watched the whole event from our 47th floor apartment that overlooks the water, Peggy waited by the phone for my single permitted phone call. When I called, she came down to the station and bailed me out for $50.

It turned out that I had the same court date as the transvestites. We were good old laugh-it-up buddies by then. Determined to clear the charges against me, my friend and attorney, Chris Cohen, strategically pulled out numerous articles and began working the courtroom before the judge came in. He showed the Clerk of the Court pictures of me and newspaper articles about an earlier attempt to swim the English Channel. When the Judge came in and my case came up, Chris pulled out the articles and starting chatting with the Judge about my attempts to swim the English Channel. Finally the Judge said, 'What's going on here? I've heard enough, just get outta here!' My case was dismissed. If only swimming the English Channel was that easy . . .

Since 1875, when the merchant navy captain Matthew Webb was the first to swim from England to France, thousands have tried to swim the English Channel and only about 400 have succeeded. Swimming the English Channel is about as physically demanding a thing as a person can do. Because of the threat of hypothermia, the sheer distance and the constant need for energy replacement, the English Channel is considered by most to be an ultimate endurance challenge.

The strict rules enforced by the Channel Swimming Association, which presides over each attempt, do much to see that swimming the English Channel remains one of the most difficult of tests. Wetsuits are strictly prohibited. The only equipment permitted is a non-insulating swimsuit, a bathing cap, goggles, nose clip, earplugs, grease and a light stick for swimming at night. The swimmer is allowed no contact with the boat crew or the mandatory escort boat and is required to provide their own food for the day, which is fed to them at intervals by the boat crew from a pole. At no time, including during feedings, can a swimmer touch the escort boat as doing so results in disqualification.

It took me four attempts before I successfully swam all the way across the English Channel. On my first try, I learned just how important it was that the captain of the escort boat knows what he's doing. The boat captain has the critical job of keeping the swimmer on track. He must be familiar with the strong tides that rip up and down the Channel, flooding into and out of the North Sea every six hours. Stories abound of swimmers who have been ever so close to the French coast after twelve hours in the water only to struggle for another four hours with a flood tide carrying them sideways. My first attempt ended after the strong tides had shifted on me and the driver of my escort boat, unaware of what he was doing, led me in the wrong direction and I was horribly out of position to complete the swim.

My second attempt in 1982 was aborted due to windy conditions, which generated very high seas from the onset of my swim. The waves were so high that as I swam well to the side of the escort boat, I was often unable to see it beyond the crest of the waves that blocked my view. The relentless motion of rising over the high waves and falling into the low troughs was making me seasick. Because I grew increasingly nauseous, which impeded my ability to keep some food down for nourishment, I decided to abandon my attempt after a few hours. My third failed attempt was perhaps the most frustrating for me as the outcome could've easily been avoided. My swim ended not because of my performance but the incorrect information provided by the boat captain. Nearly 9 hours into my crossing, the captain informed me that I was only a third of the way across, when in fact I had been halfway. Based on his estimation, which I accepted at the time, there was no way I could've stayed in the water for another 18 hours. Back on shore, where I reviewed the chart, I realized that instead of a third of the way, I had made it to half way across! I was incensed! I could've easily endured another nine hours in the water to swim the remaining half. The Channel crossing had been firmly within my reach but was terminated due to error. For a person like me who always does his homework, who thoroughly calculates the facts and figures, this careless mistake was hard for me to swallow.

For my fourth attempt in September 1985, I left no room for error. This time, I brought along my climbing partner Dick Stockment and Bo Kemper, a personal friend in Chicago, to ride on the escort boat to manage my feedings but also to make sure I had accurate information on the progress of the swim. With Channel water ranging from 58 to 62 degrees F (14.5 to 16.5 degrees C) during the warmest month, hypothermia is a big risk. My defense was to swim hard at 70 strokes per minute to maintain body heat. This worked until early in the evening when fatigue set in and the sun set below the horizon. My limbs started feeling heavy and slightly numb due to the reduced circulation in these extremities. To make matters worse, the tide had turned against me, a setback that would lengthen the time of my swim and my battle with the cold. As the hours ticked by, both Dick and Bo kept a constant eye on my condition. Despite the cold's effects on my body and the moisture from the sea spray that accumulated in my lungs, I could still count my fingers and remember my name. This is a test that open-water swimmers use to ensure that hypothermia doesn't become life-threatening.

In the hours that followed, I swam by pure will and with the satisfaction of knowing that I had gone the farthest of any of my Channel-crossing attempts. Mentally, I was optimistic. Having made it that far, I wasn't going to give up. I couldn't give up. When we stopped for my regular feeding breaks, Dick and Bo did their best to cheer me on. Along with the new stats of how much distance I had covered and still had yet to go, the words of encouragement they offered helped to buoy my resolve and warm my spirit.

By the 20th hour, I knew I was getting both close to the finish and close to my breaking point. As I glanced up to the escort boat, the incandescent glow of the spotlight against the austere black backdrop of the night radiated a peaceful effulgence that I hadn't noticed before. By then, the cold had seeped into the core of my being. The constant numbness and exhaustion had driven a dangerous wedge between my mind and body. My body felt like a machine, my strokes mechanical. My mind's job was simply to keep it operating at all costs.

Twenty-two hours 15 minutes after having left Cap Gris Nez on the French side, I dragged myself out of the surf and stood on the rounded stone gravel of Shakespeare Beach. I swam the 21-mile crossing in one of the slowest-ever times. Yet all that mattered to me was that I had made it to the other side and had finally accomplished this very long-range goal. I recalled how, back in 1965, when I was a junior in college, I had wanted to swim the English Channel. Exactly 20 years later I achieved this feat. Although I was thrilled to have made a successful crossing, my immediate concern was my state of health. My body was shaking uncontrollably. I could hardly stand. I had to swim back to the boat where I was pulled in. With my body limp from exhaustion, I cracked a rib in the process. Quickly the escort boat took me to the port of Folkestone where an ambulance was waiting to take me to Ashford Hospital. Once there, my condition was so bad as to be a curiosity to the staff. In addition to hypothermia and a broken rib, I had accumulated water in my lungs from breathing the sea spray all day. The pH of my blood was closer to that of a fish from all the salt water ingested. Surprisingly, the next day I was fine. My steely determination and endurance was acknowledged at the end of the season when the Channel Swimming Association awarded me the Van Audernaerde Endurance Trophy—for making the slowest swim of the year.

THE SEVEN SUMMITS

Another of my greatest ambitions of this time period was to climb the highest peaks on each of the seven continents. In the late 1970s, Seattle climber Jim Henriot spoke of his personal goal to climb the highest mountain on all seven continents. Since then, that dream has captured the imaginations of some of the world's greatest mountaineers who have adopted that quest. I, too, had thought, 'What an interesting achievement that would be!' Had I come up with this in the latest decade, I would have launched into the fray to be the first. But in 1980 I was somewhat circumspect and merely tiptoed into the competition to see how far I could get.

The concept of climbing the highest peak on every continent did not come to the forefront until the Seven Summits were established. We now recognize the Seven Summits as Mt Everest in Asia; Aconcagua in South America; Mt McKinley in North America; Kilimanjaro in Africa; Mt Elbrus in Europe; Vinson Massif in Antarctica, and Carstensz Pyramid in Australasia. The highest peak in the intimidating ice wilderness of Antarctica, Vinson Massif, was not discovered until 1957 and wasn't recognized as the highest summit until aerial and ground surveys were completed in 1961. For many years, climbers flocked to Switzerland's Mont Blanc in the mistaken belief that this was the highest peak in Europe. However, geographers knew that Europe extended part way into Russia and that Mt Elbrus, in the Caucasus mountain range, stood 2400 ft higher than Mont Blanc, making it indisputably the highest peak on the European continent.

MCKINLEY

My foray into this pursuit began with McKinley, which at 20,320 ft is the highest peak in North America and presents a formidable challenge due to its northern latitude and severe weather conditions. The weather in Alaska is severe and, as I would learn, the storms that hit McKinley are frequent and brutal, so much so that it is a rarity to climb this mountain in decent weather the entire way. Even staying at the high camps, which are unprotected and thus vulnerable to winds that can reach hurricane strength, is a risk. The secret of successfully reaching the summit of McKinley is to be prepared to go for the summit right when an amenable weather window opens. In the event of being unexpectedly besieged by a storm while on the route, McKinley first-timers are directed to hunker down and defend their tents from being destroyed by the wind.

My partner on this trip was Dick Stockment, a fellow climber and former colleague at the Chicago Board Options Exchange in the late 1970s. My adventure on McKinley began when we arrived by train in Talkeetna, Alaska in May of 1980 with our 70 lb packs. It takes a lot of gear to climb McKinley. As one Alaskan told me with grandiose understatement, 'bring a hat and maybe some gloves'. In addition to some seriously warm clothing and boots, you need ice climbing equipment for the steep slopes and in the event of having to rescue your climbing companion from a fall into a crevasse. Most expeditions are planned for about 21 days, so climbing this summit necessitates bringing a lot of food.

After our standard bush pilot flight on to the Kahiltna Glacier, we had planned to trek up the glacier on snowshoes. Nobody had told us that mountaineering skis were the new standard equipment. Since we decided not to hire a guide, one of the Talkeetna bush pilots, Kitty Banner, still kids me about how nobody thought we had a chance of making the summit without a guide.

After being flown in by bush pilot Cliff Hudson, we started the long process of carrying our gear up the mountain. One day we would haul our excess supplies up to the site of the next camp where we would leave it in a cache, then return to our tent at the lower camp. The following day we would break camp and hike to the cache and pitch the tent. Thus, two days were needed to make a move to each camp up the mountain. That's okay because if a climber proceeded with only one day per camp to the high camp, he would be virtually certain of getting altitude sickness. It takes some time to acclimatize to altitude and to build the supply of red blood cells that carry oxygen through the body.

After eight days we reached the high camp situated at 17,200 ft, an extreme place for a host of reasons. In addition to the altitude, the temperature was in the vicinity of 0°F (-18°C) with a wind that kept most of the climbers tent-bound. We carried with us the knowledge that many climbers have died on this mountain. This is the psychological baggage one climbs with. One person had died the previous week and while we were at the high camp, another climber was waiting for evacuation due to cerebral oedema.

After a day's wait at high camp for the right weather conditions, Dick and I saw our chance and took it. We left for the summit early before the light of day. On the steep slope to Denali Pass, I was afraid I would have to turn back because my toes were numb and getting colder, and if they froze solid I would have severe frostbite. Once the sun rose and my toes started to thaw, I knew I was good to go to the top. The steep gradient of the snow-laden slopes made for slow and plodded climbing up past Archdeacon's Tower and on to the summit.

Standing on this highest North American point, I marveled at how the Chicago trading floor seemed a universe away. One of the great advantages of working for myself was that I could take six weeks' holiday a year to pursue adventures like this. Although the view was fogged with the ice crystals of an approaching storm front, it was an inspiration to be here. With the threatening weather pattern moving our way, we did not linger on the summit. As we started our descent in tandem with the sun that was moving from its zenith toward the adjacent peaks to the west, the temperature dropped precipitously. Part way down, we encountered a German couple who were making their ascent for the summit. In addition to their steadfast determination, what immediately struck me about them was how extremely fatigued they appeared. In 1980 it was not normal for mountain climbers to use weather forecasting and besides there was virtually no way to receive weather information high on the mountain. What you see is what you've got, so none of us knew that we were racing a storm on that summit day. As we stopped and talked to them, I offered them a candy bar which they gratefully accepted before we parted and went our separate ways.

We arrived safely at high camp that afternoon as the weather was closing in. A blizzard hit the mountain that night which deposited enough fresh snow to make McKinley effectively impossible to climb for many days to come. The next morning, two frostbitten climbers struggled through waist deep snow to get back to base camp looking very much the image of death. They had made a late start with the intention of a bivouac without a tent that night then proceeding to the summit the following day. Luckily, they had not been too high on the mountain and were able to make it down that morning. The German couple did not come down and we sensed that they had not survived. There was no way to mount a rescue attempt in these deep snow conditions. When climbing resumed 10 days later, Austrian climber Peter Habeler was first to reach their lifeless bodies. He told me later that he dragged them out of the trail and gave them a mountaineer's burial: He dropped them into a crevasse. It was the only way to remove them from the main climbing route, out of the path of other climbers.

VINSON MASSIF

My next of the Seven Summits was an epic project that involved going to Antarctica. Having heard about an expedition going there, I got on the phone to introduce myself to Pat Morrow. He referred me to Steve Drogin, the expedition organizer. I offered to pay one person's pro rata share and he was happy to have me join the expedition.

It was around this time that the competition to complete the Seven Summits was heating up. Dick Bass, owner of Snowbird Ski Resort, and Frank Wells, President of Disney, were making a headlong effort to be the first to accomplish this feat. In 1982, they hired a unique polar transport plane that was a converted DC-3, which had skis and three, instead of two, engines. The engines were turbocharged for extra takeoff power. Using this aircraft to take them to the remote region of the Antarctica, the Bass/Wells expedition succeeded in making the ascent of Vinson, which was only the third ever. The first ascent had been made by an American expedition in 1966, nine years after the peak was discovered in 1957.

Quietly in the competition to be first on the Seven Summits was Pat Morrow. Pat had already climbed the hardest one: in 1982 he became the first Canadian to climb Mt Everest. Our expedition to Antarctica targeted getting Pat to the top of Vinson Massif.

The obstacles of Vinson Massif are encountered way before one ever reaches Antarctica. The US Congress has designated the National Science Foundation (NSF) to control all American Antarctic activity. The NSF is only concerned with scientific research and does not condone adventure activities. They do not want the liability of conducting rescues of stranded adventurers. The bottom line is that adventurers cannot visit American bases in Antarctica or receive any cooperation from the NSF. We sought and got cooperation from Chile and Argentina instead. Both countries allowed us to land at their bases in Antarctica and were willing to supply other services, such as dropping off airplane fuel by parachute.

Although the ascent up Vinson is uncomplicated and technically minimal, the remote location, extreme cold and harsh wind make it both costly to travel to and dangerous to climb. Only 750 miles from the South Pole, the lower atmospheric pressure at the poles sucks in air masses into these regions at high altitudes. Once the air cools over the South Pole, it descends rapidly and blasts outwards at high speeds that can reach over 100 mph. These are the katabatic winds. Getting caught in these high winds on Vinson is the most serious aspect of the climb.

It had taken 18 months of unwavering persistence and planning on Pat's part to secure the necessary governmental permissions and to make the other arrangements for our attempt on Vinson Massif. All the effort that it took to get us there was wasted when our plan just to reach the base of Vinson Massif in November 1984 was destroyed by a severe windstorm. On the first day, we landed on the glacier next to the Argentinean base of Esperanza in our Tri-Turbo DC-3 and we were the guests of the base staff for dinner. That night a katabatic wind developed that pounded our camp with winds gusting 100 mph. In the morning, we discovered that our plane had broken its tie-downs and started sliding down the glacier toward the cliff overlooking the Southern Ocean. Luckily, a snow machine had gotten jammed under the wing of the plane and only this stopped the plane from sliding down the glacier and over the edge into the sea.

Although the plane had been saved, its fuselage and wing had been damaged. Luckily, our English pilots were able to get the plane in good enough shape to fly to Rio Gallegos, Argentina for repairs. With fresh memories of the Falklands War, the Argentine military met the plane and put the pilots under house arrest while the necessary repairs were made. Meanwhile our climbing team sat in the walk-in-freezer-style cabins for five days, worrying whether the plane would make it back or whether we would have to wait two months for evacuation by the supply ship that was scheduled to come to the base at the end of the summer season. Despite the anxiety over our future, it was fascinating being there. I never tired of visiting the Adelie penguin colony next to the base. Fortunately the TriTurbo did return and took us back to Punta Arenas, Chile where we reconsidered our options. We decided to try again. This time we only made it as far south as Rothera, the British base. There we experienced an oil pressure problem with one of the engines and we had to retreat to Punta Arenas once again. Our season was over.

In late November 1985, Pat Morrow and I kept our appointment to have another try at Vinson Massif. It was during the Southern Hemisphere's austral summer season, the best time to climb in the

Antarctic as the 24 hours of daylight there take an edge off the perennial cold. Our group of seven climbers landed on the 3-ft sastrugi, which are waves formed by the winds on the hardened snow, and quickly went about setting up the first of our four camps. Even though the weather was on our side at that moment, we felt vulnerable next to the huge swathe of barren ice upon which our camp bordered. Our last experience had made us extra wary of the danger of high winds. Because our isolated location would have precluded any outside intervention if we happened to need it, we cut snow blocks to build protective snow walls around each of our camps as a precautionary measure.

Eager to take advantage of the amenable weather and the constant daylight, we opted to begin our three-hour hike to deliver supplies to the foot of the mountain. Two days later from camp one, we set out for the top of Shinn Ridge, the ridgeline descending from the continent's third highest mountain Mt Shinn. Here, we caught our first spectacular view of Vinson Massif. When we reached camp two, situated on the edge of a glacially carved bowl, we bedded down for some much needed sleep before we were awoken several hours later by a bellowing wind that kept us camp bound the following day. When the winds subsided, we set out for camp three, a climb of 2000 vertical feet that featured a crevassed icefall. Since falling into one of the mountain's many deep crevasses posed a constant threat, we climbed roped together lest one of us fell into one of these icy abysses.

Roped together necessitated that we modify our speed ever so slightly as we climbed. I have always been a paced type of mountain climber. From all my experience on mountain trails, I had developed a pretty good feel as to what pace I can set without needing rest stops. I always had an accurate sense of how much energy my body was using. Over the course of honing my pace, I learned to maintain an even energy expenditure. For instance, I would go much slower up a steep hill and much faster on flat terrain. I opted to set a conservative speed, which allowed me to be successful overall. My speed wouldn't be impressive if one was just looking at an isolated segment of a climb, however the end result was relatively rapid ascents.

By the time the sun dawned on the eighth day, we were determined to put the remaining 4000 vertical feet to the summit behind us. Reaching the base of the 700 ft summit pyramid several hours later, we all stopped to put on our crampons for the final steep climb. Within the hour, I was standing on Vinson Massif's corniced summit smiling from ear to ear with the rest of the team as we posed for our summit picture. As we gathered together before the camera, we unfurled the United Nations flag, which we took turns carrying to the top. This gesture emphasized the autonomy of the Antarctic, which should be open to all the world's people. With the click of the shutter, we broke our pose as we shouted out in celebration. Everyone hugged one another. Then we turned to take in the unobstructed 360-degree view, which served to substantiate our accomplishment. It had been nine days since we had left the base camp. As I looked out over the vista below, I just shook my head in wondrous amazement that we had become just the fourth group to ascend this mountain.

CARSTENSZ PYRAMID

My next Seven Summits climb was both similar to and completely different from Vinson Massif. In May 1986, Pat Morrow and I teamed up again to climb Carstensz Pyramid, the highest mountain in the Australasian area. While we Americans regard Australia as a continent, geographers consider the continent to be Australasia, which includes New Guinea, and the other surrounding islands. Since our climb of Vinson, Dick Bass had made a successful ascent of Mt Everest and laid claim to being the first to climb the Seven Summits based on climbing the highest mountain in Australia: Mt Kosciusco, a modest 7310 ft peak at the top of a ski resort. Seemingly beaten in the race for the Seven Summits, Pat Morrow still wanted to finish the project in its purest form with a climb of Carstensz Pyramid, the highest mountain in Australasia at 16,800 ft. Named after the Dutch navigator Jan Carstensz, who was ridiculed by his Dutch countrymen after having reported seeing a snow-capped mountain just 4 degrees south of the Equator, Carstensz is located on the Indonesian western half of the island of New Guinea known as Irian Jaya. It is the highest mountain existing between the Andes and the Himalayas. The snow-dusted summit of Carstensz juts out of jungles below and is buttressed by gray limestone faces. Like Vinson Massif, Carstensz is all but inaccessible. Between the government that tries to keep all visitors out due to the occasional threat of guerrilla warfare in that area and the dense wall of rainforest that acts like a fortress to the mountain, not many venture into this lost world. In 1984, when Pat Morrow and his wife Baiba traveled to Irian Jaya to climb Carstensz, they were informed that the permits they had diligently obtained before arriving meant nothing to the military authority responsible for

Irian Jaya. Since then, it had taken Pat over a year to procure the more complete permission for us to climb Carstensz. Because we wanted to enter the area from the site of a huge open pit copper mine, which was only a day's hike to the base of the mountain, I contacted Milton Ward, President of Freeport McMoRan mining company and secured his invitation to cross their Timbagapura mine site. This defused the reservations of the Indonesian government in issuing their permits to us.

The climb was very intriguing from a cultural perspective. Visiting the area, which is still largely untouched by modern civilization, was like stepping back into the Stone Age. Native porters, some wearing no clothes except for a penis gourd, led us up the mountain to the campsites. The Dani tribe that we caught a glimpse of as we traveled through their villages was fascinating. The people in this isolated part of the world still use stone axes and grow primarily potatoes for food.

The ascent to this peak required rock-climbing abilities and thus qualified Carstensz as the most technically challenging of all the Seven Summits. Unlike some of the other peaks where a climber has to deal with the dangers of capricious weather, the rain in Irian Jaya comes year round and almost daily making the weather more predictable and therefore, unavoidable. Everyday like clockwork at around noon, rain clouds rose up from the jungle basin toward the mountain, drenching any climber on the mountain.

After hiking to base camp and preparing for two additional days, on 7 May we made our ascent for the summit. That morning I would learn first-hand how the after-effects of rain could be a real detriment. I was climbing the first pitch of our long day, which was muddy and slippery from the previous night's downpour. Suddenly, I lost my foothold on a patch of mud that gave out. I abruptly slid down the steep crack until Pat stopped the fall with the rope from his belay point above.

Although the route to the summit looked extremely hard from our vantage point at the lower elevations, once we started up, we were very surprised that everywhere we reached on the abrasive rock faces, we were able to find protrusions to grip onto to climb higher. Nevertheless it was a lot of rock climbing. We made 19 roped pitches on the way up including several rappels on the knife-edge ridge. Hanging along the face of these sheer drop-offs, my adrenaline got a kick every time I looked down. The crux of the climb was chimney and overhang at rock climbing grade 5.8. Then with only a few paces left before we reached the top, Pat, Baiba, our two Indonesian climbing companions and I paused so we could clamber up the last section of rock together. This was our second summit together and an enormously special moment for Pat. Making it to the top of Carstensz concluded his Seven Summits project, which he began in June 1977 with Mt McKinley. Elated with our own sense of personal triumph, we took photographs of each other to capture the moment.

As we stood together, straining to see the view that lay beyond the enveloping thick blanket of fog, we rested for a while to gather our wits for the decent. Our climb was only half over. Rappelling the steep dangerous faces going down would prove more mentally challenging than going up. A plaque that we found near the summit that memorialized a climber who fell to his death en route to the base camp from the peak warned us of this danger.

After getting caught in a profuse rainstorm on the north face that had us carefully moving through the water streaming off the rock face, we finally completed our last three rappels in the dark and rain to the bottom at 9 pm. We were soaked and happy to finally be down off this dangerous mountain, as we headed toward the shelter of our warm tents.

MT ELBRUS

The last mountain I climbed with Pat Morrow was Mt Elbrus in Russia during August 1986. The highest peak in Europe, Mt Elbrus looms at an elevation of 18,481 ft and is a massive double-peaked extinct volcano ensconced in ice. Although Elbrus is a straightforward ascent on moderately angled snow and ice slopes, the altitude and ever-changing weather prevent many climbers from making it to the top. Once at the summit, there is little shelter from the elements. Although Pat had successfully ascended to Elbrus' east peak in 1983 during his Seven Summits bid, he was coming back to Elbrus for the 39 ft-higher west peak, which whiteout conditions had prevented him from safely realizing during his previous attempt.

Since Elbrus takes ten hours to climb from the Priutt Hut and descend back to the trailhead, we awoke the next morning before daybreak and started out for the summit. Under the stillness of a canopy of stars, we trekked together in perfect silence save for the sound of the snow compressing under the weight of our steps. In addition to the headlamps that we each wore, a near full moon shone brightly to offer further illumination and animate a retinue of abstract shadowy forms that moved with us upon the snowfields that we trod.

For the duration of our ascent up the mountain, it was pretty cloudy. We spent the day moving slowly as the sun tried persistently to penetrate through the thick cloud layer. When the curtain of clouds finally parted, we were able to take in the breathtaking view of the adjacent peaks and glaciers that had been obscured since our arrival.

Elbrus turned out to be the easiest of all three of our climbs together. It wasn't too technically difficult and we didn't have any severe weather conditions to deal with. Once we reached the higher elevations, a strong and steady wind kicked up snow limiting our visibility. It started snowing slightly as we reached the saddle of the mountain where we stopped to put on our crampons. Luckily the weather didn't turn on us and we were able to make it to the summit two hours later.

In the winter of 1985, Peggy and I traveled to Beaver Creek, Colorado where I competed in the Mountain Man Triathlon, which entails cross-country skiing, snowshoeing, and ice-skating. We were immediately enchanted with the pristine rural terrain and the year-round sports activities that this area has to offer. Once again in 1986 I entered the Mountain Man Triathalon and really started thinking about having a home in Beaver Creek. We organized a separate trip to look at houses. Due to the weak real estate market, we could drive the streets and virtually every house we would ask about, the real estate broker would say, 'Yes, it's for sale. I know where the key is to show the house.' We picked the house we liked best and bought it. We never looked anywhere else.

Although Chicago would remain our primary residence, we started going up to our house in Beaver Creek almost every weekend after that. At the end of a long busy week on the trading floor, Beaver Creek became our home away from home. I soon realized that the landscape around our home provided great training grounds for mountain climbing. At our house, the elevation is about 8200 ft, from where I could make my way directly up into the mountains to 11,000 ft. Hiking, biking, cross-country skiing, or snowshoeing, depending on the season, were great acclimatization and training for my ensuing climbing expeditions.

KILIMANJARO

Having climbed three of the Seven Summits with Pat Morrow and one with Dick Stockment, I became intent on summiting the last three—Kilimanjaro, Aconcagua and Everest. In April 1987, I set out for Kilimanjaro, the highest mountain in Africa, with Pat Arbor, a close friend of mine from Chicago. Located in Northeast Tanzania, near the Kenyan border and reaching a 19,340-ft elevation, Kilimanjaro is an extinct volcano, one of the most massive in the world. Standing alone in the surrounding plains, Kilimanjaro appears to be an island unto itself. Due to its high elevation and proximity to the Equator, Kilimanjaro is home to five climatic regions. Beginning at the lower elevations, one passes through a dense tropical rainforest, then a savanna, alpine moorland and barren desert before traversing a snowfield en route to the summit.

Heading up the mountain on our first day, Pat and I were dripping with perspiration as we moved through the humid, dense rainforest that was teeming with wildlife. There, we managed to view a few screeching colobus monkeys that were hanging on some tree branches and heard the melodic calls of the great-crested hornbill. That day, we arrived at our first camp, the Mandara Hut, at 9000 ft where we stayed for the night. In the morning, we continued on through the rainforest. As we stepped out onto the open moorlands on the southern slopes of Mwenzi, it was shocking to see how the rainforest abruptly ended. Although Pat and I didn't have any difficulties with the gradual increase in elevation, we passed some climbers who had developed altitude sickness most likely as a result of not having paced themselves up the mountain. The final camp was a hut at 15,000 ft.

We started before dawn and plodded up the long scree slope toward the crater rim. As we neared the summit, it was my nose not my eyes that let me know we were almost at the top. I could detect traces of sulfur in the air that were produced by the steaming fumaroles on the floor of the inner crater. When we reached the rim of Kilimanjaro on the fifth day, we walked along the expansive, snow-covered terrace toward the highest point. After exploring the summit, we headed back down the same day. I had really enjoyed this climb, which had been free of such hassles as government regulations and severe weather conditions.

MT EVEREST: PART I

The ease of climbing Kilimanjaro would stand out in stark contrast next to the memory of my experience on Mt Everest, indisputably the hardest of the Seven Summits to climb. My first attempt to climb Everest in the Himalayas was in September 1987. This was not the best time for me, as things at work were getting hectic as a result of the market's volatility that year. I was at the pinnacle of my business career and had all this trading activity going on that needed tending to. Although I had already made prior arrangements to climb Everest in September, I left for Asia with a lot weighing heavily on my mind.

I went to Everest with the Snowbird Everest Expedition that was trying to get the first American woman to the summit. Of course everybody on the climbing team of about ten hoped for a shot at reaching the summit. The trouble, I learned, with climbing in the Himalayas is the huge amount of time that it demands, during which one basically sits around at base camp waiting for the right weather conditions to develop and getting acclimatized to altitude. Climbing Everest is a six-week project while the final summit drive is typically only four days. While I was used to waiting a few days for favorable weather conditions before climbing other summits, on Everest the weeks of waiting tested my patience to its limit. What made it worse was that there was little else to do but wait. For instance, I would like to have used the time to get in a workout, but even that came with objective risks. If I ventured out to climb the Khumbu Icefall, I would have to risk falling into a crevasse or getting hit by a collapsing serac. If you do a hard day at this altitude like climbing the icefall, you're ready to rest the next day. When it appeared that an amenable weather window would never arrive, I finally got too impatient. At that point of my life I was clearly too impatient to succeed on Everest. I departed for home after less than a month. As it turned out, patience would not have paid in 1987—the weather never did cooperate and none of the climbers on our expedition made the summit. Less than a month later, the crash of 1987 occurred, which made me particularly glad that I had returned to the States when I did. I would have loathed returning from Everest to find my business in a shambles due to the October debacle in the stock market.

The one thing that I had figured out about the stock markets is that nearly every crash over the course of the twentieth century always happened in the month of October. This includes the Crash of 1929 and, from my personal experience, the waterfall collapses of 1978 and 1979. During the crash of 19 October 1987, my third experience of a crash, many of my traders and some of my customers lost a lot of money. So did I. It was a doozy. The Dow Jones collapsed an astounding 520 points in one day which was an unprecedented 22% of the value of the Dow Jones Average. My business of options market making was highly leveraged and the scale of that drop far exceeded what we thought we would ever need to be prepared for. Most of us in floor trading were thrown into survival mode. Had I still been on Everest, the massive and immediate position reductions necessary to survive could not have been implemented in my absence. It took me nearly a year to earn back what I had lost in October 1987. Then a spooked market on Friday 13th in October 1989 caused margin calls, which again put me in survival mode. 'Was this a vicious circle?' I wondered. More than that, the crashes of 1987 and 1989 heralded some significant changes in the trading world. MBAs were now getting greater incentive to go to work in other fields of employment. Things had changed to such a degree that the compensation contract I was offering was no longer competitive for the top graduates in the job market. By the late 1980s and early '90s the appeal of the trading business had faded enough that I had to be content with hiring graduates with four-year degrees instead of MBAs. More people understood the theoretical edge of options trading, and so each trader was making less money. Meanwhile, the rest of the economy had moved forward.

It was at this time that I took a good hard look at my involvement in the trading business. I had tired of the vicissitudes of making and losing money. I didn't want to spend my whole life focused on making money when I already had enough, especially when there were so many interesting sports projects that I could take on. In a dramatic move at the end of 1990, I turned over management of our cadre of floor traders to Bob Kirkland who had proved over the years that he could carry the responsibility. And I was outta there! I never again made a trade on the exchange floor even though I maintained my membership on the New York Stock Exchange and other exchanges. Peggy—who had retired from her job two years previously—and I became full-timers at our house in Beaver Creek, Colorado. And the lifestyle was great. Most days I would participate in two sports and sometimes three. I completed one of my goals of climbing all 54 of the peaks over 14,000 ft in Colorado. I finished the Leadville 100, an awesome 100-mile running race in the mountains at altitudes of up to 12,600 ft.

I had turned my life upside down: I made my business career secondary and made my adventure goals my primary focus. The call of adventure was still luring me and I realized that life was too short for all that I still wanted to experience outside of the corporate world. I told myself that I had the resources and it was time to pursue what I loved doing.

THE IDITAROD

The taste that I had cultivated in college for pursuing adventures that were historically significant as well as challenging sparked my interest in the Iditarod. The Iditarod Trail Sled Dog Race, usually called the 'Iditarod' is an annual dog sled race held in Alaska. The Iditarod is an enchanting tradition that celebrates dog sledding as a mode of transportation integral to the Alaskan way of life.

The Native American Yupiat and Athabaskans first established portions of the Iditarod trail long before the Russian fur traders used them during the 1800s. Between the 1880s and the mid-1920s, the trail saw heavy traffic by miners who came to Alaska for the gold. When northern ports like Nome became icebound, dog sledding was relied upon to deliver mail, firewood, mining equipment, gold ore, food, fur and other essential supplies between the trading posts and settlements that dotted the Interior and the western coast. In addition to commemorating the legacy of dog mushing in general, the Iditarod pays homage to this method of transportation for saving the children of Nome from a diphtheria epidemic. In stages like the Pony Express but with dog sleds, diphtheria serum was rushed to Nome in 1925. Today, for many Alaskans who live what is called 'bush style'—inhabiting modest cabins that lack heating systems and piped water and getting by with only the bare essentials—dog sledding is still used by some for hauling supplies from far distances. For a city dweller like me, competing in the Iditarod would feel like stepping back in time.

For years I had harbored the ambition to one day compete in the Iditarod, an aspiration that I acted on toward the end of the 1980s, when I looked into how to prepare for this race. Participating in the Iditarod involves covering approximately 1160 miles over a wide variety of terrain from the coastal areas near Anchorage, to the Alaska mountain range, to the Yukon River and over to the frozen coastline approaching Nome on the Bering Straits. With different terrain came all kinds of weather conditions from just above freezing to −50°F (−46°C), from blizzards to clear nights with the Aurora Borealis filling the sky. Entering an Iditarod can take years of preparation as mushing in such grueling conditions is not something that one casually undertakes, nor without extensive training.

Without so much as ever having a pet dog, I was determined to lead a team of dogs through the hazardous terrain of the Iditarod trail. I was introduced to a top musher named Bruce Johnson who lived with his family in a remote homestead in the Yukon. The year before I met him, he won the second most important dog sled race, the 1000-mile Yukon Quest. After talking it over with him, Bruce agreed to teach me the sport. Over the next four years, I would travel from Chicago to the Whitehorse area in the Yukon to train with him for a few weeks each year. After extensive training and feeling like I knew what I was doing, I began entering some 'middle distance' races, which were still 300 miles. In 1991 I entered my first Iditarod. It was extremely difficult, ridiculously frigid, and overly exhausting and I loved every minute of it. For my preparation, I closely studied the trail and trained with my team on parts of it. A major concern is not to get lost or deviate off the course. Although the trail is established with a snow machine track, subsequent snowstorms can make the trail difficult to decipher. Straying off course can be costly as it isn't always easy to get back on it. Although the dogs run willingly even through the harshest conditions, they lose their enthusiasm or can become confused if they have to backtrack over the same stretch of terrain.

Although the dogs have more than enough physical stamina to complete a two-week race, I learned from my 1991 attempt that keeping them motivated was a real test. That year, I got about halfway to McGrath and just couldn't manage to keep the team going. The dogs weren't so much tired as psychologically defeated. My lead dog Suzie had lots of years running trails and knew a few tricks herself. I was not her regular master and she dared to victimize me. As she was leading the team through the night, she would sometimes spot a tree or other protected area, which would logically be a good spot for a regular six-hour stop. Then at full speed she would lead the team off the packed trail and into the soft snow. This is a mess—the team becomes bunched up in the deep snow, and the natural animosity between various dogs results in a dogfight breaking out. Even without a fight, I would have to untangle the traces and pull the dogs out of the snow onto the track. Other times fights would break out during feeding breaks. These fights are an awesome sight because the dogs gang up on a 'scapegoat' and try with all their viciousness to kill the victim dog. I would have to run into this tangle kicking them with my boots to get their attention and grab the dogs by the collar to pull them away from each other. It always amazed me that in the frenzy of a dogfight they still recognized their master and did not attempt to bite me. These off-course excursions and fights quickly demoralize the dog team and motivation and performance deteriorates progressively.

Also in this 1991 attempt, my sled was not strong enough for the wicked high-speed downhills that often sent me pitching over the handlebar, or required me to tip the sled on its side to create more drag to slow the team. One broken upright detracted from the strength of the entire sled structure and more of the wood components broke. I made repeated temporary lashings, but my sled was virtually destroyed. I limped across the long 75-mile leg, which included the desolate Farwell Burn, with my broken sled and unruly dog team. Finally, I arrived at the remote village of Nicholai, where I gave my team an extra long rest while shop repairs were made to my sled. After a day I continued on to the town of McGrath but still had trouble with both the sled and my dog team. I wanted to continue, but finally I had to admit my team was wrecked psychologically. If the dogs won't go, I can't go. Although this was a huge letdown for me, I promised myself that I would come back to Alaska and complete the Iditarod the following year.

Although they found it humorous that I was out there, my first year as a rookie with my errant dog team and a completely broken down sled tied together in pieces, the people of Alaska were fully supportive of what I was trying to do. Here I was, a Chicagoan, an unusual participant indeed. I was an interloper, but they respected the fact that I didn't want to leave the race in 1991 and that I vowed to come back and finish the race next year.

In preparation for the 1992 Iditarod, I considered what I would have to do. I could no longer use the dog team of Bruce Johnson who had loyally taught me the sport over the past five years. These dogs looked to Bruce as their master and would never perform 100% for me. My plan was to form a new dog team. Many of the Alaskan mushers who are top competitors raise their dogs from puppies, thus establishing an enduring relationship with their dogs.

They must dedicate their lives to the sport of dog sled racing and the preparations. During the summer they might work on construction jobs to earn enough money to train throughout the winter with their team in preparation for the Iditarod in March. Iditarod competitors come back year after year; in fact, many who raced when I did in 1991 and 1992 are still top competitors. Having my own kennel to develop a strong team would not work for me. I proceeded to lease for the season 27 good dogs from five different racing kennels. With this mix of sources, the dogs collectively would not have a strong bonding to a prior master. I hired Mike Madden, who finished in 13th place in 1991, as the trainer. From the time the snow was on the ground until the race started in March, Mike would train the dogs for half of the time and I would come up to Fairbanks from Chicago to train them for the other half of the time.

Everything Bruce Johnson taught me worked, but I had to apply it to a new team.

The best training trip was a trial run of the final third of the Iditarod course from Shaktoolik to Nome. I loaded my dog team and sled into a small Cessna 206 and the bush pilot flew us from Fairbanks to the windswept native village of Shaktoolik. With dogs piled in willy-nilly, I imagined that I would have my hands full breaking up dogfights. But the dogs were mesmerized and sat silently throughout the flight. It was an unforgettable ethnological tour where, each night, I stayed in the home of a local family and ate their food, whether it was recently hunted caribou or home-canned salmon from the prior season. The training was great for the dogs because they would get familiar with the trail they would actually be running in the race. On the day the Iditarod started, the whole city of Anchorage came to a screeching halt as thousands of spectators turned out to see the teams lining up on Fourth Avenue to get underway at two-minute intervals that began at 10.00 am. As the race official counted down the start time, excitement electrified the air. I was a bit nervous and somewhat relieved when my best lead dog, Gus, remained unfazed by all the commotion. He was as cool and composed as could be. With all the cheering fans, flashing cameras and the proximity of the other barking dog teams, it is easy for the dogs to get overly excited and running too fast through the tight turns was a major hazard. The Iditarod course, which begins in the city of Anchorage in the southeast, extends up to Rainy Pass of the Alaska Range, then into the sparsely populated interior, and finally along the shore of the Bering Sea before finally reaching Nome in the northwest.

After departing from the first checkpoint of Knik, I headed into the Alaskan bush and the first 100 miles, which is known as 'moose alley' because of the many moose that are found in this region. This is one of the most dangerous legs of the trip as moose, in order to avoid being bogged down in deep snow in the event of an attack by wolves, their natural predator, prefer to stand on the beaten trail and will defend their position against an aggressive team of sled dogs. Invariably, the moose wins—kicking the dogs until they retreat. Susan Butcher, who would go on to win four Iditarods, had to withdraw from the 1985 race when a pregnant moose killed two of her dogs. I count myself lucky to never have had a run-in with a moose during my two Iditarod races, but I've had close calls during training runs.

On the second day I made it to the checkpoint at Skwentna—149 miles into the race—without incident. The Iditarod is a high-speed race and the mushers only carry one day of supplies. A month before the start, we would package all supplies to be transported by bush pilot to the 24 checkpoints. This consists of dog food, dog booties, personal food and changes of long underwear. We would try to time our rest stops to be at checkpoints. Here the mushers could sleep in a cabin or some other village building, but on three occasions I had to roll out my sleeping bag and camp alongside the trail, with a sled cover pulled over me for protection from the elements. As well as resting at the checkpoints we could simultaneously pick up the supply bags. At a checkpoint being used for a rest stop, I first staked out the dog team, fed them, checked their feet, then prepared my own food before getting about two hours' sleep. Then I would get up to prepare the team by hitching them up and putting booties on their feet that were fastened with Velcro straps. Although dogs can run half of the hours of the day, I trained my dog team to run six hours, rest six hours, and repeat that around the clock. The dogs can see the trail just fine in the dark and speed is not diminished in night runs.

Seeing to the safety and health of the dogs is the number one priority enforced by the Iditarod rule. Volunteer veterinarians examine the dogs at the checkpoints and look for signs of injuries and exhaustion before allowing a musher to depart again on the course. This routine was repeated twice a day throughout the race.

As I worked my team toward the mountains of the Alaska Range, the weather turned for the worse and we got caught in a storm. The wind howled and the snow stuck to everything it came in contact with. I followed the narrow trails balanced on one side by a heavily forested incline and ravines on the other side. The tree line and rocks that jut out onto the trail were a constant threat to the safety of the dogs and intactness of the sled. Moving conscientiously through this area, I managed to miss several boulders that could have otherwise been real problems had I hit them.

Having made it safely to Rainy Pass, I rested the dogs and got some badly needed sleep before heading out again up the mountain, to the divide of the Alaska Range and down Dalzell Gorge at a treacherous downhill speed. The dogs can reach 28 mph running downhill and the task here was slowing the team down just to maintain some semblance of control. I would ride the brake at the back of my sled and be ready to drop the snow hook in the snow.

This challenge to slow a dog team down was repeated on the next leg after a rest. It is the Happy River Steps, where the trail drops over a series of bluffs as it descends to a river basin. This is the scene of the most injuries in Iditarod racing. The switchback steep downhill trail is a supreme challenge in slowing down the team. As I would approach the corner of a switchback, even the brake and snow hook was not enough. Finally I would have to turn the sled on its side to create the most drag to slow the team. Descending to Happy River took a heavy toll on my sled the previous year with a broken upright. This year I was relieved to get through without injury or a broken sled. Finally I was solidly in the Alaskan Interior and in good shape. In contrast to my 1991 attempt, I was really pleased with the performance of and the attitude demonstrated by my dogs thus far. My favorite lead dog, Gus, was proving himself to be a real worker. By the time I reached McGrath where I had to scratch in 1991, the temperature had sunk to $-40°F$. This was bitter cold. I anticipated the cold and had two bales of straw sent to the McGrath checkpoint which I spread out for the dogs to sleep on. When the six-hour rest stop was finished, I prepared the team complete with booties on each paw to protect against the abrasion of this extremely cold snow. I called 'OK' for the team to start and they just stood there. After several tries I got the lead dogs to start off, albeit sluggishly. They only went 100 yards and stopped. They were miserable from the cold. I took them back to the checkpoint for an additional three hours of rest in hopes they would be eager to run when completely rested.

After this additional rest, they were willing to start but only just walked a few hundred yards, then stopped. My lead dog, Gus, just wouldn't run and, finally, would not take any steps to get the other dogs moving behind him. Despite my repeated commands, Gus refused to listen and I suddenly feared the worst. Memories flooded my mind from the year before, when I had to withdraw from the race after the team would not obey my commands. I was adamant that this would not happen to me again, especially since the team and sled were in good shape. Calming myself, I realized that the most important thing was to get Gus to move. As lead dog, if he got going, the rest would follow. Even if the other dogs wanted to run, without Gus initiating this action, this simply couldn't happen.

Since whips or any other type of prodding devices were strictly forbidden by the race rules, I had to rely solely on my voice, but my words were falling on deaf canine ears. My directives did not seem to register. I had no choice but to try a last resort strategy that I had heard of other mushers using in this situation. This tactic involved communicating to the dogs in their language.

Leaving my position on back of the sled, I marched up to Gus, and, getting down on my hands and knees, paused for a moment to look him straight in the eyes. Then I bit him on the right ear just hard enough so he squealed. It was hard enough for him to know that I was the lead 'dog', that I was the alpha male in this chain of command. He got the message that I was in charge here and he wasn't. Before Gus' revelation wore off, I hurried back to the sled from where I bellowed in my most commanding tone for Gus to move out. Without a second thought, Gus headed out, with the rest of the team obediently falling in line behind him.

The rest of the race we became tight and raced like a real team. Gus performed everything I asked on command without a hitch. I realized the extra time that I had spent training with my dogs resulted in a bonding that would make all the difference in terms of finishing the race.

The cold abated somewhat over the next two days but it was still $-20°F$ ($-29°C$). My team was entirely comfortable running in this temperature. I would then learn that it was a good thing that I didn't have a long-hair breed of dogs. I caught up to the only team of Siberian Huskies in the race. Unlike my team, where every dog had different markings and were of varying sizes, this Siberian team was beautifully matched. I followed for about one hour then the musher suddenly stopped his team to allow me to pass. 'My team is overheating and we'll take a rest here,' the musher explained as I carefully passed to the side of him. That's interesting—the general public might think the Iditarod is run with purebred arctic dogs like Malmutes or Siberian Huskies, but they are not the right dogs for distance racing. What most of us use is Alaskan Huskies which is any mix you want to breed. The result is, generally, relatively small-boned dogs in the range of 40 to 50 lbs. Just like a cross-country runner, the light build facilitates endurance running. These are also short-haired dogs because at their incredible energy burn levels of 4000–6000 calories per day, they will be able to stay warm enough in all but the most extreme cold temperatures. Usually a little 'wolf' is bred in for aggressiveness. This mixture produces top dog athletes which can, and in fact do love to run the Iditarod. You won't find these scrappy Alaskan Huskies in any dog show! Once I reached the Yukon, the trail got a little easier to follow along the river. I was regaling in the pleasure of mushing a well-prepared team in good conditions. I was reveling very optimistic about reaching the finish line. Eventually the trail led us off the Yukon and over land to Unalakleet, a checkpoint located on the shore of the Bering Straight that demarcates the turn for Nome. At this juncture, I made sure we stopped for the required hours so that all the dogs could get a chance to eat and rest. Since we were closing in on the finish line, I didn't want them to suddenly run out of energy for lack of rest or nutrition.

As we were making our way along the shores of the Bering Sea and toward Nome, the peak performance of the dogs and their heightened enthusiasm seemed to indicate that they knew we were nearing the homestretch of the race. After trekking the 42 miles to Shaktoolik, I was tired and ready to rest at this checkpoint although the team appeared anxious to keep on going. I was intent upon waiting for the following day, right before sunrise, to take off over the sea ice of the frozen Norton Bay, which comprised the next segment of the race. While at Shaktoolik, I was relieved when the native villagers relayed to me that the weather should be fine for the following day. However, after we were already on the trail the next morning and the sun had come up, the wind picked up and the temperature dropped. Hoping that the lashing winds that typically come off the coast wouldn't turn the storm into a blizzard, a common occurrence around there, I stopped to put on an extra layer of clothing under my parka and checked that all the dogs had booties on for protection from the sharp ice crystals. This is a never-ending task because many of the dogs didn't really like having the booties on and had a way of shaking them off while they ran unless I had put them on tightly.

As I left the shoreline of the Norton Sound, I was aware of the exposure I would have until reaching the other side of the frozen bay. Even with a little wind, the blowing snow makes it difficult to see the branches of spruce trees pushed into the ice to mark the route. Moving against the direction of the blowing snow, it stung my skin as it pelted my face. I squinted to see when the loss of visibility made it difficult to keep my bearings. If a full blizzard developed it would be virtually impossible to stay on the trail across ice. Fortunately, the conditions did not worsen and the blowing snow dissipated as fast as it had come up and by the time we hit the flats at the shoreline it was clear again. Gus had picked up the pace and we hoped to make it to Koyuk, the next checkpoint, by late that night.

When night arrived, I caught a glimpse of the lights of Koyuk out in the distance. I thought that I had never seen a sight so welcoming. They promised that rest and shelter were awaiting us. At Koyuk, we bedded down for the night and, having just traversed a 40-mile stretch of ice, I felt like I was in a five-star hotel. Just to be out of the wind was a luxury. After some restful sleep, I prepared the dog team and we started off before the sun came up. My dogs recognized the route from the training run the previous month and the closer we got to the finish line, the keener the dogs seemed to run.

By the time we got to White Mountain we were just 99 miles from the finish line in Nome. The reality of finishing the race gave a shot of adrenaline to my system that warmed my chilled body. I had to curb my enthusiasm because White Mountain was a mandatory six-hour rest under the rules before sprinting toward the finish line. There is intense competition in the race from White Mountain to the finish but I was content with my position. I was just inside the top 50 mushers out of the 76 starters, which was very respectable for a rookie. Once we left the final checkpoint at Safety and took off for the last 22-mile stretch of the course, my dogs could not be contained. They knew the finish was just ahead. As we got closer to Nome, I caught sight of a few spectators who started lining the trail that came into the city. Gus pushed on even harder, like a long-distance runner making a dash for the finish line. As the crowds lining the streets grew denser, the moment that I had envisioned and worked toward for so many years was finally coming to pass. I caught sight of the huge burled arch that reads 'End of the Iditarod Sled Dog Race'. I was heading right for it. As I crossed over the finish line and under the arch, the city's fire siren sounded, announcing my achievement to all in earshot. I had come in 47th place.

In addition to the euphoric feeling of finishing, I was really proud of my dog team and how they had endured through those 14½ grueling days during which we covered 1112 miles. As I stroked Gus's coat, he seemed quite satisfied too. While the press took photos of us and interviewed me, Gus sat with a composed dignity that seemed to suggest that he was born for this type of attention.

Out of all the adventures and races I undertook throughout my life, the Iditarod was the only one that involved working with animals and was somewhat of an awakening for me in this regard. I realized that dogs were much like people in that if you earned their respect and treated them fairly, they would go the distance for you. Although dog sledding races such as the Iditarod are criticized by detractors as being inhumane, the mushers, who are actually out running with their teams, will tell you that their dogs live for this type of work and enjoy pleasing their masters. Moreover, it is not just the winning musher, but also the lead dogs that are recognized at the finish line and at the awards banquet ceremony that follows. Here, in the company of their master, lead dogs of the winning team are presented with a trophy and decorated with wreaths of yellow roses as they are presented before an appreciative audience.

Since I had achieved my objective of finishing the race, this was my last Iditarod. I wasn't going to be a competitor year after year in order to try to rise up into the top 10 finishing places as many other mushers aspire to do. Of course, it seemed such a shame to quit the sport after that because I'd learned so much. I now knew how to do it, what it takes and what the entire process entails. But I had already achieved my objective, and there was no further use for all this knowledge I had accumulated. I hoped that perhaps some day I would at least be able to share my knowledge with another adventurer who was interested in competing in the Iditarod.

Later in the summer of that year, I was sleeping in the warmth and comfort of my own bed in Beaver Creek when Peggy and I were awoken by the sound of the telephone ringing. It was my friend Bob Hernreich calling from a small party across the street. He was requesting that Peggy and I come down and join the gathering. President Bill Clinton and Hillary Clinton were there on a short vacation. Evidently, over dinner that evening, the subject of me having done the Iditarod had come up and Clinton was interested in hearing more about this adventure from me first-hand. Clinton just said, 'Well, call Fossett up and have him come over.' That's when Bob got on the phone and called us. We were already asleep at that point, but we heard the message he left on our answering machine. Peggy and I got up, dressed and walked across the street. As we were walking up to the house, our neighbors, former President Gerald Ford and his wife, Betty, were leaving the party to go home. Everybody was outside saying goodnight to the Fords. Then we were invited in where we all sat around and talked.

As this was the first time we had met the Clintons, what first struck me about Hillary was how effervescent she was, especially for that late hour in the evening. After the introductions were made, President Clinton and I moved away from the group to find a comfortable place to sit. As we discussed the Iditarod, what really impressed me about Bill was his focus. We conversed at some length during which he never once looked away. He seemed completely absorbed in what I was saying. I believe that this is one of his great qualities and a huge source of his charisma. He is so self-confident that he is able to give the other person his full respect and attention.

As we discussed my experience with the Iditarod, I told him that although I had encountered many harsh conditions and challenging situations throughout my life, such as those on my mountain climbing expeditions, the two weeks I had spent racing over the Alaskan trail were special. Of all my adventures thus far, completing the Iditarod had given me the greatest satisfaction. I relayed how finishing the Iditarod my second time out was a major accomplishment since it had been a five-year project to learn how to do something which was not readily available to me. I told him how I had to go up there to the Yukon and to the Alaskan areas to train for the sport, that it wasn't easy to learn and in fact was quite difficult not only to get a dog team to respond to me as their master, but also to train in those conditions and then to race over this extraordinary terrain for an extended period of time. He listened intently as I recounted how I'd never forget racing across the harsh but strikingly beautiful Alaskan landscape, under the canopy of the Northern Lights, through tundra and spruce forests, over hills and mountain passes, along rivers and across frozen seas.

Leaning forward in his chair, President Clinton confided in me that he'd always wanted to compete in the Iditarod, and that he still intended to do so. This response by the President caught me by surprise, but this was definitely a man to be taken seriously. I told him that I would be more than happy to introduce him to the sport. If I could do it, no doubt he was also capable. We spoke of training during two subsequent meetings, but how would he ever find the time? Perhaps this is the advantage I have over many others who would love to be involved in a fascinating adventure like the Iditarod: I take the time and go out and do it.

Part II

FOR THE RECORD: 1992–2005

5. GETTING MY FEET WET

Steve's the most determined guy that sets out to do anything that I know. It's like the kid in him that he didn't grow out of. It's what's charming about him. It's a characteristic he's got that I admire.

Joe Ritchie, Mission Control Director

MT EVEREST: PART II

Within a few weeks of finishing the Iditarod, I returned to Mt Everest for another try at the summit. Having just come off the grueling Alaskan race trail, my decision to attempt Everest in such quick succession turned out to be overly ambitious. I hadn't realized how burned out I was until I reached the base camp for our ascent. It started with an intestinal problem contracted during the trek into Everest Base Camp—a very common problem for climbers. After recovery, I found myself at Camp 2 at 22,000 ft coughing through the night and thinking I was coming down with pulmonary edema. Pulmonary edema is a life-threatening build-up of fluid in the lungs, which requires immediate descent for recovery. It didn't help that my childhood asthma left me with a 20% obstruction of the bronchial tubes making it necessary for me to breathe more to get the same amount of oxygen into my lungs. With the prospect of serious health problems and my impatience with the lack of activity of an Everest expedition, I decided to forgo my attempt. I was disappointed that I did not persist because that expedition was very successful and several of the climbers on our expedition made it to the top of Everest. One of the guides, Vern Tejas, who did come down with pulmonary edema, retreated to lower altitude for a couple of weeks to recover, then proceeded to reach the summit.

It surprised me that I wasn't able to endure and climb Everest. Mountain climbing was my original sport starting at age twelve and over the years I have climbed approximately 350 mountains. In my early years, I thought it was my destiny to climb Everest but now I understand that it is not going to happen. I am not so well suited for Himalayan expeditions: my vulnerability to high-altitude health problems and most importantly my impatience stands in the way. Climbing Mt Everest is supremely difficult. With over 2000 ascents, Everest is a surprisingly common achievement compared to other explorations and adventures. It was around this time that I began to seek out new kinds of adventures, particularly those that I could excel at. I was inspired to do things that nobody had done before. Although I would continue to climb mountains for enjoyment, I found myself heading off to the sea and sky where I could realize more unique achievements in terms of being the fastest or the first.

FIRST-EVER SAILING RACE

By 1992 Peggy and I lived primarily in Beaver Creek and I commuted to Chicago when I needed to look in on the business. I was living the ski resort lifestyle, engaging in some type of physical activity every day and keeping up with business over the phones and Internet. It was a pivotal time for me. I was searching for something new—something that could challenge me in ways that I hadn't been challenged before. Competing in the Iditarod taught me to think outside of the box in terms of what was possible: it had been a long-term, five-year project that involved learning to do something that wasn't readily accessible to me. It necessitated that I cultivate a new skill. Finishing that race proved to me that I didn't need to limit myself to sports that I knew or was familiar with. I was inspired to make a quantum leap in my adventures.

I was 48 years old and had already completed a number of adventures. However, that was when I sat down and asked myself, 'What are the most interesting adventures I can take on?' I identified two new feats: one was to sail solo across the Atlantic and the other was to make the first balloon flight around the world. Moreover, sailing and ballooning had a practical appeal since they were sports that were eminently doable for me as I approached my fifties.

I had never flown a balloon before and had done only a small amount of recreational sailing. With little background in these sports, I know my goals sounded audacious but that's what I wanted. Characteristically, I decide what I want and only then do I figure out if it is something I could accomplish. Then, I set goals within a probable time frame and start taking the steps to achieve those goals. Other people might work differently, but this approach seems to work for me.

In considering the goal of sailing a singlehand (solo) race across the Atlantic, I quickly learned that multihull sailboats are much faster than monohulls. I figured it would take me about 21 days in a monohull or about 14 days in a multihull, either catamaran or trimaran. That's an easy decision: being out in the Atlantic alone for 14 days is a lot better than 21 days! I put out the word to some Chicago sailors that I was interested in sailing a multihull across the Atlantic and all of them immediately pointed to David Scully. Dave, a true adventurer in his own right, was in the process of moving to France to participate in the extraordinary multihull sailing scene. I was formally introduced to Scully by his then girlfriend Lynne Howard, who was one of the floor traders for my company. Dave in turn arranged for me to sail a two-day leg in the Mediterranean with Mike Birch, a Canadian who achieved great success sailing in the French races. It was on *Fujicolor*, the 60-ft trimaran, which was one of the fastest sailboats in the world. I was sold—I had to have one of those French trimarans. Over the next year, Dave helped make the contacts to negotiate to buy one of the top boats. The trouble was there were only six 60-ft trimarans that were of the current generation and highly competitive—and none was actively for sale. After submitting bids over a period of six months to Groupe Pierre Premiere on their boat of the same name, I got the word that the company was closing its sailing program. I made sure I was sitting in their office in Paris the next morning with my new bid. The Managing Director replied, 'Come back this afternoon and we will discuss it further.' Unable to find a French buyer to match my bid in order to keep the boat in the country, he agreed to sell me the boat. One of the finest multihulls in the world was mine.

The first step I took was to rename the boat. To break away from its reputation as a French boat, I wanted an American name. What could be more American than an American Indian tribe—it would be *Lakota*. I still get the occasional French question: 'What is a

Kota?' In a reverse of normal, I renamed my business Lakota Trading Company after my boat.

Our first race was in six weeks and gave us little time to prepare. It was the Two Handed Round Britain & Ireland. This was a 2000-mile race around the British Isles relieved by four stops of 48 hours each. It was just Dave Scully and me to handle this powerful boat: a tall order for me since I had never been in a sailing race, much less sail a big multihull in tough conditions.

As race day approached in early July, I had all the expected jitters and insecurity of a first- time competitor. But once the race began I had more important things to worry about than first-time nerves. Early into the course, I received a lesson in what it means to sail in severe weather conditions. On the first night in the Celtic Sea between England and Ireland we were hit by a storm that churned up huge and fierce waves. The seas rose up like huge mountains all around the boat before crashing over the deck when *Lakota* pitched into them. We were drenched by the waves whenever we had to leave the protection of the cabin to go up to the deck to make the necessary sail changes. We clipped our tethers to the jack lines of the boat to prevent being washed overboard by a surprise wave. Because *Lakota*'s sails were old, they tore under the strain of the gale-force winds and had to be constantly repaired en route. We would have to wait for sea conditions to subside then drop the sails to the deck where we could do some of the sewing. However, most of the repairs had to wait for the next stopover where a sailmaker could make a competent repair. We had another setback when our radar shorted out and we were forced to keep a sharp eye out for shipping traffic and the shoreline until reaching a stopover where we could get a replacement of the radar circuit board. In the end, *Lakota* proved that she had what the best racing sailing boats are made of: Strength and speed. Even while battling the precarious weather, we were able to sail fast most of the time, often hitting speeds of 30 knots. Not only that, but we managed, despite all the various equipment problems and sail changes, to take first place. Winning my first-ever sailing race was a pivotal moment for me and it gave me a taste for the extreme adventure that competitive speed sailing offers.

Now I was starting to think beyond my initial goal of sailing a singlehanded TransAtlantic race. I was sitting on one of the fastest sailboats in the world. With the full-time effort of Dave Scully it was possible to organize a broader program in speed sailing. There are some barriers to multihulls: we are not allowed in most sailing races. In the early 1990s the most common reason given by race organizers was that multihulls were unsafe. Actually, all sailing is high-risk. It is true that if a multihull flips upside down, it can't be righted. But on the positive side, it will not sink because there is no lead keel and this makes rescue easy. Monohulls have different but equal risks: if they fill with water they sink and the crew will find themselves in a life raft.

The real reason for excluding multihulls from races is that they are too fast and therefore have an unfair advantage over the monohulls. Being a newcomer to sailing, I didn't get all the handicapping and restrictions. My idea of sport was that you should try to have the fastest equipment and be the first to the finish line.

We thought we had the Fastnet Race committee warmed up to the idea of admitting a multihull and moved Lakota to Southampton near the start. The legendary Fastnet Race starts at the Isle of Wight, sails out to Fastnet Rock at the southeast corner of Ireland, then back to a finish at Plymouth, England. In the end, the Race Committee did not admit us. We still wanted to see how we would do, so we crossed the start line 10 minutes after the last class of boats started. Fifty minutes later we had passed all but the first couple of boats and had sailed out of the Solent into the open water of the English Channel. Our speed was extraordinary: on the 150-mile stretch returning from Fastnet Rock to Bishop Lighthouse in England, we averaged exactly 25 knots for 6 hours. Up to that time in 1993, I don't think a sailboat had ever sailed that fast for that long a stretch. We finished in a time of 52 hours 10 minutes, which was 8 hours faster than the race had ever been sailed before, but we could not make a record claim because we were not officially in the race. We had a fine celebration dinner at the China House Restaurant that night. At daybreak the next morning, I was sitting on the balcony of my room with a cup of coffee in hand, watching Dennis Conner's Winston cross the finish line as the official First to Finish.

My very first official world record was coming soon. I saw a storm tracking directly for Ireland. As it crossed Ireland the winds would circulate counter-clockwise the entire 704-mile circumference of the island. We could sail downwind all the way. On one day's notice, we stowed our provisions and pulled Brian Thompson out of a wedding party to join us. I had met Brian on the Two-Handed Round Britain and Ireland race, where he had finished in second place. Brian is a truly excellent sailor whom I wanted to sail with us whenever possible. We sailed from Plymouth to Dublin to get into position. In Dublin, we were joined by Irish sailors Cathy MacAleavy and Con Murphy and we took a start the next day. The downwind strategy worked. We set a record time of 44 hours 42 minutes compared to the previous record of 75 hours. The Cork Dry Gin Trophy still sits in the National Yacht Club of Ireland waiting for someone to break our record.

In spring 1993, I had already identified that flying a balloon around the world was something I wanted to do, but I hadn't done much about it. On my trip to Paris to negotiate on the purchase of *Lakota* I was looking for a gift for Peggy. I glanced in the window of the Hermès design house and there was a scarf on display that depicted these great historic aviators. On it, of course, were the Wright Brothers, the first to fly an airplane; Charles Lindbergh, who made the first solo TransAtlantic flight; Chuck Yeager, who was first to break the sound barrier; and Neil Armstrong and Buzz Aldrin, who landed on the moon in 1969. But there were also more recent aviators like Dick Rutan and Jeana Yeager, pilots of Voyager, the first non-stop non-refueled flight around the globe. And I thought, yes, these are great figures in aviation history, but there are still unprecedented feats which could earn a place in Hermès' or anyone else's list of historic aviators. One would be to make the first balloon flight around the world. I realized this was important and that I should get off my duff and go for it. I went in and bought a scarf for Peggy, but I wasn't about to tell her why. She learned soon enough.

When I had looked into ballooning as a possible new adventure I had read about the Hilton Earthwinds project which was having plenty of problems just getting their unwieldy balloon launched for a round the world attempt. I figured it wasn't too late for me to become a competitor. I decided to jump in wholeheartedly.

When I got back to Beaver Creek, I started taking balloon pilot training. I contacted Ed Sagon, who goes by the name of 'Merlin'. He was the wizard of hot air ballooning in the Vail Valley near my home in Beaver Creek. Predictably, he asked why I wanted to get a balloon pilot's license. Thinking it a bit audacious to show up for my first lesson and state that I wanted to make the first balloon flight around the world, I said, 'I just want to make some nice flights.' We laugh about that whenever we get together now. Over the course of the summer and after 11 flights with Merlin, I had earned my hot air balloon pilot license.

As my ballooning goals required flying long distances, it was lucky that I got involved with the sport at the right time, when the technology was being developed to make such a flight viable, specifically the development of the Rozière balloon in the early 1980s.

A hot air balloon requires a great deal of fuel to keep it airborne, which means that it can't be flown even for more than three days. The performance of a gas balloon, which usually uses helium, is compromised when the helium cools and shrinks at night. When the sun's rays no longer warm the balloon, it begins to sink toward the ground. To counteract this movement, a pilot has to 'ballast', which simply means lightening the load by throwing excess weight overboard in order to arrest the descent. However, when the sun comes up again the next day and warms the helium, it causes the balloon to rise. Now without the weight that was ballasted, the balloon starts to fly too high, forcing the pilot to open the valve to let out helium to keep the balloon at a reasonable altitude. As such, flying a gas balloon constantly involves letting out helium to stop daytime climbs and lower the altitude, and ballasting to stop night-time descents. Practically speaking, it is impossible to build a manned gas balloon big enough to allow a pilot to continue this cycle for more than about five days. A circumnavigation flight would take about three weeks.

The Rozière balloon is the best answer to flying long distances. Designed and tested by Donald Cameron of Cameron Balloons in the late 1980s, the Rozière uses a combination of helium gas and hot air. Although basically a gas balloon, instead of using ballast, a Rozière is equipped with a hot air burner to warm the helium at night in order to keep the balloon from descending. This is obviously much more efficient than carrying and jettisoning ballast and means that a balloon can stay in the air much longer.

After becoming a balloon pilot, my license still contained a 'restriction', which basically said that I could only fly a hot air balloon. Therefore, in order to be licensed to fly the new state-of-the-art Rozière balloons, I had to go out and obtain flight instruction to learn the theory and the practical laws of how a gas balloon operates.

In January 1994, to get my rating, I contacted John Kugler, a gas balloon pilot and instructor. During our conversation over the phone, he invited me to a ballooning rally, which he was holding with some of his friends and other gas balloon pilots in McCook, Nebraska. He said if I came out, he'd be able to take me up and check me out in gas balloons so I could get the restriction removed from my balloon license. Taking John up on his invitation, I made my way to McCook. His crowd of friends had convened in the hangar after a long morning flight. They'd been caught in a snowstorm and were now enjoying some beers—probably to take the edge off. As I stood off to the side watching the festivities, John noticed me and strolled over to introduce himself. He was so tall I wondered why he wasn't on a basketball court. He told me if I was crazy enough to fly in this cold and unpredictable weather he'd take me up the following day. I took him up on his offer. Meanwhile he introduced me to his balloonist friends who included Tim Cole, Bruce Comstock, Nick Saum, and Dennis Brown, all of whom would later be key team members on my distance balloon attempts.

The next morning, it was quite windy. The weather was nasty with temperatures close to zero. I could tell that John wasn't keen on going up, but his passion for the sport got the best of him. Despite the weather, I was also determined to carry out our plan and he wasn't the type of guy to discourage anyone especially when it came to ballooning. Despite 15 knots of wind and snow showers, we made our daring launch, which was virtually horizontal due to the wind. After he briefly explained to me the basics of the technique, John turned things over to me. After a six- hour flight across Nebraska and into Kansas, we set up for a landing near Hayes, Kansas. We chose our landing site and valved out gas for the approach. It would be a tough one in 25 knots of wind. As we descended to about 100 ft above the ground, we released our trail ropes, which stabilized the descent as they dragged on the ground. 'Don't worry about those power lines, the ropes don't conduct electricity,' John shouted. My eyes must have been as big as saucers as we hit the ground just beyond the power lines. As we dragged horizontally through the snow and over hummocks, we pulled the rip lines to quickly release the gas. Finally we were stopped! 'We cheated death again,' John quipped. I don't know about these gas balloonists! Anyhow John was impressed with my ability to operate the balloon and that was good enough for him to sign me off for gas balloons. But that was not all John outfitted me with.

Looking at me with a quirky grin, he said, 'Well everyone who gets a license with me gets a nickname.'

'Okay, what's mine?' I asked him.

Pausing to think for a moment, he smiled again and replied, 'Cucumber, yeah, Cucumber, that's it. You're as cool as a cucumber.'

Somehow I thought this was just like being a military pilot and I was pleased to have my own pilot nickname, and quickly said, 'Well, if you think the shoe fits . . .'

PRIVATE JET: CITATION X

The last of my new adventurous pursuits was aviation. Although I had got my pilot's license in 1967, when I was still in graduate school, I didn't buy my first plane until 1987 when I wanted to get to and from our new home in Beaver Creek in a couple of hours instead of a half day that would be required on the airlines. It was a Falcon 10, which is a small but fast private jet. However, I never flew the plane because I didn't have the required rating. A management company piloted it. I got rid of it in 1990, but in 1992 I decided to buy another Falcon 10 and this time I was going to be the one to fly it. It seemed crazy to sit in the back and let hired pilots have all the fun flying it. I decided to upgrade my credentials.

I already had my instrument rating, but lacked my commercial and multi-engine ratings. It was a most enjoyable experience having and flying a private jet. Flying my jet became such an important part of my life that after two years I wanted to have the best. After a little research, I concluded that the new Citation X was the best owner-pilot airplane on the market. If an owner wants to ride in the passenger compartment, there are bigger and more luxurious jets. But if the owner wants to be the pilot, there is nothing faster or more advanced technologically than the Citation X.

When I ordered the airplane and met the President of the company, Russ Meyer, I told him of my interest in flying it for world records. He said he would accommodate me, although I don't think he thought for a second that I was serious. Now he knows—I was serious. Since I took delivery of the plane in March 1999, I have set 10 important world records including US Transcontinental, Australian Transcontinental, and Round the World in both directions. I have been the primary demonstrator that the Citation X is the fastest private jet and Russ Meyer writes effusively to congratulate me each time I break a record.

It was sad and ironic that my expansion into sailing, ballooning and aviation was occurring around the same time that my father was experiencing profound contraction and limitation in his life. At the beginning of the 1990s, we noticed that my father was beginning to lose his memory. At first, the signs were subtle. He would have trouble finding the words when he spoke. As his condition worsened over the following years, my mother and he moved up to Portola where my sister, Linda, lives. Linda and her husband Steve Dansby shouldered most of the load of caring for him. By the time my father was taken to a doctor for formal diagnosis, he had already reached stage three Alzheimer's disease.

In 1994, when the care he needed exceeded what my mother and Linda could provide, he was moved into a nursing home in nearby Reno.

My father was an exceptionally intelligent man. I thought it some strange cosmic joke that my father, a man who delighted in using his mind and exercising his intellect, would come down with a disease that attacked this faculty. He of course resisted the move into the nursing home, although he knew he had no choice but to resign himself to it. I couldn't help but feel when I visited him there that he had given up on everything altogether.

6. A T-SHIRT AND A BOTTLE OF WINE: MY FIRST TRANSATLANTIC BALLOON FLIGHT, AUGUST 1994

You owe us a bottle of wine and a T-shirt.

Air traffic controller in Birmingham

Having secured my gas balloon license, I was keen to get some long-distance ballooning underway. In March of 1994, I contacted Tim Cole and asked him if he would like to be my co-pilot on a TransAtlantic flight. I had met Tim at John Kugler's ballooning event at the end of January and he seemed very knowledgeable. Logically I should have considered John Kugler since he helped me get my gas balloon qualification, but he was so big and tall I suspected the weight of pilots would become a limitation on a successful TransAtlantic.

As we talked about ballooning across the Atlantic, Tim was very enthusiastic as this was an adventure he'd apparently always wanted to undertake and the Atlantic was the premier flight that a balloonist could do. Before committing himself, he told me that he would first need to discuss it with his wife. Tim called me back pretty quickly and said that he was game for the adventure but that he didn't have the finances to pay for his share of the balloon. I was excited that the project was moving on and I told him, 'You take care of your personal travel expenses, and I'll take care of the rest.'

I went to Bristol, England to visit Cameron Balloons Ltd., the manufacturers of the Rozière prototype balloon. In 1992, Cameron put together a race across the Atlantic with five identical Rozière balloons. It was named the Chrysler Race after the sponsorship by the Chrysler distributor in Europe. I was impressed that although two of the Chrysler balloons ditched, three had made it. The fact that these Rozière balloons had proven capable of flying across the Atlantic made them the obvious choice for me. Since there was enough risk in this TransAtlantic endeavor without taking on untested balloon technology with some other balloon manufacturer, I ordered a Rozière balloon identical to the balloons used in the Chrysler TransAtlantic Race. While at the factory, I spent a couple of days learning the concepts of flight, oxygen and communication systems, and the flight controls. We would need to have a H-F radio on board to communicate with air traffic control to make position reports each hour just like commercial airlines. There was no distinction between balloons and airline flights for this purpose.

After some long discussions about the equipment, I asked Bruce Comstock to design an autopilot for me. Bruce must have wondered why I wanted an autopilot since there would be two pilots to fly the balloon. But I wasn't about to disclose my real ambition yet which was to make the first Round the World Balloon Flight and to make it Solo. To fly Solo, an autopilot would be required not just because of the flying workload but because it would be absolutely necessary to allow the pilot to get some sleep. Bruce Comstock finally agreed to design and build what would be the first working balloon autopilot. The autopilot's job is to maintain the balloon system at a constant altitude by controlling the burners. It was effectively an altitude stabilizer with a pressure-sensitive relay that reads variations in barometric pressure at certain altitudes. When altimeter and barometer data were evaluated with a computer algorithm, the autopilot determined the correct period and frequency of burner firing in order to maintain level flight.

Perhaps more than any other sport, ballooning is solely at the mercy of the winds. For a balloon, the wind is the only source for horizontal locomotion. Because balloons are just like dust in the atmosphere: the balloon will move almost exactly with the wind, steering is achieved by changing altitude where the wind is moving at a somewhat different speed and direction. Since a balloon has no steering mechanism, it depends solely on the skill of the meteorologist who must find the right wind pattern, which is moving in the desired direction at the fastest speed possible, and the pilot, who must stay with it. A balloon pilot flies with the right wind currents by altering his altitude.

Having the best meteorologist is extremely important. Bob Rice is the dean of adventure meteorology. Bob was simultaneously regarded as the top weatherman for both sailing and ballooning and we had already had success working together on some of my previous sailing projects. Bob Rice was the meteorologist for substantially all the important balloon flights to date: the first Atlantic and Pacific crossings, the first Solo Atlantic, and the early abortive Round the World attempts by the Hilton Earthwinds project. In recent years Bob had worked with the National Oceanic and Atmospheric Administration (NOAA) in the application of a Trajectory Model to ballooning. NOAA's reason for development of the Trajectory Model was primarily to track the path of volcanic dust and radioactive particles from nuclear explosions. By using the balloon-adapted trajectory model, Bob was able to forecast where the balloon would travel at given altitudes. He was a canny forecaster of bad weather who would anticipate what the weather models would show on the next computer run. I asked Bob Rice to be the meteorologist for this flight and I was delighted when he accepted. Early in the summer of 1994, I went to St John's, Newfoundland to organize facilities for our launch, which we planned for late summer. I was introduced around by local attorney Paul Stokes and was able to line up everything that we needed. After consulting with Tim Cole, I chose Fielding Grounds, a soccer park located near the center of town as the launch site. As it was somewhat sheltered from the winds, we thought it would serve as a suitable private area to launch from. Several previous TransAtlantic balloon attempts had been made from St John's and the people there were familiar with what was going on and offered to handle a lot of the local logistics for us.

Tim Cole arrived in St John's at the same time as the balloon equipment. He brought with him his regular gas balloon-flying partner Dennis Brown. Bruce Comstock also arrived for the preparations. After a few weeks of equipment organizing and just plain waiting, Bob Rice saw the weather pattern we wanted, which was a 'zonal flow' or straight winds without the disturbance of low-pressure systems or storm fronts. This would also allow us to stay out of the clouds. Bob issued a 'Code Green' for 8 August. The three stages in Bob's coding system are 'Code Red' which means the weather pattern is unacceptable, 'Code Yellow' meaning that the weather pattern is being seriously considered, and 'Code Green', which means 'Go' and we plan to launch on the specified day.

On the morning of 8 August 1994, after the balloon was inflated and everything checked out by the team, Tim and I climbed into the capsule. The weigh-off was performed, which first required removing sandbags until the balloon was in exact equilibrium, then taking off an additional precalculated weight of sandbags to give us the climb rate we wanted. We released the steel hawsers and the balloon shot up like a rocket. We took off at 11.30 am local time. We were less than a mile from the ocean and the swift wind propelled us over Cabot Tower on the hill above the harbor of St John's and toward the coastline. As we moved out over the sea, there was no turning back. Our next landfall wouldn't be until Ireland. As intimidating as it seemed, we were both looking forward to the unknown.

Our climb up to about 8000 ft was smooth. That evening a valve warning light came on alerting us that the valve in the top of the balloon was open. If this were the case, the gas would escape and we would lose altitude. 'I don't care what the valve light is saying, I put the valve in. That valve is not open,' Tim insisted.

Taking him at his word, I calmly reached up and unplugged the circuit breaker on the light. Tim was a little shocked that I trusted him so implicitly at this early stage but I would learn over the course of my experiences that it is this sort of trust in one another that makes for an effective partnership. This malfunctioning valve light was not flight-critical but it had startled us briefly and was a nuisance.

Sharing the tight quarters of our capsule probably did much to break the ice. At 5 ft high, 5 ft wide and about 6 ft long, the space we shared wasn't big enough to hold a queen-size bed. Stretching out in any direction was limiting and since we couldn't stand all the way up, we both developed neck aches. We could only see outside if we opened the hatch and stood up or sat on top of the capsule. The capsule was rather Spartan and much of the space was taken up with food, water and other gear. There was no heater on board although we did have good sleeping bags.

Despite this small living space, we adapted quite well and settled in for an excellent flight. During the first night, one of the two liquid oxygen tanks over-pressurized and started to spew liquid oxygen outside the capsule. This could have been a problem because we needed the oxygen to breathe at the higher altitudes and couldn't afford to lose too much. Although oxygen isn't flammable, it will induce greater flames if exposed to a fire source. So as a safety measure, we shut down the pilot lights and the burners. To reduce the pressure in the tank, we bled most of the oxygen out of the tank. With this weight reduction, we felt the balloon rise slowly to a new equilibrium altitude.

After a cold night, we welcomed our first sunrise which was just starting to warm us up a little bit. Once the sun warmed our balloon, it rose to a natural equilibrium level and did not require the pilots to fire the burners. Thus daytime was a welcome break from piloting duties. Seizing this opportunity, Tim heated up some water for coffee. Just as he was about to hand me my cup, all of a sudden, the capsule shook violently, followed by this phenomenal roaring sound. We feared the worst—that something must have broken. However, it was just the sonic boom of the Concorde on its daily flight from London. That woke us up a lot faster than our coffee.

Before we took off, I filed our international flight plan with air traffic control. I specified Bristol in western England as our primary destination and Hamburg, in northern Germany as the alternative. However, this would not be the last of our responsibilities to air traffic control. We had to comply with all rules. It does not matter whether you are flying in a balloon, small airplane or an airliner, hourly position reports must be called in to Oceanic Control. This was the most tedious part of the trip. We would record our latitude and longitude and calculate our position for the next two hours. Then we would take turns calling on our HF radio to get the attention of the busy Oceanic Controllers. We would read out our position, altitude, and speed then the estimated positions for the next two hours. The airline pilots must have been curious about this mysterious aircraft at only 10,000 ft flying at only 35 mph!

We were fortunate to have had good weather throughout our flight. Our Mission Control Center was at Cameron Balloons in Bristol. Using our satellite email system, called Inmarsat C, we sent questions and automated position reports. We were also com-municating regularly with Bob Rice who was in his Boston office around the clock. As we neared the southwest coast of Ireland, the wind pattern curved to take us too far north, which prompted us to climb much higher to get a straighter track. As we climbed, we thought we'd set a new world altitude record for the Rozière type of balloon at 19,431 ft. Unfortunately, after the flight, we learned that a 25,994-ft flight had been done in Australia just two months earlier.

As we crossed the Irish coast we were delighted. We had made it across the Atlantic! We had reached our goal. Since the flight was going so well we decided to fly farther. We were feeling great and decided to relax with a cup of coffee. Tim stood in the hatch and fired up our camp stove. We did all of our cooking on top of the capsule to avoid a fire risk inside the confined capsule. Since we didn't need the burners to provide lift during the heat of the day, we had the pilot lights turned off. In a huge oversight, we had forgotten to turn off the autopilot. As the sun descended lower in the sky and the balloon began to cool off and descend, the autopilot said to itself, 'Hey, we're descending. I need to turn the burners on.' The autopilot opened up the valves that funneled the propane through the burners, but because there was no pilot light operating to ignite the fuel, a huge puff of raw propane was released up inside the envelope. Since propane is heavier than air, it came back down and formed a huge cloud around Tim and the stove. The flame from the stove instantly ignited the propane. Tim was caught in the middle of a huge fireball.

I knew there was a fire, but I couldn't see what was going on or help because Tim was standing in the 2 ft-wide hatch. I grabbed the fire extinguisher and braced myself in case Tim was overcome and fell back into the capsule. I would be next to go out and fight the fire. Everything stopped and Tim didn't move. He just stood there in shock for a moment. I quickly turned on the burner to stop our descent. Luckily, Tim was okay. He burned off his eyebrows and some of his clothes were singed. Doing the best I could to calm him down, we sat down and immediately reviewed all that happened so we would not experience it again. Tim finally recovered and we laughed upon sharing the realization that bizarre things tended to happen every time we attempted to have some coffee.

Around four o'clock that afternoon, when the sun was starting to go down, we got a call from air traffic control in Birmingham. They were livid that our balloon had come through their airspace without permission. I argued that we had filed all the flight plans for entering into their system. But finally I asked them if they would contact Don Cameron at the Cameron Balloon Factory. Well known in British aviation circles for his close but unsuccessful attempts to make the first TransAtlantic balloon flight, we thought Don could iron this out. Sure enough, he did. When air traffic control got a hold of Don, he was able to confirm that what I had said was true and they found out where the problem had arisen. What had happened was that when the balloon came over the coast of Ireland, the Oceanic Control Center 'dropped the ball'. They had not passed our information onto the next air traffic control center to let them know that we were heading in their direction.

Another air traffic controller radioed us back and said, 'I'll handle it for you but it's going to cost you.'

'Cost me what?!' I moaned to myself, trying to mask my displeasure.

'You owe me a T-shirt and a bottle of wine.'

This saying is ubiquitous among balloonists and the bribe will get you anything, anywhere in the ballooning world. This fellow was a balloonist! We knew from then on we would have no more problems. He went on to say that, 'We got this all sorted out, and we'll arrange things so that as you go into airspace toward Amsterdam, we'll make sure that the information gets passed on for you. But don't forget you owe me a bottle of wine and a T-shirt.' I assured him that as soon as we landed that we would send it right over.

We were above the clouds for all but about 30 minutes of the 50-plus hours over the ocean. As we were coming in close to Ireland, the sky was clear. It was the first time that we got a spectacular view. As we peered out from atop the capsule, we could see the ragged coastline followed by the emerald green farmland. Later over the North Sea we saw the oil rigs and could see the ships going out to service them. Isolated as we were, thousands of feet up in the sky, observing people working and carrying on their lives below evoked a warm feeling in me.

That night, the air temperature was above freezing and I sat for hours on top of the capsule looking at the city lights as we crossed over Holland and continued toward Germany. At dawn there were again low-level clouds as we entered into the northwestern portion of Germany. As this was the end of our third day, we were looking to land soon. I was sleeping while Tim was flying, and then, tearing through the quietness was a sharp 'beep-beep-beep-beep'. This was the GPS (Global Position System) alarm indicating that we just crossed a waypoint. We were directly overhead the Hamburg VOR which I had filed as our alternative destination before we took off from Canada. To the credit of our router Bob Rice, this was surely the most accurate distance balloon flight ever.

We started our descent from 14,000 ft and the brightening morning sky allowed us to locate where we wanted to come down. We'd already made contact through Mission Control with some of our team members that were following us. During our descent, because the air was quite a bit cooler than the balloon it took us three attempts to break through the cloud layer: when hitting colder air like that, the balloon, relatively warmer than the clouds, wants to go back up again. It took a while for the balloon to cool off enough to overcome this dynamic. On the third approach, we were able to penetrate the clouds and then maintain a controlled rate of descent. Finally we dropped down below the cloud layer and were low enough to get an idea of what the ground conditions were like. We then dropped down to 100 ft off the ground just to get a feel for the surface winds, surface track and surface speeds as these differ significantly from those higher up. Once we determined exactly what our track was going to be, we prepared for a landing. Moving closer to the ground, we saw all these cars maneuvering below us. A helicopter approached us from behind and was taking footage of our landing. We came in and set the balloon down in this field. There was no wind at all and it was a beautiful standup landing. Our chase team arrived within fifteen minutes of the time of our landing. We packed up the balloon and then drove to Berlin. During those 75 hours, we probably got less than about five hours of sleep each. But it wasn't like we were tired during our flight—we had been running on adrenaline. That afternoon, our German friends invited us on a balloon flight, but Tim and I needed a little sleep. The rest of the team had gone flying, but we joined the German balloonists that night for a tremendous party.

I was really jazzed to have made that successful flight over the Atlantic. It was only the ninth TransAtlantic balloon flight ever. I realized that ballooning was a great adventure and offered opportunities for important achievements. It was a sport that I was about to become very involved in.

During the TransAtlantic flight, I had already been planning how to take my ballooning program to the next level. I had flourished while sailing and ballooning with a partner, now I felt ready to undertake these adventures on my own.

I had no sooner returned home than I told Peggy that I was going to plan another balloon trip. She looked at me quizzically and said, 'Sure, honey, where do you want to go?'

I told her, 'I'm going to fly solo across the Pacific Ocean.'

She gave me a long look and in that instant she knew that I was serious. Then she pressed, 'Why the Pacific?' I could tell that she was worried about my decision and she knew that I was determined and nothing would change my mind.

I simply said, 'Because someone has already flown solo over the Atlantic, but no one has flown solo over the Pacific.'

I think there is something unique about being the first to achieve a feat, especially if it is done alone. Perhaps it's more romantically heroic or something. First solo flights tend to be more memorable than team flights. Everyone remembers Charles Lindbergh's solo flight across the Atlantic Ocean, but few recall the first team flight across the Atlantic made by Alcock and Brown eight years earlier in 1919.

7. SAILING *LAKOTA* SINGLEHANDED IN THE ROUTE DU RHUM, NOVEMBER 1994

The substance of the winds is too thin for human eyes; their written
language is too difficult for human minds, and their spoken language
mostly too faint for the ears.

John Muir, A *Thousand-Mile Walk to the Gulf*

Soon after my TransAtlantic balloon flight, I flew to England for a celebration dinner in Bristol at Cameron Balloons with Don Cameron, Alan Noble and the team members who had manned Mission Control for my flight. As the evening progressed, Don and I discussed my next flight. I told him I wanted to order a new balloon for the purpose of flying solo across the Pacific Ocean. Don looked at me wide-eyed. He realized that I had become a committed balloonist. I also talked to Bruce Comstock and we went over some of the ideas that he had come up with for improving the autopilot.

After a refit in La Rochelle, France during the winter of 1993–94, *Lakota* continued on a brilliant record-breaking streak. The Isle of Wight in southern England is one of the most illustrious speed sailing courses. Sailing clockwise around the Island in 1856, the yacht *America* established the America's Cup with a time of 11 hours 58 minutes. By 1994 the record time had whittled down to 4 hours 3 minutes. That summer of 1994 we blasted out a new time for this course with 3 hours 35 minutes. In October we took on the Round Britain & Ireland as a record rather than as a race like the previous summer. We beat the previous record by a huge margin: 32 hours with a time of 5 days 23 hours.

Finally, in November of 1994, it was time to attempt my original goal in sailing: a singlehanded TransAtlantic. It would be the Route Du Rhum, the greatest of the singlehanded TransAtlantic races. Starting in St Malo, France and running a distance of 3400 miles to the rum capital of Guadeloupe in the Caribbean, the Route du Rhum takes place once every four years in the month of November—an excellent month for arrival in the Caribbean but a horrendous month for sailing in the North Atlantic. The day before the race started the sailors all sat in an auditorium for a briefing by the meteorologists. Because they spoke French, I couldn't understand much of it. As I tried to follow the French speaker, I heard him say 'Force Neuf' several times. He described one weather pattern as 'Force Neuf' and the next again 'Force Neuf.' I recognized that Force Neuf meant Force Nine, which is the class of not just a gale but also a Strong Gale. This race was going to be a test of survival against the elements.

My team sailed with me out of the harbor and back behind the start line. We hoisted the mainsail up to the first reef, one level below Full Sail. Then they got off in a dinghy and I was on my own for the next two weeks. There I was, a rookie amongst the top singlehanded sailors in the world. Instead of feeling intimidated that most of my competitors had years of experience over me, I felt honored to be able to sail against such distinguished sailors.

Without a doubt the French have a passion for sailing. In the days preceding the start, thousands of spectators crowded through the narrow cobblestone streets of the ancient port town of St Malo en route to the harbor to see these magnificent boats and their skippers. The town was buzzing with an excitement that was infectious. It was being broadcast live on television. As an enormous number of boats crowded the edges of the start area, an estimated one million spectators lined the bluffs along the north coast of France to watch the early stages of the race. With one minute to go, I hardened up and accelerated to 20 knots. Prime Minister Chirac fired the starting gun and I crossed the line with the top competitors. Not backing off a bit, I tucked in just behind the lead boats. The television commentator asked, 'Who is this?' As he figured out it was a little-known American sailor, he was shocked. Somehow he expected all the leaders to be well-known French skippers.

It was a thrill sailing that afternoon, but I knew what was coming—the first of the storms. As the wind picked up, dark, ominous storm clouds hovered over the waters that the fleet and I were heading into. Racing into action, I hastily reefed *Lakota's* sails in preparation of what was to come. Within the hour, I was battling the fiercest storm of my life. I had to sail into the teeth of this storm in order to get sea room away from the northwest corner of France and its islands. With the waves in a steady climb from 10 ft to 25 ft, I didn't want to be on deck getting bashed. I knew I was vulnerable to seasickness, especially on the first night out before I had gotten my 'sea legs'. It was a bad time for me to get seasick when I had to perform at my best just to survive. Since I also knew that a person is practically invulnerable to seasickness while lying on his back, I braced myself on my bunk next to the navigation table so I could see all the instruments and steered the boat with the autopilot remote control in my hand. Making one-degree changes at a time to the autopilot was a tedious exercise yet necessary to keep *Lakota* at a safe angle to the wind. When the direction of the wind inevitably shifted, I had no choice but to venture outside into the storm. The waves hammered the deck as I struggled to make the required sail changes. I put on my harness and clipped the tether to the boat in the event that a wave swept me overboard. I worked as fast and furiously as I could. Pounding the deck with an unyielding force, the waves seemed intent on having their way. So chaotic was the motion of the boat that I had to fight to maintain my equilibrium as I reefed the sail and tried to maintain my command of *Lakota*.

Despite the harrowing situation, I immediately began to appreciate the self-reliance that sailing alone both fosters and necessitates. It required that I maintained a constant vigil, that I kept my wits about me at all times. I quickly estimated that the biggest concern of sailing solo, as opposed to sailing with a crew, was not to fall overboard. It's a real danger. If I did, I'd never get back to my boat for there was no one there to help me. Even wearing a harness, I must be careful that the tether is attached to a point, which still does not allow me to fall over the edge and into the water. Being dragged in the water by one of these fast moving sailboats would quickly result in my being drowned without an opportunity to pull myself on board.

At first light the next morning, the waves were still cresting at 25 ft, but the wind was dying. I ventured on deck to inspect the condition of the equipment and found that the storm jib was irreparably torn. Fortunately, I still had other headsails to switch to. I had survived the first storm with only minor damage and the loss of a night's sleep. I decided right then that I didn't want to be assaulted by one fierce storm after another. Because the shortest distance to the finish in Guadaloupe was through the storm track of the North Atlantic, those competitors who hoped to win had to sail this route. However, there was another way—the trade winds route that involved sailing south to the Canary Islands off of Morocco then turning west in the balmy trade winds all the way to the Caribbean. It's an extra 1000 miles of sailing but the winds are steady and moderate. As my goal was to finish the race and not get caught up in the extra dangers of trying to win the race, I opted for this safer alternative route. By the time I was abeam of northern Portugal conditions became mild.

After the storm my battery recharging system failed. Without battery power it wasn't practical to sail as nothing would work: the instruments, communications, or autopilot. I figured I could reach Lisbon 400 miles away before the batteries were drained. With a couple of pointers by e-mail from my boat manager, Ben Wright, I figured out it was a shorted voltage regulator. Fortunately I had a spare regulator and was finally able to change the part and point myself in the right direction again.

Two days later a new problem arose: the Inmarsat C blew a fuse and I couldn't find a spare of the right size. That was my satellite e-mail system that I used to receive important routing advice from my meteorologist and maintain social communication with my team, Peggy and the rest of my friends. Without the use of this instrument, a tremendous weight of loneliness swept over me. I had been using the satellite e-mail so fluently that I seemed to hear the voices of the writers. Now I felt truly alone.

Although it was daring to be sailing across the Atlantic without any weather information, I was game. I began to improvise and work with what I had. I pored over the weather charts that I had brought onboard and tried to construct a weather picture based on what meteorological information was available to me, hoping that the weather patterns would not change drastically. I was able to locate where the trade winds were and sailed them according to the direction that they were blowing. Relying on instinct, I learned how to 'listen' to the wind to get a feel for when it was time to tack and jibe. My senses became heightened. I noticed that there's a certain time of day that worked out best for doing the jibes. The heat of the day tended to produce a slight wind shift, which prompted me to jibe in the morning and jibe back in the other direction in the afternoon.

Since the direction of the wind was coming from behind me, I was constantly working to maintain a proper sailing angle. Sails are most efficient when the air flows over them like an airplane wing producing lift. Just putting sails out like a balloon would result in dead slow sailing. These boats have to sail at an angle to the wind to achieve decent speed. When sailing downwind, I had to maintain an efficient wind angle, which necessitates sailing a longer course back and forth rather than directly on course.

Toward the end of my second week at sea, my calculations told me I was closing in on the finish line. Without my communication equipment, I could only imagine how the rest of the fleet was doing. I also became the mystery boat in the race. No one knew where I was or how fast I was going. It was conceivable that the better winds on my trade winds route would allow me to make up for the extra distance and show up at Pointe à Pitre, Guadaloupe and shock the French sailing world with a victory. I imagined that there must have been many debating that possibility over wine or espresso in the cafés of France.

Even though a surprise finish was not on the cards, my decision to go south paid off for me. As I had predicted several years earlier, I was able to sail the Atlantic in 17 days in a multihull. I was thrilled when I crossed the finish line, ecstatic that I had made it. Although I finished three days behind the winner, it was good enough to take 5th place overall, a respectable finish for a newcomer! In fact, I made the best American finish since Phil Weld's third place finish in 1978. My fellow sailors were impressed and congratulated me with sincere enthusiasm on my outstanding job. It was not that I was a threat to beat these top professional sailors, but rather that I had demonstrated that I was competent to sail the ocean in the fastest and most powerful sailboats. I appreciated their words of recognition. I had sailed against the top singlehanded sailors in the world and managed to flourish in this very competitive race. The feeling of accomplishment at having finished the Route du Rhum was influential and enduring. Relying on sheer instinct and determination, I was able to make it to the finish line on my own. Having overcome the various problems that I met with on my first singlehanded race meant that I was no longer a sailboat-racing novice. Sailing the Route du Rhum, I had come into my own as a race sailor.

Finishing the Route du Rhum fulfilled my original long-term objective to sail singlehanded across the Atlantic and satisfied the reason I bought *Lakota*. Usually, when I accomplish an ultimate goal that I set for myself in a particular sport, I tend to move on. However, this would not be the case with sailing. I realized that I had one of the fastest sailboats in the world and that we could actually break world records with her. I hadn't thought too much about world records when I bought *Lakota*. Yet, after racing her, I realized that this is what she was capable of and I was intent on tapping her full potential. As long as I could have the wind in my sails, I would use it to go after every speed sailing world record.

8. A LITTLE ON EDGE: MY FIRST SOLO BALLOON FLIGHT ACROSS THE PACIFIC, FEBRUARY 1995

My goal was to be the first to balloon solo across the Pacific. The fact that I achieved the Absolute World Distance Record was icing on the cake.
Steve Fossett

When I returned home from the Route du Rhum in November 1994, I started to lay out careful plans for my solo balloon flight across the Pacific, which I expected to attempt in January or February 1995 when the jetstreams would be at their strongest in the Northern Hemisphere. I reviewed all that I had learned on my TransAtlantic flight. I made a list of improvements to upgrade the conditions in the capsule that would help make my flight more comfortable and enduring.

Since ballooning across the Pacific Ocean involved a certain amount of risk, I was intent on doing whatever was necessary to minimize that risk. Throwing myself into the planning stages of the flight, I wanted to know every detail of the balloon system and be familiar with every piece of equipment. I checked out all the new technology that had come on the market and thoroughly researched all the ballooning magazines and manuals that briefed me on the new equipment I would be using and how to repair it in flight if need be. This way, I thought I would have the odds in my favor.

I made all preliminary arrangements from my home in Beaver Creek, where I actually trained for the flight. I had concluded early on that the greatest vulnerability to distance balloon flights was equipment failure. This led me to continue to fly with an unpressurized capsule, which would allow me to avoid the complexity of equipment required for maintaining cabin pressure at high altitudes. Since I would be flying in an unpressurized capsule, I took advantage of the elevation around our home to acclimatize myself to the decrease in oxygen at the higher altitudes. In addition to hiking at the top of the surrounding mountains, I would sometimes sleep in the ski patrol hut located at the top of the Beaver Creek ski area.

When January 1995 rolled around, I felt both mentally and physically primed to make my TransPacific solo attempt. My feelings of mental preparedness were owed in part to Bruce Comstock and Nick Saum whom I had brought on board to assist me as my support team. Both were knowledgeable gas balloon pilots. Nick was the most experienced launch director for gas balloons and Bruce possessed invaluable, in-depth knowledge regarding how to deal with the balloon equipment. He developed the autopilot I was using, which was now called the 'Comstock Autopilot'. I felt fortunate to have both of them on my team.

Mission Control was still headquartered at Cameron Balloons in Bristol, England. My balloon route ran from Seoul, Korea to North America. It was an enormously complex task to get the various permissions to launch a balloon from Seoul, Korea. We had Korean balloonist Jeun Heum Baek working for us as an agent. He was probably bribing the various government officials to get the necessary approvals. We eventually procured permission to launch from Olympic Stadium in Seoul, but I never felt secure that the permission would remain in place.

I was a little on edge about attempting my first solo flight across the Pacific, an adventure that neither I nor anyone else had pulled off before. Of all the oceans to cross the Pacific is the most dangerous because of its size and hostile weather conditions. If I had to ditch, search and rescue would be extremely difficult because of the rough seas in winter.

We set up our equipment in January at Olympic Stadium. Nick and Bruce became concerned that the air temperatures at altitude over the Pacific would be cold enough to freeze my propane fuel.

The last thing I needed on my first solo flight was to have the fuel freeze, causing me and my balloon to plunge into the icy Pacific Ocean. Nick, Bruce and I discussed the possibilities of mixing propane and ethane because they have similar burning properties and, more importantly, this mixture could withstand the cold weather better. Since the ethane's freezing point is about $-85°C$ and the propane is $-45°C$, mixing them together creates a combination that greatly reduces the gelling or freezing point. Going back to a 'Code Red', we delayed the launch. I ordered the ethane from Canada and had it air freighted to Korea. As this took two weeks, I flew home to Beaver Creek and came back in February after the ethane arrived and the balloon tanks were refueled.

By mid-February, all systems were go and 'Code Green' was issued. As the balloon was being inflated on 17 February 1995 it towered up into the sky like a giant skyscraper. Although everything was running smoothly for us logistically, politically it was a different story. We were still having some problems with permissions. Just before launch, Mr Baek and governmental officials were in a panic because I had not gotten special permission to fly over Japan. I felt that I didn't need it because I would be complying with all aviation regulations. I feared that one of the seven governmental agencies that we were dealing with might step in and stop the launch at any moment. I wasn't sure if we were going to pull it off until I lifted off. Finally, I was able to make an excellent launch from Olympic Stadium in Seoul, Korea.

Almost a day after launch, the weather turned menacing over Tokyo. I got caught in a snowstorm. Ice and snow covered the balloon. The flight was in jeopardy. Mission Control and I were very concerned that the balloon couldn't remain aloft with the weight of the snow and that I'd crash. Slowly I floated away from the snowstorm and soon connected with a jetstream to speed me on my way. After having passed the storm, I was trying to get some sleep when my altitude alarms went off. Realizing that I was quickly losing altitude, I fired the burners but nothing happened. This effort did not stop my fall. I figured that the pilot light must be out. When I hit the igniter switch to relight it, it created a huge explosion. The jolt of the blast shook the capsule. I looked up through my plexiglass hatch and saw a fireball and quickly realized what had happened. When the pilot lights blew out while I was asleep, the Comstock Autopilot continued to fire the burners in an attempt to maintain level altitude. This liquid propane mixture built up in the accumulated snow on the top of my capsule. When I lighted the pilots, the accumulated fuel burst into flame. Looking on the bright side, had I not ignited the pilot light when I did, there would have been much more propane, a bigger explosion, and a bigger fire, which would have burned through some of the important balloon components. While the risers connecting the balloon envelope to capsule were metal cables, the straps holding on the fuel tanks were 1-inch nylon webbing.

After the fire burned out, I opened the hatch and stuck my head out the top of the capsule. As I assessed the situation, I was relieved to see that there was no damage significant enough to impede my flight. I was lucky.

The next morning I started having problems with the generator. It worked fine in testing at sea level but was rather balky at 10,000 ft and wouldn't work at all above 14,000 ft where I needed to spend most of my flight. I would have to descend to run the generator in order to recharge the batteries that all my electronic equipment used. In another day, the generator would not start at all and the clock was ticking on when my batteries would run out. Going into the final night of the flight some of my equipment indicated low voltage. I knew I had to act. I promptly shut down all of my electronics: the satellite communication system to Mission Control and even my GPS navigation system. There was no time to notify my team what was going on. I would be in the dark both literally and navigationally. I would not be able to receive any directions from my meteorologist Lou Billones in case my flight path was being changed by the winds and I needed to fly at a different altitude to reach the coast of North America. I was at the complete mercy of the wind; wherever it blew I was going. I still had almost 800 miles of ocean to cross and I wouldn't know whether I had made it to land until the next morning. In the worst case I could have been looped around the low-pressure system and been carried north and west toward the Aleutian Islands.

That night was extremely uncomfortable. Without the electrical system operating, my heater didn't work. It was really cold at the 19,000-ft altitude I was flying. I put on all my dog sledding gear including the heavy boots. I wrapped my sleeping bag around me but still I shivered through the night. Although it was hard to fall asleep in the cold, as I dozed off, I dreamed of the warmth of the morning sun and being over Canada soon.

At daybreak, I opened the hatch and looked down upon a glorious sight—land! I presumed it was Vancouver Island. I went back inside to check my maps to see if I was correct—I was! I'd made it! I was the first person to cross the Pacific Ocean solo in a balloon and, ironically, had no functioning communication system by which to share this triumphant moment with anyone. Although I was scheduled to land as soon as I got into Canada, I started to do some figuring and realized that if I continued on, I had a chance of breaking the Absolute World Distance Record in ballooning which was previously set by the team Abruzzo, Newman, Aoki, and Clark who were the first to cross the Pacific Ocean in 1981. After checking to make sure that I had sufficient fuel, I couldn't think of a good reason not to go after the record.

My plan was to continue on throughout the day and see how far I could get. I used what little battery power I had saved to let Mission Control know what I was up to. I decided to fly until dark when the surface winds tend to abate and the air is calmer and more conducive for landing. One thing I was certain of—I didn't want to spend another night in the capsule without heat!

Later in the day I crossed Calgary, Alberta and did a climb to 25,000 ft because I knew that would be an altitude record for the Rozière type of balloons. I never actually filed for the record because it didn't seem significant compared to my Absolute Distance Record. I continued on to Saskatchewan where I did a perfect standup landing in a wheat field at the village of Mendham. As I exited the capsule and stepped onto solid ground, the elation I felt over achieving my objective made me feel weightless. As it turned out, my flight was a huge success. I had accomplished two major feats: one, I became the first balloonist to fly solo across the Pacific Ocean; and two, I set a new Absolute World Distance Record of 5,435.82 miles.

Shortly after I made the First Solo across the Pacific, Barron Hilton, the CEO of Hilton Hotels, contacted me to congratulate me. It was his Earthwinds project in the early 1990s that prompted my interest in entering the competition to make the first Round the World Balloon Flight. The balloon system his team was working with was innovative from the standpoint that there was a helium balloon on top and a ballast balloon hanging below the capsule with a fixed amount of regular air inside of it. The purpose of it was to stabilize the balloon's altitude so it didn't go up and down during the day or night. The project was a bust. They had a total of five launch attempts and never made it very far. One time the balloon dragged into a mountainside in Reno and ruptured the ballast balloon. The final attempt they flew only 200 and some odd miles before the ballast balloon ruptured and the pilots landed.

The Earthwinds pilot in command was Larry Newman who had been a co-pilot on both the first TransAtlantic and TransPacific flights. During the course of these attempts, I had actually contacted Larry Newman and told him that I was interested in getting on as one of the pilots of Earthwinds. Nothing came of that, which in hindsight was probably a good thing for me. I went on and pursued my own ballooning projects. Later, when Earthwinds came to an end, Barron was surprised to learn from Larry that I had wanted to get involved as one of the pilots. By then I'd done a couple of flights and was perceived to be competent as a distance balloonist.

After my successful Solo TransPacific flight, Barron Hilton invited me to attend the Victor Awards which is an Academy Awards style of television program for honoring athletes and coaches in the major sports. These awards are given every year to athletes for their outstanding success in various sports endeavors. As an aviation enthusiast, Barron made sure that there was a Victor Award for aviation. When my name was called that evening and I made my way up to the podium, I felt extremely honored to be recognized. I had won my first award as a balloonist.

It was at the awards ceremony that Barron and I became friends. That night we discussed our mutual passion and interest in aviation and ballooning. During our conversation, Barron probed, 'What is next on your ballooning agenda?'

Looking him straight in the eye, I casually said, 'I'm planning to fly solo non-stop around the world.'

9. SHAKEN UP: MY FIRST SOLO ROUND THE WORLD BALLOON ATTEMPT, JANUARY 1996

To fly a balloon around the world would be a milestone. Once it's done, somebody can do it faster or better, but only one person can do it first. It would mean a lot to me to be part of aviation history.

Steve Fossett

While still riding the high of my First Solo TransPacific balloon flight and the Absolute Distance World Record, I immediately started preparations for my first official attempt at flying round the world. I made several changes: first we moved Mission Control from Cameron Balloons in England to Loyola University in Chicago. Bo Kemper had taken on the task of directing and providing media relations for Mission Control and as he was also a public relations executive at Loyola, it made sense to have Mission Control based there. Joining Nick and Bruce on the team was Andy Elson, who is a brilliant engineer. A balloon pilot himself, Andy quickly proved to be very beneficial and helpful to our efforts. He worked on improving the burners so they fired better at high altitudes and developed a propane-fuelled cabin heater. As I found in the TransPacific flight, generators are problematic because of the air density changes at varying altitudes. Although this could be solved with a turbocharged generator that would be very heavy, I instead switched to a solar power generating system. This consisted of a solar array suspended 15 ft below the capsule, which was designed to track toward the sun for maximum energy absorption.

Because fuel consumption during the Solo TransPacific was much higher than the computer models predicted, Donald Cameron and Andy Elson sought to address this with a major design change of the balloon. There would be a silverized Mylar cover that reflected the sun, which would reduce heating the balloon during the day and let air pass through it. Keeping the balloon cooler during the daytime would, in theory, stop the balloon from rising and forcing out helium. At night, the Mylar would work as a thermo pane to keep the balloon warm so it wouldn't require as much burner fuel to maintain altitude. By keeping the balloon cool during the day and warm at night, the Mylar would enable me to reduce helium loss during the heat of the day and reduce fuel burn at night. This flight was the first application of a Mylar-covered balloon.

My launch team assembled in South Dakota immediately after Christmas to prepare the balloon system. I would be taking off from the Stratobowl near Rapid City, South Dakota. The Stratobowl is a historic ballooning site. Altitude records were set there in the 1930s and other subsequent important balloon flights were made from this venue.

We were all anxious because this was my first solo attempt around the world. Whatever feelings I had about undertaking a circumnavigation flight were complicated by the sadness I would be flying with. Shortly after Christmas and just before the New Year, my father passed away. As I prepared for my launch, I was still dealing with my own personal thoughts about his recent death. We had been close my whole life. It was extremely difficult to watch his mind deteriorate over the five years that he battled Alzheimer's. Perhaps it was fitting that I would be going on this balloon attempt soon after his death. After all, it was my father who introduced me to the world of adventure. In addition to the many wonderful things he instilled in me, my father's love of adventure and the great outdoors would always be with me.

On 8 January 1996, my launch was quite a spur-of-the-moment ordeal. My team was having trouble with leaky burner solenoids and had just repaired them when the time came to launch. My crew hurriedly threw all my equipment, food, and supplies into the capsule. It was a mess and a danger because of the difficulty of finding necessary tools to make repairs during the flight. This was the least of my worries. As I took off and climbed to 14,000 ft, I heard strange popping noises sounding from all around the balloon system indicating that something was wrong. I strained to determine the cause of this disturbing sound, to no avail. It wasn't until the plane carrying the *National Geographic* photographer Joel Sartore saw the balloon and made contact with me that I learned what was happening. Our 'Mylar theory' literally had holes in it. The material was falling apart. Actually, it was engineered incorrectly. The designers did not allow enough expansion of the balloon as it climbed in altitude. Mylar has very little stretch or elasticity. Despite the ghastly appearance, I would be able to continue the attempt but without any benefit over the traditional Rozière balloon design.

I flew eastbound across the US where a Category 5 blizzard was ravaging the East Coast. As I passed over Washington DC, I flew over a very quiet Dulles Airport, which had been shut down due to the storm. Straining to listen to every word of air traffic control, I reasoned that I would be okay if I could stick to my flight plan, which would take me over the storm.

Whenever I needed to change hoses on fuel tanks, I would climb out on top of the capsule. At first, being on top of the capsule intimidated me. Rounded at the edges, it was a mere 5 ft by 7 ft. I felt that I could slide off at any moment and would wear a harness for protection. However, unlike sailing, where the interfacing of wind, water and boat creates sudden jolts, there are no surprises when flying a balloon. Since the balloon is carried at the same speed as the wind, there is no threat of hitting anything or getting jarred off. Once I was convinced of this, I stopped wearing the harness.

As I left the United States coastline south of Atlantic City, all my instruments went out. This was a total electrical failure. The solar panels didn't work well enough to maintain a charge in the batteries. Without electrical power, I could not communicate, navigate, or even run the autopilot. Without an autopilot I would have to operate the burners at all times and would have no opportunity for sleep. Therefore, there was no possibility of flying around the world—I was now in survival mode. Too bad this electrical failure didn't happen just 50 miles earlier because I could have descended through the storm and gotten the balloon on the ground somehow.

I started to think of contingency plans and realized that maybe it would be possible to make it across the Atlantic without ditching. I could fly without burners like a traditional gas balloon just as the first TransAtlantic flight was done by Anderson, Abruzzo, and

Newman in 1978. Instead of sand ballast in a gas balloon, I had a
huge amount of fuel weight. Each night I could cut loose one or two
fuel tanks as ballast to stop the balloon from going to the surface
of the ocean and when it climbed too high during the day, I could
valve out helium. It would be a harrowing trip of about four days
to reach Europe for landing, but at least it would be survivable,
theoretically. Then I had a better idea. Since I was above the leading
edge of this huge storm and the wind circulated counter-clockwise
around a low, I could descend into the storm and ride the winds to
the north with the hopes of hitting Nova Scotia or Newfoundland
before being pulled over the open water of the North Atlantic. The
winds were propelling me at a very fast rate to the east and further
out over the sea. Since my navigational instruments were down, I
tried to remember the shape of the weather patterns and the
possibility that they could take me back up to Canada rather than
on my trajectory over the Atlantic. I wanted to get back to Canada.

The next day, I was still flying in the snowstorm over the Atlantic
and was heading up the Bay of Fundy when suddenly the balloon
cooled and started to descend. Although I tried to arrest my fall, I
couldn't. As the water rushed up to meet me, I threw back the hatch
to climb out on the capsule and ballast some fuel, but it was too
late. The capsule ricocheted off the water. The sudden impact with
the sea's surface was so violent that it dislodged the skirt of
material, which comprises the lower 10 ft of the balloon system. I
immediately pulled out my knife and cut away two fuel tanks. I
should have dropped only one because I immediately went into a
rapid climb. I valved helium all the way up and still the balloon did
not level until 15,000 ft. Things were not going well. I was in zero
visibility from the light snow showers and had no way of notifying
other aircraft of my position. I was quite shaken up but also
disappointed that I had lost control of the balloon and smacked the
water. With these flying problems and the lack of electricity to
operate the transponder so other aircraft would know I was there,
I decided to set off my EPIRB (Emergency Position Indicating Radio
Beacon) to notify the search and rescue team so they could track my
location. An EPIRB is a small, battery-powered emergency satellite
transmitting device carried on ships and aircraft for use in case of
emergencies. It may be activated automatically by water or manually to transmit signals, which assist search and rescue units in
responding to and finding persons in distress.

Later that afternoon, I was proceeding toward the north end of
the Bay of Fundy and was then pulled over the northern shore just

north of St John's in the province of New Brunswick, Canada over which I decided to descend. As I got closer to the ground, I actually saw the field that I wanted to get to if only the wind would cooperate. The winds really cooperated to the extent that I was able to fly a traditional aircraft-landing pattern of 'Downwind', 'Base' and 'Final'. My original north course was the Downwind leg, the lower level winds carried me west for the Base leg and surface winds took me south for the Final leg. I dragged in on the snow- covered hay field before I was able to summon some surprised spectators to hold the capsule until I could release enough helium from the balloon to stop it from dragging the capsule.

When Joe Ritchie learned that I had lost communication upon leaving the US coast, he got in his Cessna Conquest and came to search for me or help in any way he could. He arrived in New Brunswick soon after my landing, bringing Bill Kurtis, the documentary producer, our team photographer Kate Oeleric and Joe's daughter. It was great to have friends on hand and that set up the occasion of a celebratory dinner in St John's. I reflected how I didn't get too far in my first around the world flight attempt. I flew for just two days and for only about 2000 miles. But at least I had survived.

It is redundant to say that my father's death was hard on my mother. Although she knew his demise was inevitable and that he had suffered from Alzheimer's for five long years, his passing was hard for her to accept. As we drove from the cemetery after my father's funeral service, I wondered how she would spend her days without him. Even though my father had been confined to a nursing home, I wondered what her life would be like now. For some reason I couldn't picture it. I don't think she could, either.

My mom had always been a trooper. She was never one to play the martyr, the victim. She had this great sense of humor that was one of her most outstanding and endearing character traits. Despite whatever setbacks she encountered throughout her life, she always managed to hold her head high and carry on and see the lightness and humor in circumstances if possible. I hoped that she would do the same in this situation. To get her excited about the future, soon after the funeral, I encouraged her to plan a trip to Switzerland to visit the places where she and my father had spent many summers. I told her I would pay for her airfare and expenses. She was deeply appreciative and accepting of my offer. She booked her flight and seemed genuinely enthused about her trip.

Soon after returning home to Beaver Creek from my first around the world balloon attempt and merely six weeks after my father's death, I received some shocking and deeply saddening news: my mother had died in her sleep from carbon monoxide poisoning. My sister Linda explained to me that Mom had come home from doing some errands that day and left the car running in the garage. She, too, had become forgetful in her golden years and would sometimes get out of the car without turning off the engine. As the garage is attached to the house, when she walked in the door, her beloved cat scampered out into the garage. Since it was winter, she feared the cat would become cold out there and so she left the door connecting the house to the garage open for the cat to come back in. She never turned the car engine off or shut the door. She never made it to Switzerland. She died that night in her sleep.

Her death was initially deemed a suicide. When some family members vehemently objected, suicide was stricken from the coroner's report and it was ruled an 'accidental death'. How or why was not important to me. Either way, I understood. The weeks following my father's death, I had noticed that the light had faded from my mother's eyes. Her abundant sense of humor with which she had always embraced life was no more.

There was a solemnity at my mother's funeral that I had never experienced before. That she was laid to rest next to my father, her husband, was the greatest consolation. As I stared blankly at her casket, emotionally drained from having lost both of my parents in quick succession, I concluded that perhaps we are not always supposed to understand the meaning of events, that some things will remain a mystery and that the key to living peacefully is being comfortable with that.

What I was certain of was that my mother had been proud of me. She was my biggest fan. Any time my name was mentioned in the press for a certain feat I achieved or record I had broken, my mother took it upon herself to share this news with whomever she came in contact with. From her neighbors to strangers at the supermarket: 'That's my son!' she'd gleefully exclaim.

Standing at her graveside watching the sunlight begin to slowly recede from the winter sky, itself a reflection of the evanescence of life, I made a promise to myself that day. I would continue to make my mother proud of me.

10. OVERJOYED: A NEW PACIFIC OCEAN SINGLEHANDED WORLD RECORD, AUGUST 1996

He is the best sailor who can steer within fewest points of the wind, and exact a motive power out of the greatest obstacles.
　　　Henry Thoreau, *A Week on the Concord and Merrimack Rivers*

S ince I always sailed with very good sailors and not as a profession, I made a point of continuing to sail singlehanded to debunk the possible misconception that I didn't know anything, that I was just a city boy and new to the sport. It was important for me to demonstrate that I just wasn't along for the ride, that I could sail the boat and do it alone if necessary. In fact, I felt cut out for this type of challenge. Singlehanded sailing is also very much an endurance test and endurance is my best attribute. I was in my element.

Although I had the choice of entering singlehanded sailing races, I much preferred breaking world records. The feeling of going after a record is distinctly different than competing in a race. Since one isn't racing against other boats, it becomes purely a race against time, a feeling that is much more exhilarating for me. It forces me to make the best use of every second to beat the standing record time. Besides, a record is more prestigious than a race win: there is a race winner every time the race is held but there is only one record holder. By definition the record represents the fastest that a course has ever been sailed.

In May 1996, my crew—Brian Thompson, Ben Wright, Peter Hogg and I—delivered *Lakota* to Yokohama, Japan, from where I would sail back to the States alone. I was going after the West to East Pacific Ocean Record, which is sailed from Yokohama to San Francisco. Funny thing, in getting the boat to Japan we also put up the East to West TransPacific record. The reason there are two different records for sailing across the Pacific is the difference in speed; the West–East route is faster than the East–West route because of the prevailing wind. Finally, after repairs from the delivery trip were completed, *Lakota* was fully prepared for the voyage. Bob Rice, as meteorologist, sent me off from Yokohama on 5 August 1996. As I sailed away from the Japanese coastline, *Lakota* was in top form.

Throughout the trip, I never encountered a serious problem or breakage that I couldn't repair alone. In fact, it was one of the most eventless journeys that I had since starting sailing three years earlier. The worst parts of the trip were the holes of no wind that I encountered. Twice I ran out of wind for nearly a day. Later in the trip I were virtually becalmed for an agonizing three days. The most frustrating thing for me is when the wind disappears and I can't do anything about it.

I used the time constructively to check and recheck the boat's equipment. I also planned out future ballooning and sailing adventures and waited for the conditions to change. I was already in the throes of preparing for my next around the world balloon attempt. After my first attempt my team and I realized in retrospect that the launch was a bust from the start. This didn't deter me. I was more than willing to learn from my mistakes. That attempt taught me that I would need to go back to the drawing board and effect some design changes to the balloon, electrical system and capsule. We needed to redesign the balloon insulation factor so that none of the reflective Mylar on the outside of the fabric would be directly attached to any load-bearing portion of the balloon, such as the webbing. This would enable the Mylar to maintain independence of, and not be affected by, any change in the balloon. All these problems sifted through my mind as I sat becalmed on *Lakota* in the Pacific Ocean.

I also used my windless hours to catch up on sleep, which tended to elude me when I sailed singlehanded. Sleeping was always a little scary when the boat was sailing, especially downwind. If a sudden gust of wind came up at a surprising wind angle, the sails could load up and pull the boat over—and, once upside down, these big multihulls don't come back right side up. My routine before getting ready to sleep was to take an extra reef. Reefing is lowering and re-securing the mainsail on the mast in order to reduce sail area. I would set alarms for boat speed and wind angle to alert me to dangerous changes in the wind. Because the alarm was so loud there was no danger of sleeping through it. In fact, I would have to turn off the alarm first before solving whatever sailing problem caused it. With all of my attention focused on the boat and the wind, there wasn't much time for sleep in singlehanded sailing. I've never gotten any sleep on the first and last nights of a singlehanded record attempt. Four hours per night was the average for the rest of the days on the water.

As if to underscore its mercurial nature, when the wind finally came back, it did so with a fury. All of a sudden I found myself scrambling to get the sails reefed in order to keep under control. Just as the wind filled in the slacken sails, so, too, did it lift my spirits. As I reefed and jibed, I was reveling in my increased speed, thankful to be clipping along again, making up for lost time. With two reefs in the main and the staysail up, I was soon hitting speeds of more than 30 knots. *Lakota* came alive as she shot through the water with ease. The day was perfect. The sailing was perfect. The sun glistened on the deep blue water. I smiled as we surfed down gentle, undulating waves, picking up more speed. The wind and the heat from the sun felt great on my face. Wide-open seas, great waves, a beautiful day; I thought to myself that it couldn't get any better than this.

After 20 days 9 hours 52 minutes 59 seconds I sailed under the Golden Gate Bridge in San Francisco—shrouded in dense fog—and crossed the finish line. I crossed the finish line under at around midnight after traveling 4525 miles. I was overjoyed. I had established a new Pacific Ocean Singlehanded World Record. It was a moment of epiphany for me personally. This was the first World Record I had broken sailing on my own.

Breaking this singlehanded World Record went a long way to building my confidence level and proving to the media and sailing community my competency as a speed sailor. At that time I never expected my World Record to last for more than a couple of years. Yet even today, my record time has still not been superseded.

My next singlehanded record was the 1998 Singlehanded Trans-Pac Race from San Francisco to Kauai, Hawaii in *Lakota*. Although the weather was favorable, on the first night I damaged the daggerboard. A daggerboard is a retractable centerboard that is lowered downward through the hull to give the boat straighter tracking, especially upwind. It hit something in the water and the daggerboard had split and started to peel. The breakage generated a lot of noise for the rest of the trip. Despite the extra drag, the winds from California to Hawaii were sufficient to make for great and swift sailing. I sailed as opportunistically as I could. Throughout the trip, I made plenty of sail changes in response to any meaningful shift in direction or force of the wind. It was beautiful sailing, culminating with a dawn arrival at Honalei Bay on the island of Kauai. I was First to Finish and set the course record with a time of 7 days 22 hours 38 minutes.

11. QADDAFI CHANGES HIS MIND: MY SECOND SOLO ROUND THE WORLD BALLOON ATTEMPT, JANUARY 1997

It is only in adventure that some people succeed in knowing themselves—in finding themselves.

André Gide, *Journals*

In addition to the harshness of the elements, harshness expressed by humans can pose an equal if not greater threat to the lives and safety of balloonists. In September 1996 two American balloon pilots, Alan Fraenckel and John Stuart-Jervis, were shot down and killed by a helicopter gunship when they flew over military airspace in the former Soviet republic of Belarus. They were participating in the Gordon Bennett International Balloon Race, which is the most renowned balloon race in the world.

Responding to the onslaught of international criticism this inhumane act incited, the Belarus Ministry of Defense had alleged that the pilots of the balloons had committed violations of international norms and customs. The US State Department rejected this excuse as 'totally unacceptable'. According to the race organizers, the balloonists had filed flight plans and had received permission to overfly Belarus airspace. Moreover, one of the balloonists was by profession an airline pilot and was very well versed in international air traffic procedures. When I launched my second round the world balloon attempt little did I know that I would be faced with having to avoid this outcome myself.

While Mission Control remained at Loyola University in Chicago, I changed my location for the launch. After some friends of mine, who had recently bought the St Louis baseball Cardinals team, offered me Busch Stadium as a launch site, I seized the opportunity to have a stadium launch which had worked so well for my TransPacific Solo, when I took off from Olympic Stadium in Seoul, Korea. I relished St Louis as the place for the launch partly because I had attended graduate business school at Washington University in St Louis and I was still involved as a member of the university's Board of Trustees. This location also appealed to me for a tactical reason. To establish my around the world balloon flight as official, I would have to cross the North–South line, the longitude from where I took off. Starting on the East Coast meant that, when I came back to land at this longitude, the winds could easily carry my balloon past its landing target and out over the sea. Therefore, I thought that central US was a safer and more logical area from which to launch and St Louis, Missouri satisfied this criterion. The evening of the balloon inflation on 12 January 1997 the wind was active, swirling in the stadium during this critical early phase of the launch. We had hoped for calm cold air but that night there was 10 mph of wind flowing down the Mississippi River and coursing through the arches of Busch Stadium. When the balloon is first rising to stand upright, it is vulnerable to twisting and tearing. Although the capsule was well secured to stadium vehicles, the balloon was being buffeted in the wind and once made a complete twist. Bruce Comstock stood in the capsule trying to finish the checklists as the fuel tanks were clanking against each other and the entire balloon system was being pulled precariously over to one side. Finally, when there was enough helium in the balloon to make it firm and stable, I hurriedly boarded the capsule and released the system and took off out of there. Since it was the wee hours of the morning of 13 January, few people saw the launch. Luckily, I was able to escape without damage to the balloon. As I climbed into the cloudless night, it was an awe-inspiring sight to see the stadium and the skyline of downtown St Louis.

The Atlantic crossing went well, during which I opportunistically cut away empty fuel tanks after opening valves to ensure that they would fill with seawater and sink into the ocean. Gas balloonists are always looking for ways to ditch superfluous weight so the balloon can fly higher to take advantage of the faster winds. That was not the only thing I unloaded. I was required to carry an HF Radio for long-distance communication with Air Traffic Control, which I hated because of the scratchy transmissions and the interminable repetition necessary to make myself understood. As I approached the eastern side of the Atlantic, I took the delightful opportunity of tossing the radio into the sea 18,000 ft below. From this point onward I could use the shorter range VHF radio instead.

After having successfully made it across the Atlantic, my plans changed. I had expected to join the Polar Jetstream which would have pulled me north into Europe then across Eastern Europe and possibly on through Russia. Yet the turn north did not happen as I completed the Atlantic crossing. Instead, I tracked due East over the Straits of Gibraltar and missed my ride in the Polar Jetstream. To make matters worse, I was heading directly for Libya, one of the last countries in the world that I wanted to go to.

As I proceeded over Morocco and into Algeria, the wind looked like it was going to deliver me to Libya's doorstep. At that time, US–Libyan relations were less than cordial. Since flying over Libya was not on my itinerary, my team at Mission Control frantically tried to figure out how we were going to procure overflight permission from Libya. Efforts to find winds in this area to carry me away south of the Libyan border were futile. My meteorologist, Lou Billones, informed me that there just weren't any. Entering Libyan airspace without permission meant that I'd face the grim risk of being shot down. In order to buy some time to get a contingency plan worked out, I flew low to reduce my speed. Also, at the lower altitudes, the wind direction carried me farther south over the countries of Mali and Chad and, if I waited long enough maybe, hope against hope, I could even get far enough south to round the southern point of Libya.

Circumnavigating the globe by any kind of aircraft necessitates obtaining overflight permission to pass over foreign countries' airspace. The unpredictable nature of ballooning means it's best to get permission from as many countries as possible in case you should fly over them. Most of the information submitted is routine identification but with a unique flight like a balloon each country generally wants to know more: Am I a threat? Is my flight for political reasons? Once the authorities were assured that I wasn't going to photograph anything and that I was just a die-hard adventurer, getting permission usually wasn't a problem. In the course of applying for overflight clearance from every possible country before my launch, Libya had denied us permission to enter their airspace. Obtaining permission at this stage of the game would be nothing short of a miracle.

Responding to our overflight request, Colonel Qaddafi brought up the UN embargo against Libya which in part prohibited Libyan airliners from flying over other countries. These sanctions were imposed when Libya refused to hand over suspects in the 1988 bombing of Pan Am Flight 103 over Lockerbie, Scotland. Qaddafi told CNN Cairo to tell me, 'Because our country has an air embargo, you cannot come through the airspace of Libya. You should contact your government and ask them to lift the embargo on our republic.'

Making the situation more complex, my flight occurred at the same time as Ramadan, the Moslem holy period. Because of the holiday, the Libyans that Mission Control had dealt with before the flight were not working and had been replaced by people of less authority who hadn't been briefed on our earlier correspondences with their country.

After ceaseless appeals from Mission Control, Libya finally granted me permission to enter their airspace. Obviously the UN embargo on Libya had not been lifted, therefore I was curious to know what the deciding factor was that swayed Qaddafi to change his mind. I learned that he did a background check on me and found out that I was an Eagle Scout in the Boy Scouts and that, indeed, I really was an adventurer. As it turned out, this bit of information built instant rapport with him. Evidently, Qaddafi had been a scout and was a supporter of scouting in his country. It may have been the boy scout in Qaddafi that influenced him to change his position on the matter! Even with Qaddafi's permission, I was admittedly still relieved when I was eventually able to fly far enough south to avoid most of Libya's military airspace.

With overflight permission, I climbed up in altitude to 25,000 ft and caught the jetstream that propelled me straight across the southern tip of Libya and onward. As I made my way across Egypt, I was surprised when I began to make tremendous progress. I was in the Subtropical Jetstream, which enabled me to make a straight track to the east and travel at speeds of over 110 mph. Until I experienced this, I had always assumed that the Northern Hemisphere's Polar Jetstream was the best flight pattern. Now I had found by chance rather than by analysis that the Subtropical

Jetstream was better. This discovery set a new precedent. From that day forward, any contender for the first Round the World Balloon Flight, including myself, would base their route on aiming to achieve long periods of flying in the Subtropical Jetstream instead of the Polar Jetstream.

While making great progress across the Middle East, a new problem rose to the forefront: I had burned one-third more fuel than the theoretical balloon model had predicted. Maybe I was inefficient in my flying, especially with my slow routing to get south of Libya, but, more likely, I suspected the model was wrong. Whatever the reason, what was clear was that now I didn't have enough fuel to make it back to St Louis or even to the West Coast of the United States. I just wasn't going to make it round the world.

As I was heading for China, the overflight issue came up again and would become a prime determinant in where I would land. China had been absolutely rigid about denying overflight permission. Their position was that since a balloon cannot turn and cannot fly on the designated airways, it would infringe on their military airspace. I had tried every channel to get an overflight permit from them. Despite the efforts of the US Ambassador to China and even former President Jimmy Carter, who wrote a personal request to Premier Li Peng with whom he had a warm relationship, China would not budge. Since I couldn't make it across the Pacific Ocean and I would have needed to land in China before starting the Pacific crossing, I started thinking backward. Since China would have probably arrested and thrown me in prison if I landed there, I thought I had better land before crossing their border. I decided to put this big balloon down on the ground in India.

As I came into India, it was still nighttime and storm activities were brewing against the southwest side of the Himalaya. Although I could have landed at sunrise, I decided to stay aloft until midday. I wanted to beat the Absolute Duration World Record for ballooning, which was six days, and set by Richard Abruzzo and Troy Bradley on their TransAtlantic Balloon Race victory in 1992. After being aloft for more than their six-day time, finally, I was able to make my descent with a new record in hand.

The funny thing was, up until that time, I'd always done these impeccably beautiful balloon landings. As I was approaching the ground in India, I was having a hard time positioning myself. Extending my trail ropes, I anticipated a smooth landing in a clearing beyond the trees. However, I was moving too fast and couldn't descend. The two 150-ft ropes were being dragged through the numerous mini-villages embedded in the forest. Fearing that I would start pulling down their power lines or otherwise cause damage in the area, I cut away the trail ropes and lost this method of stabilizing the balloon. When my next landing attempt was out of control, I pulled back up. On yet a subsequent attempt, the balloon system dragged through some trees before bouncing aloft again. Embarrassed by the situation, I turned off the video cameras so nothing more of my bad approaches would be recorded for the television documentary being prepared by a Scottish TV company on the subject of Round the World Balloon Flight attempts.

As the situation grew more desperate, I resolved to touch down in a clearing that I spotted in the immediate distance. As I descended, the deflation ports failed to deploy again just as they had on previous flights. The balloon collided with the edge of a forest where it was ensnared and draped over the 50-ft tall trees and consequently, severely damaged. For a pilot who had prided himself on executing impeccably graceful landings, this comedy of errors was terribly humiliating. However, in hindsight, after having realized that we never have been able to recover or reuse one of these big balloons, I've decided that this is an effective and safe landing to make—put the balloon down into a clearing and allow it to drag to a safe stop in the trees.

I had set down in the Indian province of Uttar Pradesh, a rural area heavily populated with small villages scattered amongst the trees and meadows. When I finally opened the hatch and climbed out, I was met with a surreal sight—200 curious villagers were staring at me with a bewildering mixture of fear and awe. Being somewhat familiar with Hinduism, I was aware of the rich and epic mythology that boasts numerous pantheons of deities native to this tradition. Now I was about to experience a lesson in how these people still keep their beloved myths alive.

Soon a Hindu priest, sporting red and yellow body paint and carrying a shallow bucket of warm milk, showed up on the scene. Offering me a cup of the warm milk, I figured that maybe this was a command performance and that I'd better not let him down. I accepted his gift. To the delight of the gathered crowd, he proclaimed me to be Hunaman, the Monkey God. Upon reincarnation, Hanuman would return to earth in a flying temple. With my balloon's silverized Mylar covering and strange shape, nothing could be more convincingly a 'flying temple', especially to people who had never seen a balloon fly overhead. My balloon system was 'the shiny object that had fallen from sky'. Once again, I had brought a measure of excitement to a remote location where I had landed my distance balloon flight.

Finally, an English-speaking military officer appeared, arranged guards for my equipment, and took me to the local police station to review my papers. He then took me to the equivalent of the Mayor of the nearest substantial town, Sultanpur. After having chased me halfway around the world in his Cessna Conquest turboprop, Joe Ritchie tracked me down that evening in Sultanpur. With him were his daughter Molly, several photographers, and a cameraman from the documentary company. In the morning we went back out to recover the equipment and there was no longer any way to hide my 'tree'd' balloon from the news media. Joe proceeded to organize a couple hundred locals to help us load the remains of the balloon on carts pulled by tractors. We left the silver Mylar cover hanging in the trees, imagining that the silvery balloon fabric would be made into tents, dresses and other stylish apparel by the villagers. *National Geographic*, which was covering the event, offered to get the balloon capsule back to the US. Having always been a big fan of *National Geographic*, I appreciated their help in this matter. When the remainder of the balloon system returned to the United States, the capsule was outfitted for display at the Explorers' Hall at the *National Geographic's* world headquarters in Washington, DC. As requested, we agreed to exhibit it there for a period of time as a way of saying 'thank you' for their bringing the capsule back to the States. After the exhibition was over, the capsule was then transported to the Smithsonian's National Air and Space Museum, where it was displayed for four weeks.

Although I wasn't successful on my second attempt, I was pleased to have gotten a lot farther, gained two new Absolute World Records and had a fun time standing in for a monkey god, if only for a moment. I broke my own Absolute World Distance Record with a distance of 10,360.61 miles. I also broke the Absolute World Duration Record for balloons staying aloft a total of 6 days 2 hours 44 minutes. I achieved the latter by hovering an extra six hours above India before my landing. I had traveled further than anyone in a balloon and felt confident that, with the correct amount of fuel, I would accomplish my goal next time. When I returned home, I immediately called up Cameron Balloons and ordered another balloon.

12. RUSSIAN HOSPITALITY: MY THIRD SOLO ROUND THE WORLD BALLOON ATTEMPT, JANUARY 1998

If the sheer will of millions of supporters could keep him aloft, there would be no doubt of his success.
                    e-mail from a woman to the St Louis University's website

'We must talk' were the first words August Busch III said to me when former FBI Director William Webster introduced us. The three of us were putting on our academic caps and gowns just prior to the dedication of the new Law School building at Washington University in St Louis. 'Judge' Webster, as he prefers to be addressed, and I were on the Board of Trustees of Washington University and August Busch was the Chief Executive Officer of Anheuser-Busch, the beer company, which was donating this building, to be named Busch Hall. I said, 'Okay,' to which he said, 'I'll call you to arrange something.'

That brief exchange of words led to me touching down my Falcon 10 in November 1997 in St Louis to go duck hunting. Once on the ground, I immediately boarded the Anheuser-Busch helicopter. After lift-off, August surprised me by saying 'Now you fly it,' another adventure, since I had never flown a helicopter before. After landing at the farm west of St Louis where he lived, we put on our camouflage and went out to a duck blind. After a lot of shooting, he indicated that Anheuser-Busch was interested in becoming the sponsor of my next attempt to fly around the world by balloon. I had to explain that I had already gone on record that I would fly without advertising and in the pure spirit of adventure. 'Then how can we be involved,' he pressed. I suggested the idea being discussed by the competitors that there should be a prize for the first successful Round the World Balloon Flight. This would be great advertising for the sponsor regardless of who won the competition. I reminded him that in the early twentieth century, there were typically cash prizes for the various 'firsts' in Aviation, the most famous being the $25,000 Orteig Prize that Charles Lindbergh eventually won with his TransAtlantic flight from New York to Paris. August mulled it over awhile. We shot at a few more ducks. Then he asked, 'How much would we need to put up for this Prize?'

'These days, it would need to be a million bucks,' I replied.

Back at the house we enjoyed some hors d'oeuvres that his wife Virginia had prepared while we sat around the bar testing a new batch of Bud Light made with a new source of hops. He asked his son August IV, who was the Vice President of Marketing, what he thought of the Prize idea. August IV responded that he thought it would work. After a few more sips August III announced, 'Here's what we are going to do. We'll put up a million-dollar prize for the first Round the World Balloon Flight. One half of the money will go to the Pilot but the other half has to go to charity.' I had just witnessed one of corporate America's most decisive executives in action. I thought it was a sweetheart deal for me since I was having far more success than my competitors and I was clearly the favorite to win the race for the first Round the World. Raising our glasses to toast August's decision, I was already calculating in my mind, 'The charity half to Washington University; now how should I split the Pilot half with my team?'

The launch site for my third attempt would again be Busch Stadium in St. Louis. This time the entire effort would be based at this locale. Mission Control would be at Washington University in a dramatic-looking room with a vaulted ceiling, which originally functioned as the Chapel. Students were selected to man Mission Control and handle the multitude of media inquiries. I put Tim Cole in charge of the preparation of the capsule systems and launch team. He brought back in my gas balloon instructor John Kugler and former team member Dennis Brown. Bert Padelt, a balloon builder from Pennsylvania, also joined the team. This would be my crack launch team for all my subsequent RTW balloon attempts. These guys were some of the best gas balloonists in the United States and I felt each one added a special expertise when it came to preparing the balloon for launch.

During pre-flight preparations, Professor Ray Arvidson, Head of the Earth and Planetary Sciences Department at Washington University, got a call from NASA's Jet Propulsion Laboratory (JPL) asking us if we would do them a favor. They wanted me to carry a science package: a payload that was designed to take measurements of the Earth's atmosphere so that NASA could practice telemetry procedures for a future plan to put a robotic balloon called an 'aerobot' in orbit in the atmospheres of Mars or Venus. An automated satellite communication system would transmit the data simultaneously back to JPL and to Washington University for posting on the website. The infrared sensors that would collect this data were relatively light in weight and would not interfere with my operating the balloon system optimally. We had our science project! The students in Earth and Planetary Sciences immediately went to work with the JPL engineers in Pasadena designing and implementing the project.

On 1 January 1998, I stood in the infield of Busch Stadium in St Louis with my head thrown back gazing at my inflated balloon towering into the sky above. The lights from the ballpark reflected off the silvery balloon fabric in a bedazzling way that was not at all incongruous with New Year's Day. Adding to the festive atmosphere were television media from all networks plus a few hundred enthusiastic well-wishers who had come out to the stadium to see me off. As I made my way to the capsule, I felt like a baseball player approaching the plate intent on hitting a homerun. If I were successful, my homerun would take me around the world, not just around the bases.

I had heard that Richard Branson, the British business mogul and now a competitor to make the first around the world balloon flight, had arrived to see me off and was somewhere on the field. It only took me a minute to find him standing near the capsule; I approached him and started chatting nonchalantly. Unbeknownst to us, the television cameras were rolling, capturing our exchange.

'Well, this Steve Fossett is really an amazing guy. I can't believe he's doing this,' Branson gushed.

Realizing that he didn't recognize me and I had better tell him I said, 'I am Steve Fossett.'

Richard's face turned crimson red as he attempted to laugh off his gaffe. This, I would learn, was vintage Richard Branson. He ventures out into the unknown and unprotected environments as the promoter of the 'Virgin' brand and his image. But his venturesomeness leads to spectacular gaffes and humiliating scenes. Our meeting would run memorably on British television to the huge amusement of the audience, but Richard is always unfazed. These little embarrassments come with the territory.

Looking around to see who was watching, Richard saw that the cameras were rolling and nervously ran a hand through his wavy blond hair. He explained that he had come out to wish me luck and to watch my launch. As we were both competing to be the first to balloon around the world, I appreciated this generous and sportsmanlike gesture. Over the ensuing years when I got to know Richard Branson better, my first impression of him as being good-natured and genuine has endured untarnished.

A few hours later, my balloon swiftly lifted me up into the St Louis nighttime sky as I began my third attempt to balloon around the world. As I crossed South Carolina and headed out over the Atlantic Ocean, I was clipping along, making good speed and thinking that this time I had a chance to hit a 'homerun'. Prior to my takeoff, my team and I had made the necessary upgrades to the existing technology and equipment that would facilitate my flight. For instance, I was no longer using a gas generator or solar panels that had failed me in previous attempts. Instead, I carried 21 blocks of fifteen lithium batteries that hung on the outside of the capsule. Each block of batteries lasted nearly one day, after which I'd ballast them into the sea below. I was also flying with Bruce Comstock's improved autopilot. Each year Bruce had made improvements to the 'Comstock Autopilot', to the point where I had now felt that he had perfected the system. After enduring frigid capsule temperatures on all my previous flights, I finally had a heater that worked. Professors in the Engineering School designed a heat exchanger that ran on my balloon burner fuel, then Tim Cole had it built and tested.

Once over the Atlantic, my speed accelerated and the flying was spectacular. I was caught by surprise to see a field of city lights rapidly approaching. A quick look at my chart indicated that I was making a direct pass over Bermuda. The next day, things got dicey. Lou Billones sounded the first alarm: the wind that was carrying me across the Atlantic toward England was going to make a big left turn toward Greenland. The only hope was to climb higher where the jetstream was going straight to England. If I got high enough, I would make the turn east into Europe. Tim Cole did the calculations and told me I needed to drop two fuel tanks into the ocean in order to get to 23,000 ft. I put up a brief argument that this was 15% of my fuel, a sacrifice that would seriously jeopardize my chances of making it around the world. Tim came back saying that there was no choice but to do it. Since dropping this much weight would cause a rapid climb and risk rupturing the balloon, I gingerly valved some helium to set up a descent, then cut the nylon webbing holding a tank. The ensuing climb was 800 ft per minute, which was at the upper limit of safety. I waited to level off at a safe altitude then repeated the process with the second tank. When I reached 23,000 ft, I got a call from Donald Cameron, the balloon designer, who warned not even to consider landing in the British Isles. The jetstream had brought in the biggest windstorm of the year, which would drag a balloon landing there across the ground at 50 mph with likely fatal results. I stayed at 23,000 ft where I was able to just skim the tops of the storm clouds and endured being swept up and down by a thousand feet as my balloon followed the waves of the upper level winds.

Bad news just kept piling up. When my new trajectory was calculated we realized that it was going to take me over Libya. Not Libya again! Rapid enquiries into how to remedy this situation revealed that there was no way I was going to get overflight permission in time. Unlike my previous crossing on the southern tip of Libya, permission for which was only granted at the last moment, this time I would be entering from the Mediterranean straight over the capital of Tripoli. Visualizing a welcoming party of fighter jets was enough to persuade me not to risk it. I decided to fly low across Germany to pick up enough west winds at lower flight levels to change my trajectory to Egypt and then join the subtropical jetstream there. This plan didn't work as I had hoped and I found myself on a trajectory through Eastern Europe with no possibility of getting back south to the subtropical jetstream. Ironically, the Libya overflight permission was received, but 12 hours too late for me to make any use of it.

My next setback came by way of a faulty solenoid and, subsequently, the loss of a burner. Each of the four burners has a solenoid, which allows the burners to be fired electrically from inside the capsule by either pushing a button or by the autopilot.

Since I only used two burners at a time while in level flight, I reasoned that maybe I could continue effectively with the loss of just one burner. Despite my optimism, my circumstances were, frankly, getting desperate. I was down 15% of fuel due to having dropped the fuel tanks, I was off course and now I had lost a burner. My only hope was that I could pull off a longshot which involved crossing southern Russia, a strictly forbidden country to overfly, get to Kazahkstan where I did have overflight permission, and from there get back into the jetstream for a swift crossing of forbidden China.

It is ironic that the morning twilight was my darkest hour for this attempt. After crossing Bucharest, Romania and approaching the coast of the Black Sea, a second solenoid failed. My flight was definitely busted. Since it was too late to set up a landing from my altitude of 18,000 ft before getting out over the Black Sea, I considered where I could land. It became apparent that I would have to fly another day and night to get to southern Russia and then land in this hostile country.

As the wind pushed me toward Russia, Mission Control received calls from our US Embassy in Moscow, which wanted to know where I was and reiterating to Mission Control staff that I could not under any circumstances enter Russian airspace because I didn't have permission to do so. Tim Cole responded to this directive by saying, 'he's flying in a balloon and must go where the wind takes him'. Evidently, the Embassy didn't care where the wind took me as long as it wasn't Russia. I was not to enter this country.

Nearing Krasnador, a province in the southern region of Russia, evoked an uncomfortable feeling within me that nonetheless motivated me into action. I decided to take the matter into my own hands. I contacted the air traffic controllers in Krasnador and requested permission to enter their airspace. During the long pause while I waited for their response, I braced myself for denial. Then, to my utter astonishment, the air traffic controller came back and said, 'Absolutely.' I immediately got on the phone to Tim to give him the update, which he then relayed to the US Embassy. Although I had received permission to enter and land in Russia, the Embassy came back with, 'But we don't have permission, so he can't go into Russia.' What they meant was that Moscow wouldn't grant permission to enter Russian airspace.

As I crossed the border into Russia, I hoped that the Krasnador authority to grant me permission to enter their country was legitimate. Since I had no choice in the matter, I decided to take their word for it. Once I reached the coastline, I prepared to land. I knew that the area was farm country that had livestock and wheat fields, so at least I could hope for flat ground for landing. Having chosen my field for landing, I worried when I encountered a 15 mph wind, which is very fast for this huge balloon. Coming in for the landing and at the moment of touchdown, I pulled the deflation line to deploy the deflation port. It opened and I stuck the landing like a Russian gymnast. The balloon did not drag a bit. This was the first and the last time of all my balloon flights that the deflation system worked—a haunting thought when considering the danger of being dragged across the ground by one of these huge balloons.

Once safely on the ground, I waited for some people to help me. Some of the local farmers soon approached me and I was surprised when it became apparent that these people knew who I was. They had heard about my balloon flight on the international news. Soon thereafter the Russian military arrived and offered to guard my equipment and give me a ride into the city of Krasnador. Once we reached the city, they put me in the best hotel suite.

Joe Ritchie, who was working in Mission Control, knew I was going to need help. Joe owned a computer services company in Russia and was able to arrange for his favorite translator, Mikhail Homasuik, to fly down from Moscow to help me.

In the morning, a rack of dark Russian business suits arrived at my hotel suite for me to choose the best fit. I was told there would be a reception for me with the Governor of the Krasnador region, followed by a Press Conference with the Moscow International Press Corps, which had just arrived by chartered airline flight.

Despite all the bureaucratic impediments that attended my balloon landing, it was a pleasure for me to experience first-hand the degree to which the people in Russia are captivated by a good adventure. Perhaps this had something to do with the fact that I was in the Cossack region of Russia. Typifying boldness and bravery, the Cossacks are the traditional horsemen warriors who spanned out from this region to make conquests throughout Russia. It didn't take me long to conclude that someone who would try to fly a balloon around the world and be forced to land in Russia without any support crew was just their kind of guy. My theory was validated when the Governor presented me with a traditional Cossack long coat and other regalia. Over the next two days, there was one party after another held in my honor. At each event, I partook in the customary three successive vodka toasts and discovered what is perhaps the key to international cooperation. As the effects of the vodka took hold, either I learned Russian or they learned English. In other words, the alcohol effectively melted all barriers.

The Russian hospitality and excitement made an indelible impression on me. I vividly remember one older man stopping me in a store and expressing with animated enthusiasm how excited he was about my flight. He went on to explain that his ambition was to bicycle around the world but sadly he had never fulfilled his dream. His disclosure awoke me to the fact that what I was trying to do was fascinating and uplifting to many people throughout the world and that, more importantly, I should not fold up my balloon and quit. Despite the risk and the costs, I was more determined than ever to pursue this goal until I finally succeeded.

13. BREAKING RECORDS: SAILING SINGLEHANDED, 1998–99

To be alive involves some risks.

Harold Macmillan, *The New York Times*

1998 turned out to be a busy and enormously successful year for my sailing programme. We were First to Finish in all six races entered that year: Chicago–Mackinac; Newport–Ensenada; San Diego–Puerto Vallarta; Port Huron–Mackinac; Swiftsure; and the Singlehanded Transpac. Four of those victories were also Race Records. The most extraordinary results were achieved with the *Stars & Stripes* catamaran which I had bought from America's Cup legend Dennis Conner in 1996. With *Stars & Stripes* we put up a couple of 'lifetime' records. By lifetime I mean that I don't expect these records to be broken in my lifetime: Chicago–Mackinac where we took 7 hours off the previous record for a time of 18 hours 50 minutes and the Newport–Ensenada where we finished in 6 hours 46 minutes, about 50 minutes faster than the previous record by Dennis Conner in the same boat. Two of the Race Records were also set using the durable *Lakota* trimaran in San Diego–Puerto Vallarta at just 62 hours 20 minutes and the Singlehanded Transpac from San Francisco to Kauai in 7 days 22 hours. These two open ocean races required the durability and strength of *Lakota* since the sea conditions would be too rough for the lightweight *Stars & Stripes*. With all this activity, my ballooning and sailing programs were reaching their pinnacles simultaneously.

After the Singlehanded Transpac, my next opportunity to sail a record solo came in June, 1999. This was not a race but rather an independent world record attempt on the same course as the celebrated biannual Newport–Bermuda Race. My start date was determined by a good wind forecast as determined by my sailing meteorologist Chris Bedford.

Lakota was in top condition and I felt more mentally prepared than ever before. My crew helped me hoist the mainsail in the harbor of Newport, Rhode Island then disembarked onto a dinghy. They would be getting to Bermuda by airplane. I trimmed the sails and hardened up to cross the official start line of the Newport–Bermuda course.

I was fortunate to sail throughout in good weather conditions. However, this is not to say that such conditions made for effortless sailing. Although there were no major storms to contend with, the capricious wind kept changing speed and direction, forcing me to make endless sail changes. In the 41 hours that I sailed, I made 17 sail changes. It was hard and unrelenting work, which resulted in virtually no sleep for me. The finish on the second night in Bermuda was absolutely spooky. It was pitch dark on a moonless night and I approached the reef-surrounded island at over 20 mph. One mistake in navigation would leave me grounded and *Lakota* destroyed. Fortunately I got it right and crossed the finish line in good form. Out of the darkness an inflatable pulled toward me and Brian Thompson jumped on board to give me a hand bringing *Lakota* through the narrow channel to the dock at St George's. The result was remarkable: my time was 40 hours 51 minutes—a full 12 hours faster than the previous record by fully crewed boats. I had just set an Outright World Record—the fastest record regardless of the class of boat or number of crew—and had done it singlehanded. So much for the perception of me being just a rich guy who hired good sailors to sail for him.

14. GOING SOUTH: MY FOURTH SOLO ROUND THE WORLD BALLOON ATTEMPT, AUGUST 1998

My name is Katherine and I am writing to say how brave I think you are. I hope you do not run out of gas.

from a nine-year-old girl

I approached my fourth around the world attempt knowing I had to do some things differently. We had presumed that a successful flight would be 20–23 days, but theoretically it could be done between 12 and 14 days. In order to get around the globe closer to the theoretical minimum, I would have to fly higher where the jetstream winds are faster. One way to do that was to fly with a larger balloon, which would offer greater flexibility in both elevation and duration. Therefore, we upgraded the balloon envelope to a size of 450,000 cubic ft, which was significantly larger than the previous balloon envelope, which was only 270,000 cubic ft. Of course, a larger balloon would require more fuel, but the lifting capability was nearly doubled so now I would be able to carry 40 cylinders of fuel as opposed to only 20 in the smaller balloon. I could climb immediately to 22,000 ft which would get me in the bottom of the jetstream. The balloon would have an estimated duration of 19 days.

Up until then, all my flights had taken place during the Northern Hemisphere's winter season, a time of year when the faster jetstreams are present. Aware that there was competition for the Round the World record, my strategy was to get a jump-start on the other teams by not waiting until winter. Or at least not winter in the north. I planned to launch from the Southern Hemisphere in July or August 1998 where it was winter. My flight path would take me 80% of the way over water. While the jetstreams wouldn't be as fast as they are in the Northern Hemisphere, my meteorologist, Bob Rice, assured me that winds should be more favorable down there, with cooler and more stable air and no large swings in day and nighttime temperatures. I wouldn't have to fly so high to catch the jetstream in the southern latitudes and the jetstream would not be disturbed by the continental effects of rising warm air. In addition, I would only have to fly over four countries: Argentina, Australia, New Zealand and Chile. This would greatly reduce the complexity of overflight permissions and the risk of military interceptions. The problem with the Southern Hemisphere is the water. A water landing is far more dangerous because of the risk of the capsule sinking, and being in the cold water where survival would be measured in minutes or hours, not days. Then there is the problem of rescue. There is virtually no shipping traffic over most of the southern oceans. For most of my route, if I went down, it would be days before a ship reached me for a rescue. The Southern Hemisphere is no place to be making a distance balloon flight unless you plan to succeed. I concluded that we were close enough to having the balloon system working and that I would make it this time. I would take the risk.

In June, we shipped the balloon system to our launch site, the Malvinas Football Stadium in Mendoza, Argentina at the foot of the highest part of the Andes. For the next two months Bob and I studied the weather patterns until we believed that we finally had the wind pattern to make a successful flight. In the evening of 7 August, I lifted off from the stadium. My launch was flawless. I ascended by the light of a full moon into a crystal clear sky. Everything looked good. I felt confident with my undertaking. Our planning and preparation had been meticulous.

At dawn, while flying at 21,000 ft, I was switching the fuel hoses that run from the fuel tanks on the side of the capsule to the burners overhead. At the instant that I disconnected the TEMA automatic shutoff fitting, fuel spewed out at high pressure. The fitting had failed to close, the burners above immediately ignited the fuel, and the hose was whipping about like a garden water hose turned full on. I grabbed it to gain control, but I was now holding a flame thrower that was shooting the burning propane 15 ft under high pressure. A fire in the confines of my balloon was horrifying! My heart was pounding! I had to think of an immediate solution before another fuel hose burned through. Instinctively knew I had to turn off the fuel at the tank, but I wasn't sure which one in the tangle of hoses. I just started turning off every tank that I could reach with one hand while I held the flame-throwing hose in the other. Unfortunately, it was the very last tank that finally stopped the fuel. I then put my oxygen mask back on and assessed the damage. My eyebrows had been singed and I had a small burn on my left wrist, but the balloon was not damaged. Despite the fire, this flight was going smoother than any other previous flight. I still felt confident of success.

As I headed out across the Indian Ocean, I was suddenly given a reason to rescind that appraisal. It was a slow but steady three days across the Southern Atlantic Ocean, then as I got deeper into the Indian Ocean I really lost the wind. I had been captured by the high-pressure system and was creeping at a snail's pace counter-clockwise to the north. Thinking way ahead, if I couldn't get free, I should try to get as close as possible to Diego Garcia Island where there is an Air Force base, then ditch. Nervously, I kept asking Bob Rice when I would get some relief. He confidently assured me that a jetstream would move south to my location and I could climb up into it when the time was right. My life seemed to hang on a weather forecast. After an impatient 36 hours at low altitudes of about 15,000 ft, Bob told me the winds were overhead. I climbed to 24,000 ft and I was moving again and in the right direction. Life was good again. Mother Nature was being kind. As I crossed Australia, my speed just kept accelerating until I was screaming at 100 mph across the central portion of the continent. I had intended to cross close to Sydney and then traverse the North Island of New Zealand, but the wind currents had taken me significantly farther north. As I crossed north of Bundaberg on the East Coast and started out across the Coral Sea, Mission Control thought that I was home free. I had sped over Australia in only 19 hours and the wind forecast indicated reaching the finish in Argentina in only five days. Based on that estimate, my round the world flight would take me just 13 days in total. Since the weather reports depicted good wind forecasts all the way to Argentina, Mission Control felt the rest of the flight was just a matter of putting in the time. They were so thrilled and confident that I was going to make it, they actually broke out bottles of champagne to celebrate.

I wasn't in the frame of mind to celebrate. My main emotion was one of concern. Because the jetstream continued to carry me a bit too far north, my balloon was on the threshold of entering the tropics and confronting a line of thunderstorms positioned there. I flew as high as I dared, which was 29,000 ft, as I crossed over the thunderstorms. Feeling like I had made it out of the danger zone, I thought my chances for completing the trip had improved again and that all was secure. I lay down to get some badly needed sleep, an essential that had evaded me over the last few days. It wasn't long until I awoke to the reality that there was more to that line of thunderstorms than I had reckoned. The altitude alarm woke me up, alerting me to the fact that the balloon was descending rapidly. I bolted out of the sleeping bag and manually took over the controls. Obviously, the autopilot wasn't holding the altitude any more. I fired the burners enough to arrest the descent and was relieved when the balloon started to climb again. I felt that I had just averted a sure disaster.

I continued to fire the burners from inside the capsule to maintain a safe altitude. Things were working fine this way until I fired the burners and the balloon climbed for only a brief moment and then started to descend again into the thunderstorm. The storm comprised upward and downward drafts of air that created this same dynamic with the balloon. When I'd dropped into the top of a thunderstorm, in contrast to the hot tropical air, the balloon was relatively cool and continued to sink against my will into the maelstrom. My fervent efforts to rise back above the storm were looking futile.

When I gave a good blast to the burners, the balloon shot up sharply, this time to 29,000 ft. Suddenly the balloon started falling rapidly from the sky like a hawk diving to catch its prey. At a loss to know why this was happening, I desperately blasted all burners to full capacity but to no avail. It was at this point that I knew something was seriously wrong with the system. I suspected the balloon was ruptured. My first thought was the crushing disappointment that now I wouldn't be able to finish the Round the World Flight. Of course, things were much worse than that—I had better worry about my survival. I instinctively grabbed for my parachute but realized that bailing out wasn't an option—I was over the ocean in a storm in the middle of the night! Separating myself from the balloon system and the emergency equipment therein wouldn't accomplish anything, except perhaps for pleasing a few sharks in the Coral Sea.

Somehow, I had to fly the balloon down in this violent thunderstorm and land softly. This was my only chance to survive. Big sheets of hail were pounding the capsule, I felt like I was under enemy fire. Time seemed to stand still. All I could think about was arresting my descent. I again fired all the burners, all four at once, nonstop. Perhaps the hot air passing through the streamered balloon would slow the descent somewhat.

It was wrong of me to think that the situation couldn't be any more dramatic. Opening the hatch and climbing out onto the capsule, I looked up and saw a huge ball of fire. This was not good. My balloon was being thrown from side to side and the lower edges of the balloon were burning! Adding fuel to this conflagration were the burners that were going at full blast. If there was ever a vision of hell, I was looking at it. I quietly said, 'I'm going to die.' My rate of descent was about 3500 ft per minute. I'd be killed from the impact of the capsule hitting the surface of the sea.

I had been schooled that the hardest landing anybody had ever survived in a balloon was a 2000 ft per minute fall. I figured my only chance of survival was to somehow slow the balloon down to that speed of descent. With very little time left to determine how to do that, I realized what I could do. I slid back into the capsule and decided to wait until the final minute before the balloon hit the sea surface and then cut away as much weight as I could. Decreasing the weight of the balloon might offset the speed of my fall and enable me to achieve a survivable impact.

With my gaze riveted on the altimeter, which spun down 5000, 4000, 3000, 2000 ft, I lunged up through the hatch, grabbed the knife sheathed on a riser, then cut the webbing straps on all the tanks that were not currently attached by hose to the burners. I cut away 5 full fuel tanks plus the liquid oxygen dewar. I quickly darted back into the capsule and tried to pull the hatch cover down. It was jammed between the risers in the up position. I wasn't going to have a waterproof capsule. With less than a minute to secure myself before the balloon collided with the sea, I forgot about the hatch and lay down on the bench. Although this might seem like some grandiose gesture of submission to forces beyond one's control, this was purely a practical move. Taking the impact standing up would have crushed my spine. Lying down mitigated this probability.

From my vantage point I could still clearly read the altimeter. The strange thing was, because of the discrepancy between the standard altimeter setting and what the pressure was at sea level, the altimeter spun right past 0 and I was still waiting for the impact! That was the last thought that crossed my mind before I hit the water.

The crash knocked me out briefly. When I woke up, I was a bit dazed. One thing I was certain of was that I was alive. I had survived the crash. The balloon had dragged the capsule sideways and upside down. Because I was unable to secure the hatch, the capsule was half-full of water as it lay upside down. Torn fuel hoses were still burning high-pressure propane and in fact starting to burn through my Kevlar composite capsule creating an acrid smoke in the half of the interior that was not under water. It was time to get out. Quickly I thought about what I needed to survive: I had to have my EPIRB, which would send my position satellite to the Rescue Control Center. The yellow EPIRB was conveniently floating in the capsule because I had already gotten it out during the descent. My life raft was stored in the back lower compartment and I had to think a moment an upside-down capsule in the dark: it must be upper right. I grabbed the briefcase-style raft in one hand, EPIRB in the other, and stuck a 2-liter bottle of water under my arm and dove down through the open hatch.

Making my way to the surface, I had dropped the water bottle but, without another thought, I pulled the lanyard on the life raft and it inflated. I pitched the EPIRB into the inflated life raft and climbed in. I was going to survive. I wouldn't expect to do something like that two times and be around to tell about it. The odds had definitely not been on my side. Now I was uninjured and minimally equipped, albeit only in my long underwear. Luckily the Coral Sea wasn't cold.

With the burning capsule next to me, I was worried that a propane tank would explode, so I moved hand over hand along the partially inflated recumbent balloon. Bobbing like a cork in my life raft on the chaotic sea, I tried hanging onto the balloon for some stability. Suddenly the wind blew forcefully and rolled the balloon over the top of the raft, suffocating me. Some of the propane was burning and some of it, having not been ignited, was just spewing out as pure gas. I held my breath as I desperately clawed with both hands and feet out from under the huge swathe of material. I was thinking: wouldn't it be ironic that after surviving this fall from 29,000 ft that I would die from asphyxiation under the balloon? As

I finally reached the side of the balloon, it was totally dark because the capsule and tanks must have sunk. I reached to grab the side of the balloon but my hands only found air. I could not even see the balloon in the total darkness. I was permanently separated from the balloon and adrift in my little open life raft. The sudden darkness of the night seemed to magnify my aloneness. There was nothing to do but wait for rescue.

My attention turned to my EPIRB, my only source of communication with the world. It was probably still on from when I urgently flipped the switch during my 8 ½-minute descent. However, because it was so dark and I couldn't see the controls, I decided to wait until daylight to make sure that I didn't misuse it in some unforeseen way that would disable or damage it.

Violent thunderstorms raged through the night, creating inches of rain in my raft and kicking up 6-ft wind waves. It was quite a ride and the roughness, together with the nausea of inhaling the propane gases, caused me to vomit—which I considered no inconvenience after all I had been through. As the morning sun began to rise, I checked my EPIRB and realized that it was on the test setting, not the emergency alert. I corrected that and then rested, assured that some boat would be sent to pick me up before the 72-hour battery of the EPIRB expired. I then spotted an island—I was in the midst of the Chatham Islands, an uninhabited grouping of coral atolls. I imagined waiting under a palm tree until the rescue arrived! I started paddling my raft by hand toward the tree-covered coral reef. After 1 ½ hours of strenuous paddling, I saw the waves breaking over the protective reef offshore of the island. I quickly realized my raft would be deflated when washed over the reef and I'd be shredded by the coral, I had better stay at sea, but now the sea current was dragging me toward the reef at one end of the island. I paddled furiously seaward until I could see that I would clear the reef as the current pulled me by.

At about 9 am, I heard the faint sounds of an aircraft. I looked around with anticipation as the whirr of the jet engines grew louder. Finally, I saw a French Search and Rescue plane from New Caledonia pass over. I waved but they didn't seem to see me and flew on by. My heart sank. About five minutes later they cruised back over and this time I knew they had spotted me. They circled back around and dropped a full-sized raft. The drop was so accurate it came within a few feet of hitting me. A few moments later, I climbed into my new eight-man covered raft. I felt like I had gone from a canoe to a sailboat. There were no supplies, though, and I desperately wanted a drink of water. The French airplane contacted the Australian Air Force who then took over the search and rescue operation.

At first a C-130 maintained a watch overhead, then later in the day a P-3 took over. This watch was maintained continuously in order to be sure they wouldn't lose track of me. The day was spent making drops of survival supplies to me, some of which I could get to, others of which were lost because I could not paddle the big raft. The nearest ship was the New Zealand warship *Endeavour*. It was called a warship but technically it was a refueling tanker. Interestingly, New Zealand only has one ship in its Navy and that 'warship' was it. The *Endeavour* operates in conjunction with the Australian Navy refueling the other ships. Since I was in this inaccurately charted region of shallow water and coral reefs, my rescue would be delayed due to the hazards posed to this vessel in negotiating its way to me. They could not send a 430-ft tanker into these dangerous waters.

Fortunately, there happened to be this fellow close by named Laurie Piper, who is an adventurer in his own right. He was out there with three friends in his 60-ft wood schooner *Atalanta*, which he was sailing around the world in several legs. He heard about my disaster over the radio and radioed back that he was near and was willing to pick me up. After floating in the ocean for 23 hours, it was Piper who rescued me at midnight. I was asleep in a raft and the *Atalanta* pulled up and called to me. Once I was on board, Piper and his company of friends looked at me and started to laugh. I couldn't imagine what was funny about surviving a near-death encounter. As I looked down, I suddenly realized what the source of their amusement was—I was of course still wearing just my long underwear. In my rare state of mind, I couldn't help but laugh, too. After giving me denims and a shirt to wear, we enjoyed a simple but satisfying meal. I was more than grateful to the winds of fate that Piper had been out at sea when he was.

The next morning, the *Endeavour* sent a high-speed launch to pick me up from Piper's yacht. A news team airplane was sent out to the crash site where they searched for the balloon and capsule. The entire thing must have sunk because there was nothing to be found. The *Endeavour* was en route to Townsville, Australia three days away, so that was where I was going. Richard Branson was quick to call me on the ship's satellite telephone, and expressed his relief that I was okay. He was also angling to get me on his team. The competition to make the first RTW Flight was in full swing and

Left As a baby

Below High School
Yearbook photo, 1961

Right On the summit of Vinson Massif, Antarctica, in November 1985

Below left Cross-country skiing, 1994

Below right With Dogsled Racing Team, 1991

Above Paris-Dakar Rally, 1994

Left Le Mans, 1993, with sponsors

Below With crew at Daytona 24-Hour, 1994

Above At the start of Route du Rhum, November 1994 (Thierry Martinez)

Below Celebrating the Round Ireland
Sailing Record, 1993, with David Scully

Below At the helm of *Lakota*, August
1993

Right PlayStation
arrives in New York
City, September 1999
(Empics)

Left On the mast
of *PlayStation*, with
Richard Branson
(Empics)

Above Over the coast
of Australia, June 2002
(Reuters/CORBIS)

Right In the *Bud Light
Spirit of Freedom* capsule
at the Smithsonian's
National Air and Space
Museum, 2002 (Getty)

Right With wife, Peggy

Right Landing of First
Solo RTW Balloon
Flight. July 4, 2002

Top *GlobalFlyer* over
Morocco, March 2005
(AP/Empics)

Above Departing
Kennedy Space Center,
Florida, February 2006
(AP/Empics)

Right Shuttle Landing
runway, Kennedy
Space Center, Florida.
February 2006

there were four teams preparing for attempts that winter, including Richard Branson. My race to be first had now ended because there was no way to build a new capsule and balloon in time to fly in the rapidly approaching winter season in the Northern Hemisphere. My first reaction to Richard on the telephone was, 'I'm not sure any of us should be trying this. The danger is really over the top.' It was an interesting offer, though, to be one of the pilots and it wouldn't cost me anything!

Over the course of the next two weeks, my memory replayed this near-death episode in hair-raising detail as I tried to get my mind around the implications of everything that had occurred. At one point I had concluded that, had I known the risk that I was taking, I would never have tried it. Although I was aware of the inherent danger of such extreme sports, I never imagined something like that happening, or perhaps I thought it would never happen to me.

Finally, time distanced me from the past, and I found myself reflecting on the positive aspects of the attempt. Before my wrestle with the thunderstorm and my subsequent plummet into the sea, I was having a really good flight. Having traveled 14,235.33 miles, I set a new World Distance Record for balloons. I was pleased with all the work my team had done in the development of our distance balloon system. We had things pretty well dialed in. The technology we had developed was efficacious, as were the envelope design and equipment.

Perhaps it is like giving birth, where time fades the memory of the attendant pain enough for a woman to be willing to do it again. Or maybe the aforementioned positive aspects of my blighted adventure began to eclipse the abject fear that I had experienced during my crash into the Coral Sea. I can't say for sure.

Time changed my perspective on the events when I received the follow-up phone call from Richard Branson, repeating his invitation to join him on his flight around the world as the third pilot with him and his co-pilot Per Lindstrand. I relented and agreed to come onboard and we set a meeting to work out the details and discuss the flight arrangements.

Despite almost dying on this latest attempt, I realized that it is just like most things in life. If you fall off, you either walk away or get up and climb back on.

15. FLYING WITH RICHARD BRANSON: ROUND THE WORLD BALLOON ATTEMPT, DECEMBER 1998

We kindly advise that it is not possible to land now without severely endangering the lives of the crew and any persons on the ground. We cannot steer the balloon as it goes where the wind takes it.
Sir Richard Branson, in a letter to Chinese air traffic control

After first meeting Richard Branson in January 1997, moments before my third around the world balloon attempt, we stayed in touch. At that time, Richard was a rival competitor; however, that changed. Nearly two years later, we joined forces after I accepted his invitation to join him and balloon builder Per Lindstrand in an attempt to be the first to balloon around the world. Richard and Per had been long-time ballooning partners, but had been unsuccessful in one around the world balloon attempt, plus had one failed launch where the balloon was lost after having pulled from its moorings during the inflation. As we prepared for our flight, the Budweiser Cup was still up for grabs and together we hoped to win it.

After flying to London for team briefings where the estimated performance of the balloon system was discussed, I realised that the technology of Branson's team was impressive. They probably knew more than anyone in the world about how the hot air circulated in the hot air cone and transmitted heat into the helium cell. Based on their extensive modelling of the thermodynamics, they estimated the fuel required for the round the world flight. The only problem was that the resulting answer was wrong. I was staying at Richard and his wife Joan's house in Holland Park, London. The next morning over tea, I expressed my concern over the issue, explaining to Richard that my fuel consumption on prior attempts had been one-third higher than our model predicted and that, due to similar inefficiencies, his balloon would only have nine days' fuel duration where an RTW flight required an estimated 13–15 days. We would be launching on a flight that would get us only halfway round the world! Heeding my warning, the next day Richard ordered each of his four huge fuel tanks to be cut off at the top and new sections welded in to expand the capacity by one-third. Having made this critical correction, there was hope that we now would have just enough to make the flight a success.

I quickly learned from working with Richard that everything on a Virgin project is approached in grandiose style. On a training trip to Marrakech, Morocco, the launch site for all of Richard Branson's RTW efforts, the team was so large that we substantially filled the Sheraton Hotel. In the evenings we enjoyed fine parties, including a stellar event held at a castle called the Kasbah Tamadot near a Berber village at the foot of the Atlas Mountains. Richard would eventually buy the Kasbah and make it a luxury resort. I was glad that Peggy came on this trip because we had a wonderful time.

Despite the festive atmosphere, I was unsure about how this flight team would work out. Per Lindstrand was one of the great balloonists and held the Hot Air balloon altitude record among other records. Per was also the balloon designer and was very competent working in this capacity, even though his ideas were expensive. Where Cameron Balloons was building envelopes out of coated polyester fabric, Per was using stronger but vastly more expensive Kevlar. Where Cameron used aluminized Mylar for the hot air cone, Per was pushing for gold coating to achieve a small increment in reflectivity, albeit at a huge cost. Although Richard and Per had made very successful hot air balloon crossings of the Atlantic and the Pacific, in the end there were disputes over Per's extraordinary expenditures. It didn't take long for me to figure out that the fact that I got along with both of them was apparently a key reason why I was brought in as a third pilot. It certainly wouldn't help Virgin's image if a feud broke out between Per and Richard high in the air!

The balloon system that Richard and Per flew was much more sophisticated than mine. It was a pressurized capsule with windows that was outfitted with a single bunk for sleeping. With a separate area for food preparation, it was certainly more extravagant than what I was used to. Because the capsule was pressurized there was no need to wear cumbersome oxygen masks and procedures onboard were significantly streamlined. There would be no opening the hatch, climbing up onto the capsule, and repairing equipment or changing burners during the flight. On the flip side, this meant that the balloon system had better not require repairs or else we would have to descend to about 14,000 ft where we could depressurize and breathe ambient air.

At launch time, as I made my way through the dense throng of onlookers and took my turn climbing into the capsule, I realized how long it had been since I had flown with anyone. Our liftoff was a major media event. We occupied the center of a huge circle that consisted of the press, fans, family members and the launch team. As we lifted off, trouble confronted us immediately. The initial pop off the ground was quickly followed by a descent toward the airport parking lot. On the controls was Per who fired the burners at full blast to avert disaster. Just as the balloon descended to within 30 ft above the parked cars, it leveled out, then finally began to climb again. However we did not escape without some damage. The emergency burn burned big holes in the lower skirt of the balloon. Although that wouldn't be a show stopper, we took off knowing that the performance of the balloon was slightly degraded for the rest of the trip because the heat could not be held in the hot air cone as well.

After recovering from this crisis, we quickly assumed our flying routine. We took turns on the flight controls, with two of us always on deck. During his watch, Richard took any opportunity to turn off the primitive autopilot in order to get some hand-flying time. Watching him as he piloted the balloon, I began to appreciate the upside of flying with other balloonists, which was that I had a lot less to do. Since we all shared the responsibility of flying the balloon, I actually got a chance to take in the spectacular views below us by peering through the windows and also got a lot more hours' sleep than I did flying solo.

Our chief concern after making a safe launch was the political climate that threatened to affect our trip. The United States and

Britain had just started bombing Iraq and there was a good chance that the wind currents would carry us into that troubled airspace, or at least close to it. Our trusted meteorologist and good friend, Bob Rice, assured us that he would do everything in his power to route us safely around Iraq.

As we were approaching Libya, we were alarmed when we learned that they were reneging on the overflight permission we had already secured from them. Although they had granted us permission to enter their airspace before we took off, now they were suddenly rescinding it. The three of us convened for an urgent brainstorming session. What should we do? Should we land before crossing out of Algeria into Libya? That wasn't very appealing, either, when you consider being in the middle of Sahara in Algeria. When we realized that all we could really do was change altitudes in hopes of slowing the balloon down and buying some much-needed time, Richard's mind shifted gears. He thought of whom he knew who were friends with Colonel Qaddafi. When Richard got on the satellite phone to try to get through to Nelson Mandela in South Africa and King Hussein of Jordan in the middle of the night, I could hardly believe what I was seeing. He also wrote a message to be directly delivered to Qaddafi.

Richard is bold enough to try anything that might work. Indeed, I can only imagine that his extraordinary success as a businessman may, in part, be due to this boldness. I'm not sure whether it was the letter, or whether a mutual friend in high places got through to Colonel Qaddafi, but without much time to spare, the permission to overfly Libya came through. Looking at one another wearily, we breathed a big sigh of relief at having overcome our first major obstacle. Taking a healthy stride to enter our 'kitchen', I prepared some soup, both to celebrate and to replenish the energy we had lost during the ordeal.

I was piloting the balloon out of Libya and into the Mediterranean when a meteorological report from Bob came through alerting us to a high-altitude thunderstorm on our route over Cyprus. Having nearly lost my life to a thunderstorm only months prior, my instincts took over. As we approached the volatile weather system, I suggested to Per and Richard that we get our parachutes on. Complicating the situation and narrowing our choices in how to respond to the matter was that we had to maintain a delicate trajectory to avoid crossing Iraq. If we climbed the balloon above the storm, the wind currents at that altitude would carry us into Iraq. Our decision swiftly came to us. We opted not to climb, and to face the risk of a thunderstorm instead. Fortunately, the thunderstorm had dissipated before we crossed Cyprus.

As we had been unable to obtain overflight permission from Russia, flying through the narrow corridor running between Russia and Iraq demanded precision on Bob's and our parts. Bob assured us that he was confident that he could thread us through 'the needle'. We considered it a miracle when Bob was able to successfully route us through that tight course. In the end we were able to miss Iraq by 50 miles, Russia by 50 miles and Iran by seven miles.

After crossing a number of the 'stans'—Turkmenistan, Uzbekistan, Tajikistan, Afghanistan, and into Pakistan—we were confronted with crossing the inhospitable Himalaya. While Andy Elson and Leo Dickinson had made daring high-altitude balloon flights over Mt Everest in 1991, no one had flown a balloon over the crest of the Himalaya. Dangerous mountain waves and turbulence from a rotor, both of which could destroy a balloon, can be found even on small mountain ranges. A rotor is a swirling wind on the downwind side of a mountain that can cause severe turbulence and will often curl the wind downward. It can literally smash a balloon into the leeward or opposite side of the mountain, having traversed it. When we had laid out our flight plan, we had conscientiously mapped out a route with the clear intention of avoiding crossing the crest of the Himalaya into Chinese Tibet. With our balloon flying in the direction of Everest, our anxiety levels got turned up a notch when we realized that we were not even flying high enough to clear this 29,000 ft summit. Fortunately there was not much wind that night and we were able to fly over the crest of the Himalaya without any rotor problems. The next morning we were treated to a spectacular sight as we passed along the north side of this incredible mountain range. We gazed at the famous high peaks of Everest, Makalu and Kanchenjunga lined up one after another as we proceeded along in silent awe of this natural wonder.

When we flew into the Tibet region of China, we flew into chaos. Our overflight permission for China stipulated that we limit our entry to near the southeast quadrant of the country, then proceed roughly along the corridor of airline routes until exiting toward Japan. We missed that! We were already in Chinese territory and the air traffic controllers were hopping mad. They demanded that we fly to the Lhasa, Tibet airport and land! We politely tried to explain that a balloon flies with the wind and there was no way we could steer north to Lhasa. The Chinese did not understand this.

In an effort to assuage the anger of the Chinese, Richard worked to galvanize some political heavyweights in England to come to our aid. One of his staff was able to get through to Prime Minister Tony Blair who was willing to write a letter to Premier Zhu Rongji. The British Ambassador in Beijing also appealed on our behalf to procure our overflight permission. Although my team did get the State Department working on the problem and Secretary of State Madeline Albright was kept carefully briefed on the permission negotiations, I was sitting there feeling impotent by comparison to Richard because I couldn't just pick up the phone and get through to President Clinton.

Having exhausted his British political connections, Richard sat down and typed out a candid e-mail to the Chinese authorities. He briefly explained to them the nature of flying a balloon and how we didn't always have control in terms of where we could fly, that we were subject to the whims of the wind. He alerted them to the severe harm that would befall Chinese civilians and us if we attempted to land as requested. In essence, he explained that we would gladly comply by crossing where the Chinese specified if only we could. He kindly implored them to allow us to fly over their airspace. In the early hours of the morning, a response came through our Mission Control Center. China acknowledged us but told us to make every effort to exit their airspace as soon as possible. In any case, all this negotiation was to no avail. We just continued to maintain our routine position, reporting and repeatedly complimenting the air traffic controllers on what a wonderful job they were doing. The Chinese bureaucrats never forgave us for barging through without permission. The fact that the Chinese soon closed their doors to international balloonists, forcing subsequent RTW balloon attempts to find a way to get around the southeast corner of China, would serve as a reminder of their enduring contempt with our routing.

We left China near Shanghai and were on our way to Japan when, out of the blue, a message arrived from Mission Control informing us that North Korea had extended overflight permission to us. North Korea is one on the list of three impossible countries— Russia, China and North Korea—from which to get overflight permission. As such, we hadn't even applied to North Korea. After what we had just been through with China, we were stunned that we were welcome to fly through North Korea. Although in the end we wouldn't need it because we passed south of South Korea, it was interesting to witness that sometimes balloonists elicit very positive government reactions.

As Japan would serve as our gateway into the Pacific Ocean, we continued on without incident in the direction of this country. Upon reaching Japan, the winds picked up and we were able to hook into a jetstream that flew us as fast as 180 mph. Since we had used a lot of fuel staying aloft in the slow wind conditions of China, we were relieved to calculate that we might have enough fuel to complete the RTW if we stayed in the jetstream the rest of the way. The possibility of a rapid flight home lifted our morale after all we had been through together thus far. Richard also thanked me for being relentless in my request that we add more fuel before we took off. For the first time in the flight, I believed we might have enough to make it.

Our enthusiasm dampened when we received word from Bob of a presence of an elongated trough that stretched north-south in the middle of the Pacific. He pressed upon us the urgency of flying as fast as we could in order to get to and through the trough before it deepened and created a wind shear we could not get through. In other words, if we didn't make it in time, we would hit a wall of minimal winds and all our efforts for completing our mission would be vanquished.

Dropping our empty fuel tanks so we could fly higher, we only gained a paltry extra ten mph of speed. Reaching the higher altitude came at a huge cost in terms of consumption rates of precious fuel. From his end, Bob crunched the numbers in hopes that this speed would suffice to get us through the trough and on to the United States. However, this was not to be. In the end, the weather pattern that Bob had warned us about got the best of us. Although we tried to cross it from every altitude, we could not find passage through this wall of light winds. As it happened to be Christmas Eve, perhaps this was a present that good old Saint Nicholas just could not deliver. What could have been a one-day flight to get to the United States now looked like a slow meandering flight of four days to just hopefully get to Mexico. It was questionable whether we even had enough fuel to get to Mexico for a landing.

Now that our flight was busted, the new priority became safety. Rescue experts took charge at Mission Control and Bob Rice was effectively relieved of his routing duties and sent to his hotel room. Upon hearing this, I just shook my head. I don't know what they were thinking. Now more than ever, we needed Bob's expert routing advice.

We were 1000 miles north of Hawaii and I realized we could ride this wind shear south toward these islands. I had a plan in my mind that we could reach the Big Island of Hawaii and surprise everyone with a dry and safe landing. As I flew south, my plan was working. Unfortunately I was directed by Mission Control to fly lower. When winds at the lower altitude carried us more to the west, my new target became Oahu. As Christmas morning approached, the rescue team had gotten the support and, in fact, the public relations interest of the US Coast Guard for a sea rescue, at which point I was waved off of my path for a dry landing in northern Oahu and instructed to fly lower in the trade winds which would propel us north of the island. I could only imagine that all the experience of the ICO rescue team was with water rescues and they felt this could be done more safely. My efforts for the safety and equipment preservation of a dry landing lost out.

By the time we were ready to ditch, the Coast Guard cutter and helicopters were on the scene. The plan was to separate the balloon envelope from the capsule at first touchdown with explosive cutters so the capsule would not be dragged. During normal flight, safety pins are in place to prevent an accidental deployment while high in the sky. As the first preparation for landing was to remove the safety pins, Richard climbed out on top of the capsule and struggled for a time before returning to relay that only one of the four pins could be removed. Suspecting that Richard was not mechanically minded enough, Per sent me outside to finish the job. Once on top of the capsule I could assess that Richard was doing it right—the pins were seized due to tight tolerances and loading. They just weren't going to come out. This meant we would drag until enough helium could be valved to stop the balloon.

Per would fly the landing. Concerned that the impact with the sea would tear the balloon or otherwise cause an out-of-control condition, Richard and I strapped ourselves in for the ride. Per valved just enough for the balloon to gently touch down, then it bounced back 100 ft in the air, then he valved for another gentle touch. This routine went on for some time. When I counted 47 bounces, I finally suggested valving a lot of helium to get the capsule to settle in the water. This worked. We were dragging through the water at the swift speed of the wind. Already in our survival suits, Richard and I climbed out of the capsule. Richard jumped into the wake of the dragging and I immediately followed. Per turned off the lights and secured the capsule so it wouldn't sink, then made his jump. Bobbing up and down in the choppy water, Richard and I were relaxed and relieved that we were safely in the water. The Coast Guard 'swimmer' jumped from the hovering helicopter and swam over to me. Reaching over the water's surface to shake my hand, he shouted 'Merry Christmas'. He rigged us up to be winched into the helicopter and soon we were at Barbers Point Air Station doing a few interviews still in our survival suits.

Saying goodbye to the reporters, we walked in the direction of a limo that was waiting for us. Barron Hilton, whom I'd kept informed during the flight, had arranged for the vehicle to deliver us to the Hilton Hawaiian Village on Waikiki Beach. Barron had us installed in the Presidential Suite there. Having no articles of clothing with us other than our survival suits, we were delighted to discover that his staff had even figured out how to buy some Hawaiian clothes for us on Christmas Day, a holiday during which shops are typically closed. That night Barron orchestrated a fine celebration with fireworks in our honor. It was a festive ending to a failed balloon attempt and a Christmas I shall never forget.

16. A BIGGER AND BETTER BOAT: LEARNING THE ROPES, 1999–2000

With current technology, this PlayStation *is at the limit of human capability.*

Pete Melvin, co-designer of *PlayStation*

O ur success in breaking sailing world records in 1994 inspired me to go after bigger and better records with a bigger and better boat. Like the kid who went from riding a bicycle to trying to drive a car within the same month, I was motivated to take my speed sailing program to the next level. In my opinion, the most important sailing world records are: Round The World, number one; the TransAtlantic, number two; and the 24-Hour Sailing Record, number three. After finishing the Route du Rhum in November 1994, I gave the go-ahead to build a boat for the purpose of attacking these three sailing records, with the ultimate goal of breaking the Round the World Record.

The design and construction of my new catamaran proved to be a truly worldwide operation, spread over two years, two hemispheres and three continents. As complex as the design and build of the boat were, my specifications were simple: I wanted the best boat for sailing, fully crewed, non-stop, around the world, as fast as possible. I first gave the design project to the prominent British multihull designer, Nigel Irens. He did some conceptual drawings but after three months resigned the commission. He doubted that I could put together a team to carry off this project and opted to preserve his availability to design a huge multihull for French star Laurent Bourgnon. Ironically, that boat was never built. Somewhat amused that Nigel doubted my will and ability to follow through with a project, I quickly called up the best-known American multihull architects, Gino Morrelli and Pete Melvin of Newport Beach, California. After sharing my vision and specifications for the boat with them, they expressed their enthusiasm to apply their talents to build a new class of 100 + -ft racing multihull. The design phase was meticulously completed with Finite Element Analysis (FEA) which determines where to add extra carbon material where strength is needed and save weight in areas of low stress. I contracted Cookson Boats in Auckland, New Zealand to construct the boat because of their experience in building carbon composite boats and the low labor costs in New Zealand. I personally funded the design and construction until I could find a sponsor. Finally Sony came through for me. Actually, it was Sony's European computer entertainment division. After a meeting in their London office, Managing Director Chris Deering realized this was a good sponsorship opportunity. Because the boat was mostly completed, he faced no risk of cost overrun and the ultimate risk that the boat would never be finished.

After naming the catamaran *PlayStation*, Sony gave us free reign to pursue successes that would promote the image of their computer games. When *PlayStation* took to the water in December 1998, at 105 ft, she was the largest and most powerful ocean-racing multihull ever built.

Aside from actually attempting the Round the World record, our initial challenge was to learn how to effectively and safely handle her. As experienced as our crew was, none of us had sailed a boat this big before and subsequently had yet to discover what doing so entailed. An unfortunate accident that afflicted one of our key crewmembers early on indicated that our learning curve would be steep. We were setting out from Auckland in March 1999 on our first record attempt, which was to break the 24-Hour distance record of 540 miles. As we reached open ocean the winds picked up, making it necessary to take a reef. Directing the crew in the reef procedure was my long-time boat manager, Ben Wright, who was perched on the back of the boom as *PlayStation* heaved through waves. Ben was thrown off balance and, to steady himself, he reached for a reef line which ran through a nearby block. Aware that the line would be pulled in during the reefing procedure, Ben was careful to hold onto the safe side where the line would exit the block.

In a moment of miscommunication, the crew manning the reef line at the foot of the mast let the line out a few inches. This was enough to draw into the block Ben's little finger, which was instantaneously crushed by the ton of pressure created between the line and the wheel in the block. When Ben yelled for the crew to pull the line back in so he could free his finger, they were too far away to hear him. Fearing that they might never hear his cries for help above the din of the rushing wind and water, Ben took it upon himself to save his hand from being further pulled into the block and crushed. Forcefully, he jerked his hand away leaving the entrapped fingertip in the block. We cancelled the record attempt and immediately returned to Auckland to get him to a hospital. After this incident, we went back out without Ben the next day and captured the 24-Hour record by sailing 580.23 nautical miles. This demonstrated that *PlayStation* was the world's fastest ocean-going sailboat.

Sailing *PlayStation* safely necessitated that we rise to new levels of awareness and working consistently together as a team. As Ben's accident showed, the sheer length of *PlayStation* prevented easy communication. As a result, every maneuver had to be well thought-out beforehand, and precisely executed. The loads on a racing boat the size of *PlayStation* are enormous. On a small sailboat, the helmsman might hold the mainsheet in his hand. On *PlayStation* the mainsheet carries up to 15 tons of load and can be taken in only with a hydraulic ram. On *PlayStation*, reefing or unreefing the mainsail, which took just a few minutes on smaller boats, took over 15 minutes. Nothing could be done quickly or on a whim. When wind speeds started to increase out of control, sail reductions had to be made early before the power of the wind in the sails made them impossible to deal with. The enormous loads on *PlayStation* turned areas around sheets and lines into danger zones when the boat was in motion. If a fitting or connection broke, thousands of pounds of tension could send a line or piece of hardware careening through the air with a force that could seriously injure a crewmember who happened to be standing in its path. The crew quickly learned to be aware at all times of where they were standing, and tried to minimize time spent around such highly loaded fittings.

Our attempts at the TransAtlantic record also served as a training ground for us to discover what it meant to sail *PlayStation* with a constant measure of safety. Although the RTW record was our number one goal, we were also intent on breaking the TransAtlantic, perhaps the most difficult of all the major ocean records to claim. Beginning at Ambrose Light outside of New York Harbor, the course ends 2925 nm (nautical miles) later at Lizard Head off Cornwall, England. The original record of 12 days set by the schooner *Atlantic*, skippered by Charlie Barr in 1905, stood unbroken for a remarkable 75 years. Then, between 1980 and 1990 the TransAtlantic was broken seven times, most recently by Frenchman Serge Madec who, in 1990 onboard *Jet Services V*, finished the course in 6 days 13 hours 3 minutes 32 seconds. The difficulty of this record is attested to by the fact that since 1990, nearly 20 attempts had been made and the record still stood. This was just the type of challenge that we were looking for.

We weren't expecting to break the TransAtlantic record on our first try. We were equally keen to get a feel for *PlayStation*'s limits, to realize her full potential. Our first attempt at this record drove us to this threshold uncomfortably fast. On Thursday, 16 December 1999, we crossed the starting line on our first attempt at the TransAlantic record in squally, wintry conditions. Having waited through Fall without getting enough wind in the forecast, we were enthused to finally see a solid wind field forecast even though the trip would be cold in the second half of December. On the evening of the first night, the wind was building as we were speeding along at around 30 knots, with a single reef in mainsail and Solent jib. The speed we were sailing was exhilarating but it was time to start the process of taking another reef. The enormity of the sail and the power of the wind delayed our efforts to quickly reduce sail. Suddenly, without warning, we were hit by a powerful gust of wind that blew at 62 knots. It was pitch black. Both hulls dug deep into the sea lifting the stern out of the water and flooding the bow. We were on the verge of pitch poling. Pitch poling is when a boat capsizes from back to front sending the mast or the 'pole' forward to the irretrievable degree that it flips upside down. As the boat's point of equilibrium continued to shift forward, illustrating how very close we were to experiencing that scenario, in that moment, *PlayStation*'s fate and our lives hung in the balance.

I was working at the base of the mast when I saw that several of the other crewmembers responded to this desperate situation by unclipping their harnesses and heading for the side of the boat. In that ominous instant, *PlayStation* was rewriting the rules on how to survive capsizing. If *PlayStation* went over, anyone caught in the middle of the boat would get trapped under the nets. Since the nets ran across the enormous width of the hulls, a crewmember caught under that area would likely drown before reaching the side of the boat. If a man was thrown free of the boat from his position on the bow as *PlayStation* capsized, he would have a better chance of surviving. Unlike a monohull that will sink when capsized, a multihull will float and thus can function as a huge life raft. A man overboard might have a chance of swimming back to the boat. However, that might be impossible if the boat got caught in a wind drift and was carried away.

Luckily, Gino Morrelli, *PlayStation*'s designer, was at the helm. There are few sailors who could handle the situation better. As the squall ripped into the boat, Gino had the instincts to direct *PlayStation* directly downwind. This slowed us down. Standing midships, we felt the weight of *PlayStation* shift backward as she sat back on her transoms. Although it was hard to see the expression on each other's faces in the darkness of the night, shouts of relief could be heard from the crew. The worst had been averted. That close call really, really scared us. I knew if the boat had tipped over, it would have been catastrophic. Some of the crew would have died and I was the most vulnerable at the foot of the mast. Due to Gino's excellent manipulation of the boat, we were able to recover.

PlayStation came through but four mainsail battens were shattered as a result of an unintentional jibe while steering dead downwind. Because battens are necessary to give the mainsail its proper shape, this damage effectively put an end to our record attempt. We turned around and headed to port. The atmosphere onboard was subdued as we each tried to digest what had just occurred. Our brush with capsizing drove home the importance of getting the trim right, in addition to the danger of carrying too much sail in gale-force winds. De-powering must be done early because once loads spiral out of control on a boat this powerful, the only recourse left is to hold on. And hope. On a positive side, we learned from this incident that *PlayStation* could really fly, topping 33 knots. It was also somewhat consoling that, in having pushed *PlayStation* to and through the red line, we incurred the minimal damage of four broken battens. Such an episode as we endured would have certainly destroyed lesser machines. It was now understood that *PlayStation* could withstand a high threshold of abuse.

While *PlayStation* was being repaired and we were still learning how to sail her to her full potential, I was also exploring new aviation records that I could go after in my new airplane the Citation X, pronounced 'Citation Ten'. Once at home I started working out the details, planning which world records I'd go for first. Ultimately, I wanted to go after the Round the World record for medium size airplanes.

When the Citation X was being designed and tested they wanted it to be considered for the Collier Trophy. This award is given for the greatest achievement in aeronautics or astronautics in America, in terms of improving performance, efficiency or safety of air or space vehicles. To do that, they needed some demonstration of what this plane could do. So the test pilots of Citation did a flight from Reno to Galveston, Texas and back, a 5000-km (3107-mile) Out and Return world record. They did it at an impressive 547 mph. Based on its advanced technology and that demonstration flight, the Citation X did receive the Collier Trophy. Although my purchase of the Citation X cost me $17 million, I felt it was worth it because of its high performance standard and state of the art technology. With a maximum speed of .92 Mach, it is the fastest private jet, and with the retirement of the Concorde, is also faster than any airliner. It is the ultimate 'owner-pilot' airplane. If you want to sit in the passenger cabin, there are more spacious airplanes, but if you want to fly in the pilot's seat, there is no better airplane.

On 26 November 1999 I put my plane to the test and went after my first record, the 2000-km (1242-mile) Out and Return record which I flew at an average speed of 598.26 mph, breaking my own record which I had set a year earlier in my previous jet, a Falcon 10, with Buddy Holland as my co-pilot. The purpose of attempting this record was for me to get really comfortable with the plane and its capabilities. It was then that I started thinking about the 5000-km record. I thought about that record for a long time, but it wasn't until I broke several other world records that I went after the 5000-km record. Meanwhile I decided to go after what is perhaps the most glamorous aviation record—Round the World. Since a lot of precise planning is required for this type of attempt, I spent months organizing for the trip, which involved getting overflight permits, planning the routing and figuring out the refueling stops. I had to have credit pre-arranged to pay for the fuel and make sure that the flight plans would be re-filed each stop. Since it was imperative that I fly with the jetstreams, I looked to meteorologist Chris Bedford, who was also my meteorologist for the sailing records during this time frame, to forecast the right day for takeoff.

Once we lifted off, the Round the World record clock started ticking and didn't stop until we made it completely around the globe. Therefore, everything had to come off like clockwork. Everything was timed and we all had assignments once we touched down at our refueling stops. The refueling was critical and had to happen very quickly. We had to clear customs and immigration at each stop while the plane was refueling.

Even though only a captain and a co-pilot are required to fly the Citation X, there had to be provision to get some rest on a two-day flight. We needed three pilots for this attempt. In addition to my full-time co-pilot at the time, Darrin Adkins, I decided to ask Alex Tai, an Airbus captain who worked for Richard Branson's Virgin Atlantic Airlines, to be the other co-pilot. I had first met Alex in Marrakech when I was preparing for the round the world balloon attempt with Richard in 1998. It was on that occasion that I talked to him about my idea to fly my Citation X for a Round the World record. Alex said that he wanted to be in if he could get the time off.

As I was organizing my attempt, I called Richard and asked him if I could borrow Alex Tai for this around the world attempt. Richard was cooperative and agreed to my request. I then called Alex and said, 'Okay, we're going to go round the world. Richard said I could borrow you.' Alex was stunned and flattered to be chosen as the third pilot.

I scheduled our round the world flight attempt to take place after finishing the Outright (crewed) sailing record from Newport to Bermuda which ran from 12 to 14 January 2000. What a trip! Having sailed in rough winter conditions, we put up a fine time of 38 hours 35 minutes 53 seconds. That finish superseded my own record, after I had sailed singlehanded the previous year, making this new one the Outright record and relegating my prior one to the singlehanded record. Both records still stand today.

On 14 February 2000 Alex Tai, Darrin Adkins and I boarded my Citation X at Los Angeles International, 'LAX', for our round the world attempt. There were 50 waypoints on our pre-declared course, making it impractical to get visual or radar verification by air traffic controllers, which is the normal method used for shorter records. We needed to take an Official Observer with us to verify that we crossed all the pre-declared waypoints. As we bolted down the runway and the wheels lifted off, Mike Pablo, the Official Observer, started his stopwatch. The stopwatch would tick away until we were back at LAX and he felt the wheels touch down on the ground. At that moment he would stop the stopwatch, then calculate the average speed for the course distance.

Our flight plan involved traveling from Los Angeles to Bermuda; from Bermuda to Agadir, Morocco; from there to Luxor, Egypt and then to Calcutta, India. From Calcutta we would fly to Nagasaki, Japan; from Nagasaki to Midway Island in the middle of the Pacific, which was our last stop before flying back to LAX. Crucial to our flight plan was the timing of the entire trip that would allow us to land on Midway in the dark. Midway is a nesting colony for 3 million Leysin Albatross, one of the world's largest birds with an enormous wingspan. During the day, they fly to and from their nests. If one unfortunate albatross got sucked into one of our engines while we landed on Midway, the bird definitely would not survive and I'm not sure the engine would, either. When I eventually approached for touchdown during the night, thousands of Albatross came into view. I was pleased to see that they were watching curiously from the safety of their nests. Midway proved to be our fastest refueling stop. With no other airplane traffic, the airport had the fuel truck waiting by the runway and pumped the fuel into the Citation in 13 minutes. The entire time we spent on the island from touchdown to takeoff was only 16 minutes, 6 seconds. As we headed for Los Angeles, we reveled in how efficient this entire trip had been. We never once had to deal with a messed-up stop, lost overflight permission or mechanical problems. As we touched down, and the wheels hit the runway with a screech, Mike Pablo clicked the stopwatch. As we taxied off the runway and he informed us that we had shattered the previous record time, I basked in the new experience of having claimed my first Round the World record. We had set a new world record for the medium weight H class of jets by flying an average speed including stops of 559.89 mph and had circled the globe in only 41 hours.

A few days after setting that aviation record, I went home to Beaver Creek and got some exercise: I skied from Aspen to Eagle in a record time of 12 hours 29 minutes. Then I started planning other world records I could go after in my Citation X. I found several, and began to make my attempts at them one by one. On 23 March 2000 I flew from Los Angeles to Honolulu in 4 hours 11 minutes, which still stands as the fastest speed from California to Hawaii, at 606.84 mph.

With *PlayStation* ready to sail in April 2000, we went on weather standby for our second TransAtlantic attempt. Slated to join us onboard was Richard Branson with whom, along with Per Lindstrand, I had made a round the world balloon attempt in December 1998. Having gotten along well together on that ballooning trip, and knowing that Richard was interested in boating and had even set the TransAtlantic powerboat record in 1986, I invited him to join me and my crew for this attempt.

For weeks the weather had been temperamental, forcing us to forsake on several occasions what seemed to be decent weather patterns that, in the end, simply didn't turn out. When May arrived without a suitable weather forecast, Richard had to cancel his involvement in this attempt in order to attend to business. After waiting and waiting for the opportune conditions, we finally decided that we weren't going to learn anything by sitting on the dock. Even as we set sail, the weather picture never fully crystallized. Without really knowing whether the winds were sufficient to break the TransAtlantic record, we crossed the start line on 14 May 2000 with 12 sets of fingers crossed, hoping for the best. What was certain was that this would be a frigid trip.

Our progress over the first day and a half was promising as we were just exceeding the speed needed to break the TransAtlantic Record. Before our departure, however, we had been forewarned of a problem with the weather pattern. We were starting after the passage of a cold front, which we would eventually catch up to and need to cross. Although we were able to make it across this hole of light wind, doing so cost us precious time. Another obstacle we had to surmount was navigating through the ice fields east of Newfoundland, which we entered on our third day. Tension filled the air onboard as a collision with any ice, even a small growler (a small chunk of an iceberg), would be enough to destroy *PlayStation*. The proximity of the ill-fated *Titanic* resting on the ocean's floor a mere 150 miles to our south—a haunting reminder of the damage icebergs can render—did little to put us at ease. Picking our way through this area required that we maintain a vigilant watch on deck and that we keep a constant eye on the radar. We also utilized an infrared camera, which displays anything colder than the water, to help us identify icebergs. Twice that night, we observed icebergs seemingly pop out of the thick blanket of fog and we stood on deck staring at these pearlescent monsters glistening as we cautiously sailed silently by them.

Although we could have jibed south to avoid the iceberg region, the longer course would have left us no chance of breaking the record. Such is the decision countless TransAtlantic racers have made before us. Even with our more direct route, in the end, we just did not have adequate winds to break the record. Seven and a half days—181 hours 38 minutes, 6 seconds—after leaving New York Harbor, we crossed the finish line on 22 May 2000 at Lizard Head in England.

Despite not having achieved the result we had hoped for, it had been a very satisfying trip. It was still the third-fastest sailboat crossing ever of the Atlantic. We were also able to assess improvements that we needed to make in terms of sails and rigging. We were getting sharper on our sail changes, and the passage had been an excellent opportunity for us to work through a wide variety of conditions together. As for living together on the boat, we had been a very happy crew with good camaraderie through the rough and the smooth of things.

Because choosing the right crew in any sport is important, I was fortunate to attract top-flight sailors who kept coming back to sail with me. We ran a pretty safe boat and had a good time. I think the main reason they sailed with me is because I picked interesting sailing projects. My philosophy was, if I did interesting projects and went after the most important events in the sport, then people in the sport would want to be involved in them. The key crew from my start of sailing in 1993 was still with me. Ben Wright and Brian Thompson had stayed all the way through. Dave Scully was back after an interlude of sailing a singlehanded round the world race.

At home in Beaver Creek, my attention continued to linger on the 5000-km aviation Closed Circuit speed record that had been established a few years back while the Citation X was in final testing before being released by Cessna to the marketplace. Intent upon breaking that record, I decided that now was the time. A 'Closed Circuit' refers to a course that starts and finishes in the same place. This record is done on an Out and Return course of the pilot's choosing. Once having realized that more time is spent flying upwind than can be made up flying downwind, I searched for a high-pressure ridge to follow, where there would be little wind in either direction. Having forecast this pattern for 14 July 2000, running from Alamosa, Colorado to Daytona Beach, Florida, I decided that I would fly it. With Darrin Adkins as my co-pilot, we averaged 572 mph, which is 25 mph faster than the Citation test pilots. That was a bit of an eye-opener. Test Pilot William Dirks, who previously held the record, was quick to congratulate me on the superior planning that enabled me to get more speed out of this airplane. My record for the 5000 km still stands today.

Since our second TransAtlantic attempt served to underscore that the key to breaking this record was to avoid slow weather patterns, as we prepared for our third go at this record, I was willing to be patient enough to wait for a start date that would offer the most optimal weather conditions possible. I brought back Bob Rice as chief meteorologist to work in conjunction with my onboard navigator, Stan Honey. Having sailed under Bob's direction to win several sailing world records with *Lakota*, I was hopeful we'd have the same outcome with *PlayStation*.

On 22 August we went on 'Code Green'. According to Bob, a great weather pattern was forming. We set off on 24 August 1999 into conditions that proved the accuracy of Bob's forecast and demonstrated why he is regarded as a legend in his field. Fifteen hours after leaving the start line at Ambrose Light, New York Harbor, we put 329 nautical miles in our wake to gain a 1 hour 15 minute-lead over the current record holder. We were off to a formidable start and enjoying hour after hour of excellent 25 knots of steady breeze from the southwest. We took pleasure in the tremendous sense of speed and power of sailing *PlayStation* at her full potential.

We were able to maintain this excellent pace for the next few days. By our third day, on 26 August, we were heartened by the notion that we might actually succeed in breaking the record. Things were looking notably different than our previous TransAtlantic attempts that had us struggling with broken battens, out-of-control weather conditions, icebergs and regions with light wind. We had a solid 14 hour-lead over the previous record holder. We concluded that maintaining this pace would allow us to make a 5½-day TransAtlantic record-breaking crossing.

Trouble was brewing. An intense low, tracking north, was due to intercept our course. We still figured that if we could beat its arrival, the record was ours. If the low reached us first, our perfect winds would be gone and we would be sailing upwind in a confused sea. Only 500 miles from the finish line, our dreams of a 5-day TransAtlantic began to evaporate as the low caught us and the resulting rough sea conditions slowed our pace. With such a lead on the record, we still hoped that we could struggle through and clip the previous record. However, this was not to be. Overnight the wind conditions had weakened and put the TransAtlantic record firmly out of our reach. We lost the race with the weather. Breaking it would have required crossing Lizard Head that morning at 0752 GMT and we were still 124 miles away. What was one of the most beneficent weather patterns of the year ended in light headwinds and, banefully for us, very slow sailing. Bob Rice estimated that if only the intercepting low had been two hours slower to arrive, we would have sailed the good winds to the finish. Unlike our previous failed attempts where we chalked it up to experience, a palpable sense of disappointment was felt among the *PlayStation* crew.

For the time being I decided to re-focus on what aviation records I could set in Citation X. On 17 September 2000 I went after the East to West US TransContinental Record. With Darrin Adkins, I took off from San Diego, California to Jacksonville, Florida where we quickly refueled and flew back to San Diego. We flew from Jacksonville to San Diego in 3 hours 29 minutes with an average speed of 591.96 mph. Since we flew both directions, we also established the Round Trip Transcontinental Record at 537.36 mph including the fuel stop.

Pretty determined about setting aviation records, I planned an attempt on the RTW westbound record. Compared to the RTW Eastbound route, where you fly with the jetstream, the westbound route is slower because there are more headwinds. Our route would take us closer to the Equator to minimize headwinds and thereby add extra length to the RTW. The trip would require nine fuel stops, which called for the most precise planning. We would lose precious time because we had to land more often, therefore each stop had to come off with clockwork precision.

On 22 November 2000 I, along with my co-pilots, Alex Tai and Pierre D'Avenas, plus the Official Observer, Stan Nelson, took off from Cabo San Lucas, Mexico to Kona, Hawaii. After a scary turnaround there because we lacked the proper immigration form to fill out to enter the USA, we flew on to Majuro in the South Pacific, then on to Palau, then Singapore, then on to the Maldives, and to Nairobi, then to Abidjan, Ivory Coast, and then to Fortaleza, Brazil and then to Barranquilla, Colombia, before returning to Cabo San Lucas—a total of nine fuel stops.

Our fuel stops averaged 35 minutes. That's from the time our wheels touched down until we lifted off. We desperately wanted our record to be over 500 mph and it was close. As we approached Cabo, we got permission to land straight in and make a high speed Touch-and-Go. Touching the runway stopped the clock; however, because we were traveling too fast to brake before the end of the runway, I lifted off again to continue around in the pattern for the full stop landing and a great celebration. We had executed all aspects of the flight precisely and just made our goal with an average speed of 500.56 mph. Getting the first world record for flying a medium-weight airplane westbound round the world was a wonderful way to cap off the year.

17. MISSING THE JETSTREAM: MY FIFTH SOLO ROUND THE WORLD BALLOON ATTEMPT, AUGUST 2001

*There comes a point when even by round the world balloonists'
standards the risk is too high.*

Joe Ritchie, Mission Control Director

I n March 1999, Swiss psychiatrist Bertrand Piccard and British
pilot Brian Jones became the first persons to succeed in ballooning non-stop around the world and claimed the Budweiser Cup $1
million prize competition. Their journey in the *Breitling Orbiter 3*
lasted 19 days 21 hours. The balloon was launched from Switzerland into an unconventional wind pattern, which took them deep
into Western Africa before getting into the jetstream, whereupon
Piccard and Jones shocked all the competitors by making it all the
way around then landing in Egypt.

As Piccard and Jones took off from Chateau d'Oex in Switzerland, they had many rival competitors and the media scratching
their heads wondering what the team was doing. It seemed that they
were going the wrong way. They got into a wind pattern that took
them southwest over the Mediterranean, into Africa and all the way

to Mali in the western Sahara. However, their clever meteorologists, Luc Trullemans and Pierre Eckert, knew exactly what they were doing. They had routed the trajectory south so that Piccard and Jones could pick up the subtropical jetstream that would take them across Algeria, Libya, India and Myanmar at swift speeds and then just outside the border of China. After all the fuss to get clearances from China for overflight rights, it turned out that they didn't need them. When they lost their wind over the Pacific, it was Luc who encouraged them to have faith in a great subtropical jetstream that was going to develop but that hadn't yet. Piccard and Jones steered their balloon toward the yet unborn jetstream. When they arrived, so did the jetstream and it carried them the rest of the way across the Pacific, the Atlantic and finally to their landing in Egypt.

I was shocked that Piccard and Jones became the first to circumnavigate the globe. As both are close friends of mine, when I see them I like to lecture them in jest about the three times during their flight that their wind pattern had failed, and joke that they shouldn't have been able to make it round the world. But of course they did and, while I was happy for them, I was also at the same time intensely jealous. Before I had lost my equipment in my fall into the Coral Sea, I thought it was my destiny to be first. After all, I had made the longest balloon flight in the world in each of the previous five years. I was frustrated that after making so many attempts I wasn't the first to do it. I had to re-evaluate my options. Should I continue my effort to make the First Solo circumnavigation balloon flight? Each attempt has revealed to me that this is more difficult than we previously thought. In fact it has proved to be extraordinarily difficult. Instead of letting this difficulty deter me, I just looked at it as one reason to persist until finally successful. Even though the Budweiser Cup had been claimed, I was still determined to achieve my goal to be the first to balloon solo, non-stop around the world, which was a much harder task.

I've examined my determination and perhaps it's that I just like to figure out things. Maybe that's not so much a personality trait but rather what I've learned in life. I learned in the trading business, for instance, that sometimes you make a good trade, sometimes a bad trade, but if you have a good game plan, you can, over time, taking all the successes and all the failures together, end up on the successful side. So I'm very much aware of these probabilities. I have an appreciation of the odds of success, which might be characterized as determination. In the case of ballooning, I realized that I wouldn't necessarily succeed the first time. At the conclusion of each attempt, I evaluated that I had a sound game plan and understood improvements that needed to be made to have a better chance of success the next time. So that kept me coming back, because each time I knew I had an excellent chance. I realized that I couldn't succeed all the time, therefore I didn't expect to. Nevertheless, I did expect at some point to get it right and have that success.

Making up my mind to continue my bid for the Solo Round the World Balloon record, I decided I should wait so as not to do it within a year or perhaps two years of Piccard and Jones' success. If I were successful too close to the other flight, it could be perceived as the second around the world flight, which is not very important. I wanted my flight to have its own identity as being the First Solo. Throughout aviation history, the First Solo achievements have ranked as major milestones. Joe Kittinger's Solo TransAtlantic Balloon flight was as important as the first team flight by Maxie Anderson, Ben Abruzzo, and Larry Newman. The first TransAtlantic airplane flight by John Alcock and Arthur Whitten Brown in 1919 was paled by the solo success of Charles Lindbergh eight years later. I decided that I'd be the first to fly solo around the world in a balloon and I decided to make my next attempt in 2001.

In the meantime, Richard Abruzzo, a balloonist, had bought a balloon which had been built by Cameron Balloons in England for a prior Round the World competitor. Richard planned a solo attempt but decided not to use the balloon because he couldn't find sponsorship. I then bought the balloon.

The balloon was much larger than the systems I had previously flown in. The envelope was 550,000 cubic ft as opposed to the 450,000 cubic ft one I used in the summer of 1998. The extra lifting capacity enabled me to carry 40 large cylinders of fuel; however, the fuel consumption would be a bit higher. I had the burner system enlarged from 4 to 6 burners. Andy Elson built a new capsule, which was slightly larger than the one I lost in 1998. Tim Cole, my Project Manager, spent all of his spare time for six months installing all the capsule systems.

My August 1998 crash in the Coral Sea did not deter me from flying in the Southern Hemisphere. Since there were so many complications with overflight permissions from numerous countries in the Northern Hemisphere, I decided to fly again in the Southern Hemisphere. Bob Rice would be my meteorologist and I discussed with him at great length the best place in the Southern Hemisphere to start this flight. I favored Australia for two reasons. I liked the ease of getting things done in an English-style country and also because it was close to the Coral Sea. In 1998 my balloon ruptured and crashed due to a line of thunderstorms rising from the warm waters of the Coral Sea. This was a recurrent risk. With my launch in 1998 from Mendoza, Argentina, we had no way to forecast the Coral Sea thunderstorm risk 8 days in advance. With an Australia launch I would only be a little over a day away from the Coral Sea so that I could scrub a launch if thunderstorms were forecast there.

In September 1999, Dick Smith joined me in my Citation for a tour of possible launch sites in Australia. Dick is the founder of Dick Smith's electronic stores chain and now a prominent adventurer. He had friends and contacts all over Australia. When we arrived we toured Woomera, which is Australia's aircraft test facility and bombing range. We next visited the dominantly aboriginal town of Leigh Creek, and then continued on to Kalgoorlie in Western Australia. I loved Kalgoorlie. It was a gold mining town in the nineteenth century and is still one of the largest producers of gold in the world. It is a Wild West town of bars and brothels, with scruffy miners drinking hard and carousing until late at night. The Mayor of Kalgoorlie, Paul Robson, rolled out the red carpet for us. Australians love adventure and in the Outback their enthusiasm is unbounded. I was introduced to a local named Shorty Ryan to help me with arranging things in Kalgoorlie. With a name like 'Shorty', I figured he must be at least 6½ ft tall. Funny thing: he's actually short. When he said 'no worries' you could always rely on it. He was the ultimate 'can do' guy and it seemed he never said 'no'.

Bob Rice organized my flight plan. After launching from Kalgoorlie, I would cross southern Australia and hug the northern edge of the jetstreams across the South Pacific but keeping south of all islands. I'd then cross the high Andes in the vicinity of Santiago, Chile. From there I'd continue through Argentina and on to the South Atlantic. I would pass about 400 miles south of Cape Town, South Africa, and continue across the Indian Ocean and finally land somewhere in the remote Australian Outback.

After we decided on Kalgoorlie, Tim Cole lined up the same team from my two previous attempts. John Kugler as Inflation Manager, Bert Padelt as Systems Director and Dennis Brown as Launchmaster, to help with the final preparations. Tim oversaw the entire operation, including the team members, all the equipment, the transportation of the equipment, getting everything through customs, and all the purchasing of equipment within Australia. He was responsible for booking the hotels and rental cars. The numbers on

Tim's credit card had been pretty much worn down. We never had a budget because we didn't know how much it would cost to get the job done. I had total confidence that Tim would spend my money wisely.

I spared no cost when it came to my safety. I told Tim to make sure that we had extra backups of everything this time, as equipment failure and lack of replacement parts had been a problem on some of my previous flights. I made sure that I was familiar with all the replacement parts and learned how to change them in the event I would have to. I practiced two-minute drills, during which I replaced numerous components as quickly as possible. I did this until I mastered dealing with every imaginable equipment failure.

When Bob Rice issued a 'Code Green', everything was ready at the Kalgoorlie airport and we were excited. Both the launch conditions and the Winds Aloft looked auspicious for a successful flight. The inflation started while I was back in the hotel trying to get some final moments of sleep. The balloon envelope was being filled with helium in seemingly calm conditions. When it finally started to stand up off the ground, the launch team discovered a major wind problem. Above 50 ft there was a nocturnal jet that swept over this flat area of Australia. It was not realized at ground level but when the 140-ft balloon stood up it was squarely in 15 knots of wind. To make matter worse, the envelope was laid out upwind of the capsule and it was quickly being dragged toward the capsule. The launch team, which now included Alex Tai, Red Sheese and Andy Milk, struggled to control the balloon. In desperation, they tied off one of the two control lines to a truck. That was the fatal mistake because all the wind loading went to the attachment point of that one control line. The balloon envelope tore and all our hopes for a successful launch were gone. Red called me at the hotel to break the bad news.

Since we were early enough in the season, there was a chance that I could get it repaired. But we would have to work fast if I wanted to fly in the fast Southern Hemisphere's winter jetstream before it dissipated altogether with the arrival of spring in September. Andy Elson was able to organize a team of balloon builders from Cameron Balloons in England. They flew to Kalgoorlie with the repair materials while Andy purchased industrial sewing machines for the repairing of the balloon. After one month's work, the balloon was completely and properly repaired.

Since the wind posed a continuing threat to the launch, we had to consider other launch areas which would not be subject to this peculiar nocturnal jet and which would allow us to inflate the balloon. Shorty came up with the answer. We started inspecting inactive open pit gold mines, which were scattered around the outskirts of Kalgoorlie. Mining companies generously offered us our choice of pits to use. After we chose one, the mining company brought in equipment to level the bottom. As a final confirmation, a crewmember stayed overnight in the bottom of the pit and took wind readings. The next day Tim Cole concluded that an open pit wouldn't work. Despite the protection from the wind in the pit, when the balloon launched and rose to the edge, the surface wind hitting the upper balloon envelope would drag the capsule into the pit's edge. With two tons of propane-ethane mix, that impact would explode my fuel tanks and that would be the dramatic end of me!

We would have to abandon Kalgoorlie as a launch site. We learned that Northam, Australia, was the location of a tourist hot air balloon operation, so we explored that possibility. Northam is nestled within the Avon Valley, 300 miles away from Kalgoorlie. Its little airport is pretty well sheltered from the wind and a strong inversion sets in there, creating stable air in the morning and far better conditions than our other sites for a successful launch. After verifying the existence of calm nighttime conditions, Shorty proceeded to move all of our equipment including helium tankers to Northam.

I went home to Beaver Creek, where I resumed my acclimatiz-ation to altitude—an important preparation for high flight in an unpressurized capsule. Within a month Bob Rice spotted another potential launch date and I returned to Australia. However, when I arrived, the conditions again were not quite right and there was more waiting for weather. With this time on my hands, I started to get antsy and looked around for something interesting to do. Since I had flown myself over in my Citation X, I investigated doing the Australia Transcontinental Record. There are great jetstreams over Australia in the winter.

On 28 July 2001 I took off from Perth Airport with Alex Tai and Shaun Regan as copilots and flew across the continent to Brisbane at a blistering speed. We made it in 3 hours 8 minutes with an average speed of 705.06 mph. No airplane, supersonic or other, has ever crossed Australia faster. We heard some rumblings from the Australian Air Force that they should try to break my new record with their supersonic F-111s, but they haven't.

Bob again reported that an imminent launch was not on the cards. To relieve my frustrations, I decided to go for another airplane speed record.

On 30 July I flew from Perth to Hobart, Tasmania in the remarkable time of 2 hours 28 minutes. As I sat behind the controls of my plane, I pushed it to the limits keeping the plane flying right on the red line of Mach .92 almost the entire distance. My determination was unwavering. Since the wind was dictating what I was doing with my balloon flight, I was determined to defy its influence in terms of what I could achieve in an airplane. The result was an average speed of 742.02 mph (1,194.77 km/h) which is the fastest aviation record ever flown by a non-supersonic airplane.

This had been the longest possible wait period for a takeoff in all of my ballooning projects, so we were relieved when the time for launch finally came. My team inflated the balloon without a problem and I was ready for my fifth solo round the world balloon attempt. All the troubles with the previous launch sites suddenly seemed to be in the distant past as I released the balloon's tether and sailed effortlessly up into the air. Although I knew it was getting late in the season and that the jetstream wouldn't be as strong, I was still looking forward to decent winds. I was disappointed when I found myself plotting along much slower than I'd anticipated across Australia. I kept changing altitudes, probing for stronger winds. It was like looking for a needle in a haystack and I had no success. It seemed that my launch was just a couple of hours late and the fast winds had run off ahead of me. After swinging to the south over the Bight of Australia, my wind stream turned north and took me way too far north. What was supposed to be a jetstream route over the vacant expanses of the South Pacific was now displaced to the north where there was far less wind. Bob could not find a pattern to get me back south. This became a slow tour of tropical island territories: New Caledonia, Tonga, Niue, Cook Islands, French Polynesia, and Pitcairn Island. As I approached the island of Aitutaki, I was awakened by a radio call. Local pilots had flown up to photograph this moment. I opened the hatch to see my direct crossing of this spectacular but remote island.

In November 2005, I returned to Aitutaki in my Citation and found that the Aitutakians vividly remembered exactly what they were doing when they saw my balloon fly over four years earlier. The crossing of these idyllic coral islands was fascinating, but that was not the purpose of this flight. I was becoming increasingly frustrated with the inability to break out of the slow winds. I had been in the air over 11 days when I reached the coast of South America near Antofagasta, Chile. My spirits were low. The winds that I had hoped for never materialized. 'I waited too long,' I thought regretfully. During the time it took to mend the balloon, my window of opportunity had closed and I hadn't realized this before the launch. I mentally settled into the idea that this flight would take much longer than anticipated, but I still had enough fuel because I was able to carry enough for a 23-day flight.

Next I had to cross the Andes mountain range and this was some of the most stressful flying of the trip. The Andes are one of the longest and highest mountain ranges in the world. Located in South America, they stretch 4500 miles longitudinally along the west coast of the continent. As wind strikes perpendicularly to a mountain range it creates a mountain wave. The upper part of this wave is not so much of a problem, but the downside can cause a rapid descent. Worse still is the rotor between the wave. To avoid both of these hazards, I had to go as high as possible out of the reach of the rotor.

When I got midway over the range, I felt a sudden shift in the balloon and it started ascending. I was caught in the grip of a mountain wave that tossed my balloon upward at 500 feet per minute. Fearing that the balloon might rupture if the buffeting got much worse, I hastily buckled on my parachute. However, parachuting out onto a freezing snowy Andean mountaintop was the last thing I wanted to do. With my parachute still on, I fired the burners and climbed in altitude in hopes of finding a wind current that would take me across the range. Luckily, I found a swift and stable wind pattern that carried me across the Andes without any further trouble.

As I was clearing the Andes, the winds that had carried me across suddenly died. I was making slow progress again and was faced with a new risk—a series of unanticipated thunderstorms. For the entire next day and night I flew with the thunderstorms. As evening approached, lightning was striking everywhere. Jagged columns of light crackled within a mile of me and momentarily suffused the voluminous clouds floating in the darkened sky with a soft glow. It was a paradoxically beautiful and unnerving sight. I would have enjoyed the light show if it weren't so dangerous. In the middle of the night, as the thunderstorms dissipated, the clouds spread to engulf me and it started snowing. It was a miracle that the balloon escaped damage despite the consistent risk from lightning and snow that had accumulated on the envelope. After the fall in the Coral Sea I had resolved that I never wanted to be exposed to the risk of thunderstorms again, yet here I was going through this.

It was dawn and during the previous 24 hours I had only covered a measly 300 miles and endured incredible risk. I asked Bob Rice if I would soon break out of this and get back on track. The bad news was that the Southern Atlantic Ocean was having thunderstorms and light winds with an uncertain track for the balloon. I might make it across but it would take time.

I did some quick assessment with Tim Cole and Joe Ritchie in Mission Control. I was only halfway around the world and had spent 12½ days getting that far. My oxygen gauge indicated only one-third remaining but these gauges are notoriously unreliable. I might only have a quarter of the insulated container, called a 'dewar', of oxygen left. If I ran out of oxygen, I might be able to finish the flight but I would have to fly below 20,000 ft altitude. That's not a problem in good conditions, but it was disastrous if I needed to climb higher to cross a thunderstorm but couldn't due to lack of oxygen. The risk was extremely great.

I contacted Mission Control to go over my options. Whatever decision we made, it would have to be timely. If I was going to land, I needed to do so in the next couple hours while I was still over South America and before I flew out over the Atlantic Ocean. Going over my altitude, direction, and wind speed and after taking everything into consideration with Mission Control, I was left with making the final decision. After weighing it for another hour, I came to the dispiriting conclusion that I didn't have the wind or the oxygen to take me securely the rest of the way around the globe. Yet, I didn't have time to resent this unfortunate outcome. My immediate objective was to set the balloon down before I flew out to sea. Searching for a place to land, I descended to the estancias in southern Brazil just north of Uruguay.

There was one last major concern and that was fuel—not a lack of but rather an abundance of it. When preparing for a landing, it is protocol to empty most of the fuel tanks in an absolutely unpopulated place like the sea or the desert, then cut away the empty tanks. I didn't have that option. I wouldn't be able to drop tanks anyhow since I was floating over beautiful gaucho ranch land in southern Brazil with occasional ranch houses and horses running in the fields—the risk was too great. Since hitting the ground too hard or striking rocks with this extra fuel could cause a massive conflagration, I had to make a gentle landing and without dragging into hard obstacles. It was windier than I liked at 17 mph, but I had made a landing with that much wind in Russia, albeit with a much smaller balloon. Since my landing would require near-perfect coordination, I was aghast when I pulled the deflation line at the precise moment of touchdown to let the helium out of the balloon and nothing happened. I bounced back up 200 ft in the air.

I made another approach. This time the capsule hit the ground with a thud, leaving a distinct depression in the ground and knocking me to the floor of the capsule. Frantically I pulled again, this time with all the leverage and muscle I could muster, but it still wouldn't give. As the capsule rebounded off the ground, I stood up in the hatch to check the condition of the fuel tanks. Fortunately they had not ruptured and were still intact, but the oxygen tanks had ripped off. Running out of options, my only alternative was to hold open the helium valve to get a slow release of helium until I could get the balloon in a stable drag across the ground. With each bounce I held my breath and looked to see what was in front of me. Twice I fired the burners to avoid landing in stock ponds.

Finally I was dragged along the ground in a horizontal position. I had to cut the cables that held the capsule to the envelope. As I was jostled along the ground at the wind speed of 17 mph, I grabbed the cable cutters and applied all my strength to cut these heavy cables. I was exhausted, but finally succeeded in cutting them. I sighed in relief as I watched the balloon and fuel tanks drag away, leaving me safe in the prone capsule. The envelope and tanks dragged another half a mile before being finally snagged by a row of trees and stopping. Several of the tanks dangerously spewed fuel into the air. I waited for the fire or an explosion but nothing ignited the fuel. The only sound that prevailed was silence. All was still, like nothing had even happened. I guess this is what they mean by 'grand finale'.

18. BREAKING THE TRANSATLANTIC SAILING WORLD RECORD, OCTOBER 2001

In these times, it's wonderful to hear of great news!!!
I live in Rockaway Beach NY; most of us need to hear good news these days. We have lost so many loved ones at the WTC (World Trade Center). So as you can see, this is great news. It takes me away for a moment, from all this tragedy.
Thank you, God Bless

Sean Gillan, NYC Police Officer

B y the summer of 2001 we were hungry to get back into action and go gunning after some records. By 1 May, we had made the necessary rigging replacements in West Palm Beach, Florida and were planning to sail back up the Eastern United States seaboard to New York and, more meaningfully, to the Ambrose Light starting line. We were preparing to take on our fourth TransAtlantic attempt.

We reckoned that the need to deliver *PlayStation* to New York was a good excuse as any to attempt the Miami–New York record which was currently held by Bruno Peyron (France) and Cam Lewis (USA) who co-skippered *Explorer* across this course in 2 days 22 hours 50 minutes on 2 June 1999. Crossing the start line at South

Point Tower, Miami at 12:42 EDT on Sunday, 20 May, we went on to cover 505 nm the first day and 503 the second. We crossed the finish line at Ambrose Light, New York on the evening of Tuesday, 22 May 2001, setting a new Miami–New York World Sailing Speed Record. Our time of 2 days 5 hours 55 minutes beat Peyron and Lewis' previous mark by a considerable margin of 16 hours 55 minutes. We were really pleased. Our performance had been flawless. It had been a very good trip, not just because we pocketed a new World Record, but also because we again demonstrated *PlayStation*'s potential. Taking the Miami–New York record was a real morale-booster for me and my crew. It was the perfect exercise for putting us in the right frame of mind for taking another crack at the TransAtlantic.

Once in New York, we began gearing up for a TransAtlantic crossing. Having made three tries at this record the previous year, we approached this attempt with a determination and an augmented sense of confidence that comes from experience. We knew how important it was to choose the right weather pattern and get as far ahead of the front as possible and ride with it all the way. When August arrived, we were ready to go if a good pattern emerged and ready to wait until it did.

August came and went without us having been able to track down an acceptable weather pattern for a 'Code Green'. Our chief meteorologist, Ken Campbell of Commanders Weather, explained that September is a particularly difficult month in which to get a decent TransAtlantic weather pattern. Because the water temperatures are at the annual maximum during this month, the Azores High would be displaced too far north, requiring us to sail more miles to follow around the top of the High. In addition the hurricanes in the tropical areas, after doing their damage, re-curve into the North Atlantic and barrel through as extratropical storms, which completely disturb the weather patterns we need.

Finally, early in October, we received a forecast of weather closer to our requirements. Tom Mattus, a meteorologist at Commanders Weather, classified a potential weather pattern as a Code Red/Yellow. This is halfway between yellow, which means 'possible' and red, which is no possibility. I've learned by working with a number of outstanding meteorologists that they will do an excellent analysis but can't make the final decision whether the winds will be good enough for a record.

Because *PlayStation* was being kept in Newport, Rhode Island and would thus require one day's sailing to get to New York City, we needed to be more decisive with regards to whether or not we were going to start on this weather pattern.

I called our navigator Stan Honey. 'Did you read Tom's analysis?'

'Yes,' replied Stan.

'Isn't this exactly the weather pattern we've been waiting for?' I pressed further.

'Well, yes,' he answered.

'Then let's go!' I exclaimed.

I quickly alerted Ben Wright and the rest of the crew to sail for New York Harbor immediately. We have concluded that the perfect weather pattern for the TransAtlantic record is an approaching major storm system. But it is necessary to sail in the building wind ahead of the Cold Front of the storm system. Yet the sea state is still relatively smooth ahead of the Cold Front and the typical wind direction is ideal for maximum speed across the Atlantic. It may be paradoxical to an outsider that the fastest ocean sailing is done in moderate winds, like 30 knots, and a smooth sea—most people think that it would be faster in the teeth of a storm. However, we must stay ahead of the storm and its cold fronts or the sea will turn impossibly rough or, worse, the boat could be forced into survival mode, which is very slow.

I made a mad dash from St Louis where I was hosting a 'Thank You' party for all the Washington University students who had worked on my last RTW Balloon attempt. I landed my plane at dawn in New Jersey where I got a motor launch to take me from Sandy Point to *PlayStation*.

In addition to the weather patterns at sea, a gut-wrenching and mind-boggling event that had recently occurred ashore also determined our start time. Following the 9/11 attacks on New York City's World Trade Center's Twin Towers, restrictions on civilian craft in New York Harbor had been put into effect and stringently enforced. We needed to leave Chelsea Piers in New York City before 2 pm in order to beat the 4 pm cut-off time at Verrazano Narrows.

Being in the vicinity of Manhattan made it impossible not to think about what had recently occurred there on 9/11. On that morning, I was in Beaver Creek when my office called and told me what had happened, that this plane had crashed into the World Trade Center. Immediately, I turned on the television and watched it from there. As I took in the graphic footage, I tried to remember who I knew that worked in the Towers. I lost one friend in the accident: Bob Cruikshank was someone I had known for 25 years.

We had been on the Board of Directors of the Chicago Board Options Exchange together. He had actually moved out to Beaver Creek, where we sometimes got together socially. But his office was in the World Trade Center. That unforgettable day, he went down with the building.

As I watched the events of 9/11 on the television, it took a while for their implications to sink in. I think the magnitude of the destruction, the way it was executed and our utter lack of anticipation of it caught our nation, even the world, totally off guard. My first thoughts were about the sheer number of people who worked in that building. The initial estimation relayed by the news reporters that morning was that a few hundred people might have been killed. I thought, 'No! There could be more like 5000 people killed!' My mind reeled just thinking about the number of people who were likely to be in those buildings, even though it was before 9 am when most people were due at work.

My second thought was that 9/11 was really going to change things across the board in our civilization. Just as those involved in the commercial airline industry braced themselves for the impact that 9/11 would have on their business, I speculated what it was going to do to the stock market because I still had a very active business in stock options. Even though I was in Beaver Creek, I still had over 30 traders on the floor of the Exchange. I predicted that 9/11 was going to cause a very dramatic move in the stock market.

As we departed Chelsea Piers on Friday morning 5 October 2001, I tried to put my reflections of 9/11 aside and concentrate exclusively on the task at hand. As the wind shifted S-SW and came up to 14–15 knots, we crossed the official start line at Ambrose Light at exactly 1.19 pm local time and headed out to sea. Despite the hurriedness of our preparation, our strategy was working. With an average of 25 knots for the first $12\frac{3}{4}$ hours, we covered 315 nm in excellent weather. Conditions were fantastic. The sea state was flat and the sky perfectly clear. Such rare Atlantic conditions inspired Stan to appreciatively estimate, 'If crossing the Atlantic were always this pleasant, there would be hundreds of boats out here.'

By the end of our first day at sea, the high-velocity speeds we had been able to maintain allowed us to cover over 600 nm. By our 36th hour we had already taken a 155-mile lead over the record holder's position. Dave Scully, one of the Watch Captains, came to me: 'Steve, we have a chance for the 24-Hour Record. Would you like to harden up to maximum speed?' After a few moments of thought,

I made a fateful decision. We would stay on course and sail the Atlantic without any compromise. Hardening up to maximize boat speed would have taken us off course to the south and cost us time on our TransAtlantic. We did recapture the 24-Hour Record, which we once held at 580 nm but which since had been increased to 655.13 nm by Grant Dalton on *Club Med* during The Race. We turned a distance of 687.17 nm, which re-established *PlayStation* as the fastest sailboat in the world. However, I have often asked myself if I made the best decision. I believe that if we went after the 24-Hour that time, we could have made the first 700-mile day and still have done well enough to set the TransAtlantic Record. And yet, I think I did make the right decision. For I also believe that when you have that rare opportunity to do something to perfection, do it. And the TransAtlantic was what we were doing.

Since the start, *PlayStation* was performing perfectly. We had been able to ride strong southwesterly 30-knot winds that had been generated by the low front we managed to stay ahead of and not get ravaged by. We kept most of the sail area hoisted. With the new bows, which lengthened *PlayStation* to 125 ft, we were totally unafraid of pitch poling as a result of stuffing the bows into the 6 ft swell. Hour after hour, the speedometer read over 30 knots. 'Incredible speeds to be traveling in the darkness of night,' I thought to myself as I looked down at water passing the hulls. Yes, the water was really going by at 30 knots! With about 1600 nautical miles to reach the finish line at The Lizard, we were 383 miles ahead of the 1990 position of *Jet Services V*, the current TransAtlantic record holder.

Although winds eventually diminished to 25-knots, we were still able to maintain superb sailing speeds with 565 nm to go. Haunted by the prospect faced by other attempts of a dying wind while approaching the finish, we became very nervous that the wind would quit on us again. In a half-joking, half-serious attempt to mitigate such an outcome, David Scully came out on deck donning shorts and a T-shirt and put on sunblock, superstitiously preparing for sunny calm weather. Prepare for the worst (fair weather) and maybe it wouldn't happen! The wind continued to weaken but fortunately not too much, allowing us to maintain 15 knots of boat speed when we crossed the finish line at Lizard Head.

On 10 October 2001, just 4 days 17 hours 28 minutes 6 seconds after leaving New York Harbor, *PlayStation* finally came into her own. Having sailed her at her full potential with a top-flight crew, we set a remarkable new TransAtlantic world sailing speed record that shattered the previous record of 6 d 13 h 3 m 32 s, set 11 years ago by Serge Madec on *Jet Services V*, by an enormous margin of almost 44 hours. Having taken nearly one-third off of Madec's time, we had put up the course record in sailing by crossing the Atlantic in an average speed of 25.78 knots

That time, we had all the right factors on our side and our success was enormously satisfying. We had put it all together; an extremely fast boat in *PlayStation*, a perfectly chosen weather pattern and a crew who sailed brilliantly. Stan Honey navigated our route to perfection. We followed a Great Circle route—so called because it is the shortest distance between two points on a spherical surface such as the Earth—and we stayed right on it, tracking only a mere 9 miles more than the Great Circle distance, which is extraordinary for a sailboat. Indeed, we had learned a lot over the course of four attempts that finally ended with a successful one.

As we arrived at the dock in Plymouth, legendary ocean sailor Robin Knox-Johnston was there to meet us. When he got a closer look at the crew, he couldn't believe how fresh and relaxed we looked after sailing across the Atlantic. But then we had been at sea for less than 5 days! Moreover, it had been easy sailing that never required a tack or a jibe. It was just FAST.

That night at our crew celebration dinner, Stan Honey, as if still trying to digest the reality of our exceptionally outstanding performance, turned to me and asked: 'Do you think we did good?'

With a wide grin, I replied, 'Yes, Stan, we did good.'

In fact, we nailed it. The TransAtlantic is the ultimate course for open ocean sailors. In breaking this record, we achieved a milestone in the world of Speed Sailing.

19. *THE BUD LIGHT SPIRIT OF FREEDOM*: FIRST SOLO CIRCUMNAVIGATION OF THE GLOBE IN A BALLOON, JUNE 2001

This flight will, without doubt, merit a place in history alongside the great pioneering flights of aviators such as Bleriot, Lindbergh and Yeager. The vision and determination that you have shown is an example of the true spirit of aviation and an inspiration to all pilots.

Marc Asquith, Chairman of The Royal Aero Club

M y first balloon flight across the Atlantic Ocean with Tim Cole cost me about $150,000. The cost of my balloon and the improved equipment rose with every around the world attempt as the balloons and support teams got bigger and the logistics more complex by using countries like Argentina and then Australia for launch sites. By my fifth solo balloon attempt around the world, the cost was up to $600,000. Going over the estimates for my sixth attempt, I realized that this flight would hit close to $1,000,000.

Since I was enjoying my experience with Sony as title sponsor of *PlayStation*, I had warmed to the idea of sponsorship. Deciding to seek out a sponsor for my next flight to offset the high cost, I called August Busch III who had previously expressed an interest in sponsoring my balloon project. After I got him on the phone and explained the purpose of my call, he laughed and reminded me that he once offered me a million dollars, but that I had been too proud to take it. Still open to my request, he asked me to send him a proposal, which I did. After checking with his executives, he called me back and told me the amount Anheuser-Busch would provide. Just like that—the deal was done. I felt quite fortunate because some people spend years looking for a sponsor and I was able to land Anheuser-Busch as a sponsor after only two phone calls lasting a couple of minutes August saw that this was a win–win situation for both of us which worked out to virtually complete cost coverage for me and a good promotional opportunity for Bud Light. *Bud Light Spirit of Freedom* was now the name of my new Anheuser-Busch sponsored balloon.

In addition to sponsorship, I had to find a new meteorologist. My previous weather router, Bob Rice, was again consumed in an America's Cup project and therefore unavailable for this attempt. I took this opportunity to hire Luc Trullemans who was known for his proactive routing style of changing altitudes to stay on course, a strategy that had produced the greatest recent successes in ballooning, such as the remarkable flight of David Hempleman-Adams to the North Pole and back in May 2000. And then there was the poignant reminder of Piccard and Jones' Round the World in March 1999, which I believed succeeded because of Luc's brilliant weather routing. After meeting with Luc in Brussels to see how he worked, I invited him to be Chief Meteorologist. He brought with him his assistant at the Belgian Royal Meteorological Institute, David Dehenauw.

My long-time friend Joe Ritchie, who faithfully worked in Mission Control on my last flight, now became the Director of Mission Control. Barron Hilton generously donated $200,000 to Washington University to cover the costs of setting up Mission Control, the website and summer job funding for the students manning Mission Control.

Early in June, Luc had us at a 'Code Yellow' status, connoting impending favorable conditions for a launch. He informed Joe and me that he had found a 'hot one'. According to his current analysis, an auspicious launch window had opened, offering me a chance to complete the first 75% of the global circumnavigation in a remarkable eight days. This was, of course, if the technical aspects of my flight went perfectly. I was in Beaver Creek, training at the top of the mountain to acclimatize myself for the flight, when I received the word and quickly packed my things and headed for the airport. As I flew down to Australia, my intuition told me that this time my flight was going to be a success. My confidence level soared. Last year, my attempt to catch a formidable wind pattern and complete this mission had failed. I had launched too late in the season and missed the best of the Southern Hemisphere's winter jetstream. I ended up going too far north off of the desired trajectory and 12 days was consumed just getting half way. This time Luc intended to get me going in the Southern Hemisphere winter season and keep me in the middle of the jetstream.

Having earned the support of the locals during our last attempt, we once again chose Northam as the launch site. The folks in this area had worked with us enough to know our routine and seemed to genuinely enjoy being involved in our endeavors. As we prepared for the launch, we were immensely appreciative of the cooperation and hospitality they continued to show us. Before my flight, Mayor Paul Robson of Kalgoorlie gave me a boomerang to carry with me on my trip, in hopes that I would return just as this Australian symbol always does.

When I arrived in Northam, Tim Cole and the rest of the launch team were already there, busying themselves with the final preparations for the takeoff. Equipment logistics had already been dealt with and everything was ready and in place. All we needed was a 'Code Green'. The following day brought reassuring news of a stable weather pattern, which catalyzed our 'Code Yellow' into a 'Code Green'. All systems were 'go' for a launch. To make sure that this window of opportunity did not pass us by, Tim, Bert, Dennis, and John, who comprised my launch team, fervently worked around the clock for a smooth and punctual takeoff.

Despite the rain on the afternoon of 18 June 2002, the launch team brought the capsule out of the hangar and started the preparations. We estimated that the four-hour inflation process could begin at dusk as the rain stopped. The balloon had been laid out and covered and we were careful not to uncover the balloon until the rain stopped. A climbout in a wet balloon into freezing conditions at altitude would result in an ice-laden balloon for the entire flight.

When the rain stopped, an enthusiastic crowd of 300 locals convened on the field. The light rain was replaced with swirling wind, which eventually settled down into a 5-knot East wind. However, that still posed a problem because we could barely handle that much wind strength during the tenuous process of inflation and the wind direction was blowing opposite to the weather forecast. It is imperative that a big balloon envelope be inflated on the downwind side of the gondola or capsule, otherwise the envelope will drag into the capsule as it lifts from its prone position to upright, which runs the risk of entangling and tearing equipment. Having laid out the envelope based on the incorrect forecast of a West wind, we waited and waited and waited for the wind direction to change.

The crowd suffered through the cold night while I nervously checked over the equipment. After experiencing a torn balloon during inflation in Kalgoorlie the previous year, my Launch Director John Kugler was adamant that we should not inflate with the current wind direction. Project Manager Tim Cole concurred. Meanwhile Luc was getting increasingly nervous about losing the jetstream pattern due to this delay. Speaking via the satellite phone to Luc who was in St Louis, he gave me a deadline of early morning launch or stand down until another good pattern presented itself, which could be one or six weeks from then. After hanging up, I eagerly checked with my team again. Still no go. With our launch deadline quickly approaching, the time had come for some tough decision-making. Sometimes it is necessary to overrule the experts and just go for it. I realized that this was one of those times. I called for the inflation. My team rose to the occasion and pulled it off. When that balloon stood up and had overcome its vulnerability, John Kugler was first to come over with a big smile and shake my hand, 'Good call, Steve.'

With the inflation complete, Tim checked out all the systems and turned things over to me. I climbed into the capsule and put on my parachute and helmet. After doing the final 'weigh off' which determines the equilibrium of the balloon, my crew then held the system while 200 lbs of sandbags were removed to set the desired lift. I waved to the media and crowd and shouted my departing words, 'To a successful launch and a swift flight.' As the crew backed away, I pulled the release lever.

As my silver giant rose out of the Northam Aerodrome, I was touched to see below me the cheering fans, who had patiently waited the entire night to see me off. It was a tangible reminder that people were interested in what I was doing and wanted to be a part of it even if it simply meant wishing me 'good luck'. As the balloon continued to climb, I also reflected how very pleased I was with the level of expertise that my launch team demonstrated. It testified to their exceptional ability to improvise and work under various pressures, including the unknown. Their capacity to consistently rise to new challenges never ceased to amaze me.

Despite the winds, we had a great launch on 19 June. Mission Control Director, Joe Ritchie, echoed my sentiments exactly when he exclaimed that this was the 'smoothest launch we've ever had'. My ascent was at a very fast rate of 1100 ft per minute—double what I had projected—which created some nervousness that the envelope might rupture from the pressure on the top of it as it climbed. *The Bud Light Spirit of Freedom* ascended to 21,000 ft and quickly found the wind that started to carry me at 60 mph.

My flight plan entailed flying over Australia to Auckland, New Zealand, across the South Pacific to Chile, then Argentina and then onward across the Southern Atlantic Ocean. I would pass south of Cape Town, South Africa before making the final stretch over the Indian Ocean and back to Australia. Once having reached a comfortable cruising altitude, my meteorologist, Luc, told me that I could expect to reach the east coast of Australia in just over one day and cross New Zealand within the next day. The goal of reaching the coast of Chile in eight days was looking feasible. Even though these were the initial few hours of my adventure, things were already proving different from my previous attempts. When my trajectory took me over the Great Australian Bight and then about 120 miles north of Adelaide, I was able to take in the fantastic view from atop the capsule. As I approached the Australian capital of Canberra that night, clear skies gave way to the mottled sequence of lights that graced the Eastern coastline and seemed to silently announce my departure from this landmass. While taking advantage of conducive weather conditions on 20 June, I left the Australian continent and headed east over the Tasman Sea toward New Zealand. I was looking forward to seeing land again even if it were for only a brief moment until I headed out into the vastness of the great Pacific Ocean. I knew that New Zealanders were adventure enthusiasts and looked forward to me crossing their beautiful country.

Soon after crossing the International Dateline, going 80 mph at 24,500 ft, the trouble-free flight I was enjoying so far prompted Ritchie to make the oxymoron-ish comment, 'It has been excitingly boring.' Then with a touch of sarcasm, Joe added, 'The most exciting occurrence was when Steve's first fuel tank ran out of gas.' As a fuel tank lasts about a half a day before it needs to be changed, there was really no drama involved in this at all as it was par for the course!

Thanks to such boredom I was able to get some sleep, a luxury that I usually don't have at this critical stage of the journey. The thing with boredom is that it also creates room for doubt. As I lay down, I still wondered what unexpected complications awaited me at every turn. I would soon find out.

Heading toward New Zealand, my weather team notified me of a local thunderstorm system that was hovering in this area. My mind raced to the last time I encountered a storm off the coast of Australia, which left me stranded in the Coral Sea. I fervently hoped that the storm pattern would move south before my arrival. Luckily, the storm dissipated before I got to New Zealand. As I headed out into the Pacific Ocean, my thoughts turned to the bond of trust that I had firmly established with my meteorologist, Luc Trullemans, and his assistant David Dehenauw. I felt confident that they would do everything in their power from their end to route me safely across this oceanic expanse.

Aiding Luc's and David's efforts were a plethora of meteorological tools, which included computer programs that ran analyses using both the American and the European Models. Integrating weather reports and satellite information from around the world, these analyses helped one to determine what the weather would do. Even though the results are not as accurate in the Southern Hemisphere due to the fewer weather stations there, there has been a huge improvement in the quality of worldwide weather forecasting in the past decade. From my position, I was sending observations of wind, cloud and barometric pressure, which helped pinpoint where I was relative to the forecast weather. To facilitate steering me—by having me climb or descend to different altitudes where the wind directions and speeds were slightly different—we relied on the primary routing tool, the Trajectory Model of NOAA's Air Resources Laboratory. This model combines Winds Aloft forecasts to compute where a particle would travel in the wind at various altitudes. My balloon was that particle. Even though the Trajectory Model runs out to 12 days, at that distant point in time the accuracy is about 50:50, or just about worthless. We really felt we could depend upon the accuracy of the forecast route for three to five days out.

My overall strategy in the South Pacific was to pass between low-pressure systems to the south and high-pressure systems to the north. There the winds of the same westerly direction converge. By 'threading the needle' between two systems, I planned to maintain a relatively straight and swift course to Chile.

23 June was the most crucial day thus far. A low was rapidly developing in front of me, which threatened to capture and throw me to the north. Instructions came to me to descend immediately into the trade winds, which are found in the first 3000 ft above the surface of the ocean. Although the 'trades' are easterly, which meant I would be pushed backward, it would give time for this new low to move north and out of the way of my intended track. I dropped down in altitude to 1000 ft where I planned to stay throughout the day. With all the thermal activity at these low levels, the balloon would frequently be jockeyed up and down. Flying anywhere close to level required my utmost attention. At one point I got caught in an unexpected micro low-pressure zone, which caused me to lose more altitude and brought me uncomfortably close to the water's surface. My eyes were glued to the altimeter as it relayed that the balloon was dropping from 1000 ft to 700 ft in a matter of seconds. I desperately wanted to avoid touching the sea, as doing so would terminate my flight for official record purposes, or worse. As I descended to 400 ft, I could clearly sea the waves clashing below me with unbridled force. Knowing that if the burners failed, the balloon would smack into the sea, I took a deep breath and fired all the burners. A welcome jolt threw me slightly off balance, a signal that the burners had successfully halted my descent.

For the next six hours, I hovered above the water's surface. Periodic rainsqualls continued to hit the balloon with severe downdrafts. Blasting the burners to elevate the balloon every time I reached a critically low altitude, I felt like I was riding a never-ending roller coaster. Steadying the balloon the best I could, I moved south and east.

Finally Luc concluded it was time for me to exit this roller coaster ride when he gave me the go ahead to start to climb. More than ready to resume my course across the Pacific, I allowed the balloon to rise, using the heat of the sun, to a maximum altitude of 24,500 ft where I picked up 60-mph winds. As evening approached, the balloon settled down to 19,700 ft as a result of the cooling effects of the loss of sunlight. Keen to take my first opportunity in the last 12 hours to relax, I tuned the autopilot to maintain my present altitude. Just as I did this, I was stunned that the number one burner was locked in an open position, producing continuous flames and increasing the altitude of the balloon. The implications of this equipment failure could be catastrophic to flight. At full burn, it would be a matter of moments before the balloon rocketed through its ceiling, and precious helium would be forced out its appendices, the tubes to release pressure of expanding helium. Grabbing my tools, I threw open the hatch and climbed out on top of the capsule to inspect the burner. To my horror, the fuel valve to the solenoid of the burner was frozen open. With seconds ticking away, I started working feverishly to replace the seized solenoid, but it refused to budge. As the balloon was approaching its altitude ceiling, I jumped back into the capsule and snatched my food bag that contained chemical heating pouches used to heat my meals. I threw water in them to start the chemical heating process. I wrapped the heating packs around the valve and secured them with duct tape. Within moments, the pouches heated up and effortlessly defrosted the valve to the point where I could turn it off. The balloon leveled off with only a few hundred feet from the ceiling to spare. My improvisation with the food packs had averted a devastating loss of helium. From then on, I appreciated my hot food just a little bit more and relied on this process during the numerous solenoid failures during the rest of the flight.

After seven days, I was approaching Chilean airspace. Even though English is the official language for international air traffic controllers, we wanted to be sure of clear communications for this unique flight. Washington University brought into Mission Control a professor of Spanish to talk to the Chilean and Argentine controllers and together they would guide me the rest of the way over the continent. I was glad about this because the less amount of talking I had to do with air traffic control, the more I could concentrate on piloting the balloon.

I was thinking that everything was back on track and going according to plan when a sudden shift in the weather occurred. Peering outside my capsule, I noticed a thick layer of ice coating the balloon and the capsule. Checking my temperature gauge, it read a chilly −40°F. I realized that the precipitation covering the balloon was caused by the instantaneous freezing of water vapor created in the propane combustion process. In a big balloon like this, ice adds a lot of extraneous weight to be lugged around the world. Deciding that it was a good time to 'de-ice', I prepared to reduce my altitude in order to bring the balloon into warmer temperatures to thaw the ice layer. After informing Mission Control of this plan, I started lowering the balloon from 22,500 ft to 4000 ft, where the temperature was above freezing. The melting ice created a veritable rainstorm on the capsule so I stayed inside to stay dry. When the melting slowed, I started my climb in anticipation of crossing the Patagonian Andes.

I brought the balloon up to only 16,500 ft. Normally the wind speeds are better the higher one flies, but at this time flying high held little advantage and, besides, it was a good time to take a break from breathing with an oxygen mask. Although not using supplemental oxygen at 16,500 ft might sound unusual, I do have a lot of experience with altitude both in mountain climbing and distance ballooning. The primary risk at this altitude is judgment errors due to degraded brain function in a reduced oxygen environment. I recalled how on my fifth around the world balloon attempt, Joe Ritchie back at Mission Control suspected that I might be suffering from oxygen deprivation while I was talking to him on the notoriously deficient transmission of the satellite telephone because it sounded like I was slurring my words. He was just about to demand that I descend before I lost control of my faculties. His impression was corrected over the course of the next hour when I lucidly evaluated the routing situation and laid out a new plan in response to the changing wind conditions. After communicating my thoughts, Joe immediately recognized that I was still up there functioning and thinking soundly.

Although I always flew with supplemental oxygen, if I could go without it at the lower elevations, I usually opted to. For this, I had consulted with a great team of medical advisors, including altitude medicine experts Dr Brownie Schoen and early Everest climber Dr Tom Hornbein. As practiced in mountain climbing, I took Diamox tablets twice a day and drank lots of water. Diamox is a mild diuretic normally used by menstruating women that also increases the capacity of red blood cells to carry oxygen by changing the pH of the body's whole fluid system. I would frequently use a Pulse Oximeter to test the oxygen saturation of my blood as well as monitoring my pulse. When poorly acclimatized as the oxygen saturation diminished below my sea level norm of 95%, my resting pulse would climb, reflecting the distress of the body. Once in flight for a number of days, my body would acclimatize to oxygen saturation around 80%. When working on the burners or tanks did not permit keeping my oxygen mask on, I would sometimes climb back into the capsule gasping for air, while putting my oxygen mask back on. On some such occasions I had experienced 65% oxygen saturation—'don't try this at home' as the television advice goes. I remembered what the famous balloonist, Ed Yost, said after he was the first person to fly more than 2000 miles in an unpressurized balloon capsule: 'The highest I ever climbed was 14,600 ft. When my fingernails turned blue, I dropped down.' Presently, I was at 16,500 ft and my fingernails still looked fine.

I prepared for my solo flights with an extensive acclimatization program in Beaver Creek, Colorado, where just being at my home, at an altitude of 8200 ft, helps. For training I coaxed Professor Igor Gamov into building a hyperbaric chamber for me, consisting of a red cylinder just big enough for a person to lie in, albeit with the risk of claustrophobia. Once settled inside, the plexiglass front dome is pulled shut and the motor pulls out the air until the pressure is reduced by one, two or three pounds per square inch as set by the pressure relief valves. This equates to 12,000, 15,000 or 18,000 ft of altitude respectively. I had intended to sleep in the chamber, but found it difficult because of the unnatural environment and the noise of the motor. I much preferred just hiking, running, or cross-country skiing high in the ski resort, depending on the season. When I received special permission to sleep in the Beaver Creek Ski Patrol Headquarters at 11,250 ft, I would often ski up from my house in the afternoons using climbing skins on my skis, make my dinner there, get a night's sleep and then ski down at first light in the morning. That much exercise coupled with long hours at high altitude proved to be a great acclimatization program.

I chuckle when I remember the time in 2001 when I went through my spacesuit training in preparation for the Perlan glider altitude project. This was done at Beale Air Force Base in Northern California, where the U-2 fleet is based and the pilots are trained. While in a full-pressure suit, they put you through a series of emergency procedures, including explosive decompression and a final oxygen deprivation test. As the last trainee on a Friday afternoon I was preparing for this test after having completed all the other procedures. The object was to recognize my mental deterioration and pull the emergency oxygen cord, called the 'green apple', before passing out. Once inside the altitude chamber, I opened the face shield on my helmet and they raised the chamber altitude to 15,000 ft. When this didn't affect me, they took it to 20,000 ft, where I patiently answered all the questions they asked me. I was feeling fine. When they took the chamber up to 25,000 ft, I concentrated on keeping relaxed, like a scuba diver, to reduce oxygen requirements, and silently breathed deeper to compensate for the reduced oxygen environment. After eight minutes, I suggested we try 30,000 ft. Because there were two safety technicians in the chamber with me who were only wearing oxygen masks rather than the full-pressure suit I was wearing, and there was a risk they would get the bends, 28,000 ft was the limit for this procedure. So 28,000 ft it was. Thirteen and a half minutes later, the staff were all looking at their watches realizing it was past 5 pm quitting time, when the manager gave in: 'That's good enough!' he exclaimed. It was the first time they couldn't knock a pilot out with this oxygen deprivation test.

The ringing of my satellite phone brought my awareness back to the here and now. It was Richard Branson calling to wish me luck on the rest of my flight. Having both been competitors and partners on previous round the world ballooning attempts, I confessed to him that I was feeling a bit worried at the moment because I was well south of the original planned course and would have to take a huge risk flying very far south in the Southern Atlantic. To help me get a perspective on things, Richard jogged my memory of the Christmas Day 'swim' we shared in the Pacific Ocean just off the coast of Hawaii when our balloon went down. With a goodhearted laugh, he then pointed out that at least I was still airborne.

Soon I was able to hitch a ride on a jetstream that carried me on to South America four hours earlier than previously predicted. As I crossed the South American coastline in the Patagonian region and approached the Andes Mountain Range, a growing apprehension began to gnaw at me. During my 2001 attempt that ended with my landing in Brazil, I had flown over these mountains and got caught in mountain wave, which sent the balloon repeatedly soaring and descending at treacherous rates. Fortunately, the mountains in this area of the Andes loomed only at 9000 ft instead of 20,000 ft, which I had crossed previously far to the north. Although mountain waves could still be triggered with the lower mountains, it turned out that such a phenomenon would not be a problem that day.

With the Atlantic Ocean only a six hours' flight time away, I realized that if I were going to call off the attempt for any reason, I would have to do it within this timeframe. Weighing heavily on my mind was that the jetstream I was riding was heading toward the Antarctica icepack before it would turn north again and head toward Africa. The question was, 'Should I stay in it?' When Luc and I established the flight path before my launch, going over Antarctica was certainly not part of the plan. Things had changed since then and I had caught a different jetstream. Transiting the Antarctic airspace was extremely dangerous. It is much colder than any climate I had flown in before and there was no guarantee that the balloon would survive such extremely cold weather temperatures. If problems did develop and I went down in this area consisting of floating ice pans, the chance of my being rescued was none. No helicopters or ships would be around there to rescue me.

Even though my capsule floats, I would not be able to keep it afloat for a long period and I'd be frozen in mere moments upon immersion in the frigid waters. Sobering thought.

I told Joe to organize a meeting with Luc, Tim Cole, and David Dehenauw to discuss the risks of continuing beyond South America into the 'Southern Ocean', as this region is commonly called. I wanted to be sure we were making a sound decision. On the positive side, I had plenty of food, sufficient oxygen and plenty of fuel to fly me through this region. After assessing the minimum fuel flow temperatures, the pilot light and cabin heater vaporization temperatures, the main concern was whether the fuel for the pilot lights on the burners would continue to flow in temperatures that cold. If the pilot light couldn't get fuel vapor, my burners would cease to operate and my balloon would inexorably descend into the pack ice. Temperatures were going to be $-60°C$ at my altitude and if we were just using propane it would gel or freeze at $-40°C$ and there would be no vapor for the pilot lights. As with all of my solo flights, we had spiked the propane with 30% ethane, which does not freeze until $-88°C$. Even though, theoretically, our mixture shouldn't freeze in the expected air temperatures, I don't like risking my life based on engineering calculations. However, after full consideration of the matter, my team concluded that the balloon should stay aloft through this zone of frigid air.

The next concern to address was the reliability of the trajectory. What if I came under the influence of low pressure to the south and was looped right on down to the continental area of Antarctica where I'd get stuck in the winds circulating around Antarctica? The winter there enveloped the area with 24 hours of darkness, meaning there would be no way to send a ski plane to rescue me if I was forced to land. Therefore, my primary concern was my ability to stay in the jetstream that would take me back north again. For this important task, I relied on Luc who, after reviewing the weather report, which featured good weather and strong winds, expressed confidence in our flight trajectory. Luc believed that I should be able to turn north with the jetstream and get to Africa without any trouble.

Lastly, Mission Control Director, Joe Ritchie, and I went over our emergency rescue options if the balloon were to crash in the far Southern Ocean. Joe made sure he knew how to contact the search and rescue team on King George Island located in the Antarctic Peninsula near to where I was to fly. They had an airport so, in case of an emergency, my team could fly down there.

After thoroughly discussing it, we were all in agreement that I should make it. Yet, the final decision was down to me. I was the one who'd be going alone over the desolate Antarctic ice pack. In fact, I would be the first to fly a balloon into this inhospitable territory. Although it was frightfully dangerous, deep inside, I welcomed the challenge and believed that it could be done. I also believed that my new insulated capsule would keep me adequately warm.

On 27 June my confidence level got a boost when I passed the halfway mark of my trip. I was moving at great speed, going 113 mph at 25,000 ft. What a remarkable feeling! As the congratulatory e-mails poured in, I was again touched by how the world was following my adventure. It was heart-warming to know that so many thousands of people were cheering me on. I was on top of the world both physically and emotionally. Mission Control was celebrating, too. When I had spoken to them by satellite phone earlier, I could hear cheers of support in the background.

I didn't sleep a wink for those 24 hours of my swing through the Southern Ocean. I wanted to make sure the jetstream took me north again and I didn't want to be in this dangerous area any longer than I had to. Flying high and fast, my speeds reached 123 mph. Finally I made the turn north and was greatly relieved. Soon I crossed directly over Bouvet Island, which is often described as the most remote place in the world. At that point, the *Bud Light Spirit of Freedom* became the longest solo flight by any kind of aircraft, whether balloon or airplane, a feat which also felt great. I broke my own four-year-old distance record, surpassing the 14,235.3 miles I logged in 1998, when my attempt from Argentina ended with my 29,000-ft, near-death plunge into the Coral Sea.

While I was still well south of South Africa, Luc spotted a new problem far ahead of me. If I continued at these rapid speeds, I would get to the Indian Ocean as a massive line of thunderstorms was developing. I must slow down to give time for the thunderstorms to dissipate before I got there. My instructions were to descend to 10,000 ft and fly low and slow until further notice. This I didn't mind as it was nice to take off the oxygen mask, throw open the hatch and enjoy the scenery as I slowly entered and flew across the eastern portion of South Africa. Upon leaving the coast of South Africa near Durban half a day later, I turned on the burners and hooked up with a very fast jetstream at 24,000 ft. Within another half day I would have accelerated to a maximum speed of 202 mph, almost certainly the fastest a manned balloon has ever traveled. I was traveling at these fast speeds when my capsule suddenly started shaking like I was in an earthquake. Two jetstreams had intersected causing the severe turbulence. I immediately fired my burners and climbed above the clouds and snow flurries.

As I rose above 30,000 ft, I put on my pressure-demand oxygen mask, which forces air into your lungs under pressure. At high altitudes the ambient pressure is so low that oxygen does not transfer easily through the lungs into the bloodstream. This is a new style of breathing for me. To inhale, you just relax and the oxygen is forced in and then you push deliberately to exhale. Because my safety depended on rising above this turbulence, I ascended up to 34,700 ft. I calculated that this was the pressure ceiling of the balloon, the highest I could fly without forcing helium out of the appendices. I just sat there at my navigation table and concentrated on my breathing for six hours straight before I finally dared to descend to a normal flight altitude. When I did, I was relieved that the turbulence was gone and I was again in a single straight jetstream.

The anticipation of my landing had galvanized people into action. According to a message from Mission Control, news teams and camera crews had descended upon their headquarters in St Louis while my recovery team back in Australia tried to determine where I would land.

On 2 July I was approaching 117 East longitude which demarcated the finish line for my flight. Cruising at an altitude of 28,000 ft at a speed of 63 mph that afternoon, it was officially confirmed that I had crossed the finish line 400 miles south of Northam, Australia. Although I had planned to succeed eventually, I could hardly believe that after seven long years and six attempts, I had finally accomplished this dream. Sitting on top of the capsule, I gazed out over the expanse of oceans and clouds and exulted in the triumph of the moment. I silently told myself that I had just made aviation history. As I flew the *Bud Light Spirit of Freedom*, Mission Control contacted me to tell me that the Guinness World Records had accepted my flight as the first solo circumnavigation of the globe in a balloon.

At 2 am, I couldn't sleep from the excitement of the day. Wanting to share this heady feeling with someone, I called Tim, my great project manager, who was in his hotel room. He picked up and I thanked him for all his unwavering support and help over the past years that had contributed to this ultimate accomplishment. We laughed, reminiscing about our TransAtlantic balloon flight eight years earlier. We agreed that neither of us could have imagined back then, that so many years later, we'd be celebrating my success of a circumnavigation flight. I know my phone call meant an awful lot to Tim, just as much as it did to me. Together we had been through a lot and had come a long way.

Although the mission was accomplished, my flight was not over. I had crossed the finish line, but I still wasn't home free yet. I was 400 miles south of Australia, meaning there was still a lot of water between me and this landmass. Luc was very concerned about finding winds that would take me north to Australia where I could land. I was considering the possibility of having to land in the forests of Tasmania, the island at the southeast corner of Australia, or even pass south of Tasmania and fly the Tasman Sea to New Zealand. Finally, Luc called with good news. He had found a wind current that would carry me north and put me over Australia. Confident that I would make it to land, I attended to the next task at hand, which was to ballast the remaining fuel supply necessary to lighten the weight of the balloon for landing. Having drained the fuel tanks, I then opened the valves so when they fell into the sea they would fill with water and sink. As I ballasted the fuel, I just shook my head in wonderment. The fact that I had 10 days' worth of fuel left bore witness to the awesome velocity I had achieved on that trip. I had been chasing the wind for so many years by balloon and, finally, on this flight I had irrefutably caught the best winds of all my attempts.

One half day after crossing the longitude marking 'Round the World', I crossed the coastline at Ceduna, Australia. It was afternoon and the ground winds were blowing a literal gale, making a landing impossible. I would be dragged forever and surely be pulled into power lines and electrocuted or immolated by the explosion of my remaining fuel. No one had to convince me to fly for another night to give the winds time to hopefully calm down by morning.

Since this would be a long night and I didn't want to fly beyond the wide-open spaces of the Australian Outback, I brought the balloon down to 5000 ft and languished there in the slower winds for the night. In the warmer air conditions, a fuel fitting came loose and fuel started spewing. A high-pressure propane fire erupted and one of my greatest ballooning fears manifested. I couldn't believe this was happening to me now! Immediately I dove for the tank shut-off valve and quickly turned it off. Once I did, there was just a small fire burning the residual fuel in the line. Fortunately, I had been awake when it happened, otherwise the outcome could have been much worse. I realized how this had happened: during the flight I had replaced most of the solenoids while in the cold air of high altitudes. Now in very warm air, the screw fittings were loose and this one had let go. I set about checking the tightness of all the fittings.

The drama wasn't over. Shortly after that episode, I was hit with violent rising and descending air currents, which threw the balloon about. When I looked out of my capsule, I discovered the problem. I was flying over a natural gas field whose burn-off flares greatly disturbed the air at 5000 ft where I was flying. I immediately climbed up to 8000 ft, which was sufficient to keep me out of the chaos. Tiring of these setbacks, I was getting more than impatient to land, yet still had several hours of night flying before I could do so.

On the ground, my recovery team was dealing with its own challenges. The helicopters with a camera crew and two chase planes had landed for the night in a little town called Birdsville, which is a classic Outback cattle town that housed only one small six-room hotel. The team rather conspicuously arrived in town in the middle of the night with two Citations, a twin-engine plane and two helicopters. All of these aircraft needed to be refueled but there was no adequate service or fuel available for this. Once the local farmers got wind of what was going on, they came to the rescue. They went out and got their own personal reserves of fuel and generously gave it to the recovery team so they could refuel their airplanes in time for my landing.

When the morning of 4 July dawned, I was confronted with a now-or-never situation. If I didn't get my balloon on the ground by nightfall, the wind would carry me away from Australia and out over the Tasman Sea. The window of opportunity to land was quickly closing. I resolved that I was going to land come hell or high water, but not in the water. This would happen at dawn somewhere in the vicinity of Lake Yamma Yamma, Queensland.

The forecast for light winds at dawn was wrong. As I descended to 200 ft, the wind was still 20 mph. Since the fastest wind speed I had ever landed in was 15 mph, I prepared for a very dangerous landing with this giant balloon. My mind reeled, graphically imagining how much worse it could get. The deflation ports could fail again as they had in all but one of my distance balloon flights. If they could not be ripped open this time, I would bounce and drag until I could slowly release enough helium with the in-flight helium valve. While bouncing and dragging, I could easily be injured with a broken arm or knocked unconscious and soon find myself beat into hamburger meat. I involuntarily winced as I tried to put such pictures out of my head.

As the balloon neared the earth, I positioned myself for action. When it touched the ground, I gave a heavy pull with all my might on the red line of the deflation port. To my horror, nothing happened. I bounced back up to 200 ft and flew another half mile before finally touching down again. This time I pulled with all my weight and every leverage I could apply as if my life depended on it. Still nothing. On the next two bounces, I tried the red line to the other deflation port and again nothing happened. I was exhausted after a most difficult night of flying and now with using a 110% effort I was at my wits' end. The only thing I could do to release the helium was to manually open the gas valve and hold it open. This I did. I struggled to keep the valve open as the balloon bounced up and down like a rubber ball over a five-mile stretch of the Australian Outback.

When the bouncing finally stopped, the wind would not relent and dragged the balloon along the ground. When I finally got it slowed down, Shorty Ryan and Tim Cole jumped out of a helicopter and sprinted to catch up with me. Grabbing the trail ropes that I had thrown out to help stabilize the runaway balloon, they too were dragged along with the capsule. Finally, Shorty was able to deploy the deflation port by getting the line away from the balloon and pulling it from an angle. Because the line came around the side of the balloon, even several hundred pounds of pulling would not break open the sewn deflation ports because the limp balloon absorbed all the energy from the line—the design error of the deflation ports was now understood.

Finally, after 14 days 19 hours, the balloon came to a halt and I stepped onto the ground in the Outback of Australia. After Tim helped me climb out of the capsule, we hugged each other. In addition to the several people from our team, some hands from a nearby cattle station soon arrived on the scene. Later, when a news team that had flown in by helicopter approached me for an interview, Tim kindly asked them to give me a minute. I had bitten my lip during the rough landing and Tim got me some water with which to rinse it off, so that I might look a little more presentable. I took this opportunity to climb back inside the capsule to retrieve a couple of Bud Lights. Handing one to Tim, he took it and, as a tradition, we toasted my record-breaking achievement by exchanging our bottles before opening and swigging their contents.

The beer was refreshing and helped calm my nerves in the midst of all the frenetic celebratory commotion that, for a moment, interrupted the vast quietude of the Outback landscape. I was tired but so energized to have accomplished this very difficult goal. Adrenaline pulsed through every fiber of my body. The difficulties that had complicated my journey and ended my previous attempts were behind me. As my gaze moved appreciatively from face to face of the various team members present, I felt a great sense of satisfaction and pride well up within me. I was enormously grateful to everyone involved for their contribution to the successful outcome of this endeavor.

I expressed my feelings of gratitude to all who were involved in my flights at a press conference that took place that afternoon in Sydney. In attendance were Mayors Paul Robson, of Kalgoorlie, and Ray Head, of Northam, who both congratulated me. The pair had flown in to thank me for using Australia as my launch site for this incredible mission. I took that opportunity to give back the boomerang that Paul Robson gave me before my flight. In exchange, he gave me a new boomerang to keep as a reminder of my historic voyage. We held the boomerangs high as we swapped them before the crowd. I told them how thankful I was to the Australian people for the hospitality they showed my team and me. Mayor Head of Northam then spoke, telling me, 'You are our hero. We invite you to come back to Northam at any time. The door is always open.'

The press conference was completed with a toast of Bud Light.

During the days that followed my *Bud Light Spirit of Freedom* mission I received thousands of congratulatory e-mails and letters from good friends, and fans. One of the most memorable for me was from the Academy Award winning actor, Cliff Robertson:

Just about the time the entire world has 'had enough' of terrorism—murders—kidnapping—corporate corruption and 'creative bookkeeping'—out of the blue sailed the 'Spirit of Freedom' and Steve Fossett. He has reminded this troubled world that dreams are real—can be realized if the holder is willing to hold tight with the grip of belief. Thank you, Steve Fossett, for helping this weakened world to hang in there—to tighten its grip of hope—and to never give up.

—Cliff Robertson

Back in the US, I spoke with General Jack Dailey, Director of the Smithsonian's National Air and Space Museum. Before my attempt, he told me if my flight was successful they wanted to hang my capsule in the museum, along with their prestigious collection of other aviation relics, which include Charles Lindbergh's *Spirit of St. Louis*, Chuck Yeager's *X-1*, and the *Apollo 11* capsule. I was very honored by their request and to be included in this very esteemed brotherhood of aviation. For this, I was glad to give them my capsule. Besides, I didn't need it. I wouldn't be using it any more.

With the successful completion of my solo circumnavigation flight, I had accomplished all the records that I set out to do in ballooning. I was calling it quits, having fulfilled my ultimate goal. Although I would still get together with ballooning friends, my days as a serious balloon pilot had come to an end. I was grateful to have had eight adventure-packed years of ballooning and finally to have been able 'to hit my home run'. And after some very close calls, I counted myself lucky that I could literally walk away.

20. BREAKING THE ROUND THE WORLD SPEED SAILING RECORD, FEBRUARY–APRIL 2004

My burning ambition is to break the official RTW Sailing Record. This is simply the most important record in sailing and why Cheyenne was built. I am not doing it for the publicity, recognition or any financial purpose. The only goal is the RTW Sailing Record and our sole attention is focused on breaking it.

Steve Fossett

Although most of my other sailing goals had been achieved, for a variety of reasons, I had not yet attempted the Round the World ('RTW') record. Success on the RTW would be the capstone of my sailing program, which in the last ten years had set 21 official world records and 9 distance race records, most of which remain unbroken to this day. Although I had searched for a sponsor to make an RTW attempt in 2003, I could not find one. Finally I decided I could not let *Cheyenne** pass into history, or my sailing career end, without going after the most prestigious of all sailing records. I reached into my own pocket to fund my RTW attempt, which I scheduled for January 2004.

---

* After my sponsorship contract with Sony expired, I renamed *PlayStation, Cheyenne.*

The requirements for the RTW record, which are set by the World Sailing Speed Record Council, state that the course must start and finish at the same place and meet a distance requirement of 21,600 nautical miles ('nm') based on an assumed latitude of 63 degrees South while circling Antarctica and it must be sailed without assistance, such as stopping in a port. The traditional choice is to start on a line extending between Ouessant Island, France and Lizard Head in Cornwall, England then sail to the Southern Hemisphere, eastbound south of Africa, Australia and South America, then back to the start line—and just find the fastest way to sail that course! Actual mileage sailed on RTW attempts averages about 24,000 nm. The best strategy is simple—go the shortest route, stay in the best wind, keep the boat speed high, and don't break the equipment—a tough combination. Since 1992 when Bruno Peyron sailed this route in 80 days, the Jules Verne Trophy has been awarded to the holders of the official RTW record set on this course. Over the past eleven years, 13 attempts had been made to set this record, with four successful. The current record was set by Bruno Peyron and crew aboard the 110-ft catamaran *Orang*, in 2002 at 64 days 8 hours 37 minutes 24 seconds.

For our attempt, we planned to sail with a total of 13 crewmembers including myself. There would be three watch captains who would have three other crewmembers on his watch. Each watch would sail the boat for four hours preceded by four hours of 'standby' and followed by four hours of rest. This 12-hour cycle would be implemented twice a day for the entire trip. The Navigator would consult with the on-shore meteorologist and work on routing. As Skipper, I was the leader and the ultimate decision-maker. I would also stand watch some of the time and cover for the Navigator when she slept.

One of the Watch Captains, Dave Scully, was in charge of the boat during the entire preparation phase and spearheaded the effort to form a crew. In addition to drawing on a few who were current crewmembers, like Mark Featherstone, Paul Van Dyke, Nick Leggatt, and Mike Beasley, and some who sailed with us at earlier times like Brian Thompson, Damian Foxall, Fraser Brown and Adrienne Cahalan, I saw a need to add experienced RTW sailors because none of us had that experience. Therefore we eventually added the seasoned Jacques Vincent, who had sailed round the world six times; Guillermo Altadill, who had sailed round the world four times; and Justin Slattery, who had sailed once round the world. Forming this final crew did not come without a struggle:

seven crewmembers resigned before the start. Some of them had decided that they simply didn't want to sail round the world. Others, who had come out of America's Cup programs, which had huge funding, were accustomed to a much more expensive approach to preparing a boat than our budget allowed. They were used to seeing a boat in immaculate condition. At this time, *Cheyenne* was not a new boat and in fact was five years old. Many of them quit because they didn't think we were well enough prepared to sail around the world. Yet I felt that the boat was in as good a shape as it had ever been. Before we started sailing, I took it upon myself to address thoroughly every complaint that anybody made regarding the condition of the *Cheyenne*.

We went on weather stand-by in mid-December, with Ken Campbell and his team at Commanders Weather on the lookout for an optimal sailing forecast. Since it's impossible to forecast winds very far in advance, we chose a more realistic criterion for a 'Code Green': We wanted a forecast that would get us to the Equator in 8 days or less. When January 2004 arrived and the boat was ready, I was eager to go on the first available favorable weather pattern. My determination to set sail as early as possible was fueled by the possibility that we would not be alone on the course. Concurrently, Olivier de Kersauson, skippering *Geronimo*, and the current RTW record holder, Bruno Peyron, skippering *Orange II* (the 120-ft successor to *Orange*), were both gearing up for RTW attempts.

I wasn't too worried about de Kersauson even though *Geronimo* was heralded as the boat to break all records. *Geronimo* was designed after *Cheyenne*, and was built with all the knowledge of my boat and the new technology that had entered the market since then. Despite high expectations, *Geronimo* had not achieved the success the builder had hoped for. Since *Geronimo* was launched in 2001, it had set no world records, while *Cheyenne* had broken 10 in the same time frame. I was more concerned about the current RTW record holder, Bruno Peyron, and his new boat *Orange II*. Built two generations after *Cheyenne*, I expected it to be a faster boat. And yet I was skeptical that *Orange II* would be reliable enough to make it round the world before it had gone through a year of sorting out. However, I had been surprised before when *Club Med* won The Race in early 2001 less than a year after launch.

We were targeting the same season to cross the starting line, but this was not a sailboat race. This was a record attempt and we wouldn't necessarily be racing against each other. In fact, I didn't want to line up on the same day with the other boats. If we sailed all the way around the world faster than anyone had sailed the course before, I didn't want to risk the crushing disappointment if one of these boats finished first and I never got the RTW record. I reckoned that by setting sail first, even if *Geronimo* or *Orange II* broke our record, at least we would have held the record for a couple of weeks and would have made our mark on the historical progression of the RTW record.

For our start date, we waited patiently as one propitious weather pattern after another deteriorated. Although I did want to get going, I also knew that I must wait for the right conditions in order to get a good run to the Equator. Due to poor North Atlantic weather systems, a 'Code Red' was in effect for the first week and a half of January. As the weather pattern developed which resembled what we wanted, I proposed a probable start on 11 January and issued a 'Code Yellow'. In response, the crew traveled to our base in Plymouth, England and went about completing all preparations, even to the extent of loading the food onto the boat. As 11 January approached, the beneficial forecast faded and we were back to 'Code Red'. While waiting for the next good pattern, we took advantage of the extra time together to fine-tune our preparations and tighten up our coordination of working together as a team. Unpacking the boat, we resumed training with a combination of sailing and on-shore physical conditioning for the remainder of the month.

A disadvantage of trying for sailing records is waiting for the right weather. When a start date is pushed back, conflicts in schedules often arise. Moving into the month of February with a 'Code Red' resulted in losing navigator Stan Honey due to prior commitments, as his role as navigator on the new *Pyewacket* required him to be back before we would finish the RTW. Thomas Coville also had to leave due to his commitment to re-launch his 60-ft trimaran *Sebago* at the end of March. I was disappointed that, after a month of intense preparations, Stan and Thomas were not able to make the trip. Fortunately Adrienne Cahalan was available to step in for Stan. Adrienne had sailed with us before as Navigator on *PlayStation* for the Fastnet Course World Record of 35 hours 17 minutes set in March 2002.

ROUND THE WORLD SAILING—WEEK 1

On 6 February, things started to finally come together for us weather-wise. A reasonable weather scenario manifested itself for an imminent RTW start. Shortly after 4.00 pm, we departed for the

120-mile trip to the start line off Le Stiff Lighthouse on Ouessant Island.

We hadn't predicted that making it to the start line 120 miles from Plymouth would turn out to be some of the most difficult sailing that we would encounter on our trip. Battling winds up to 50 knots with the tide flowing in the opposite direction to the wind, a particularly taxing sea state was churned up. To protect the boat from damage from the waves, we had to keep the speed below 20 knots. As the evening progressed, the wind built to 40 knots and then to 50 knots and we reduced sail to only a triple-reefed main, and tried to maintain the slowest speed possible, about 10 knots, to stop the boat from flying off the short, steep seas. Normally we wouldn't have left under these conditions but we needed to make it to the start line to catch the strong wind pattern that would drive us south toward the Equator. Crossing the starting line at Ouessant at 5.10 and 35 seconds in the morning of 7 February, the official observer from WSSRC (World Sailing Speed Record Council) relayed to us the calculations of when we would have to make it to the finish in order to break Peyron's record. We needed to get to Lizard Point by 11 April, 1.46 and 59 seconds in the afternoon. We were finally on our way.

We understood that the first week was going to be challenging. Within a day of starting, we were trapped by light winds off Portugal, which wiped out the advantage of our carefully chosen departure day. To our frustration, Olivier de Kersauson and crew aboard the 110-ft trimaran *Geronimo* started just one and one half days after us and had a fine run. Breaking fast out of that year's gate, he was aiming to catch the same large pattern South that we were. They had a great start, having picked a better weather slot than we did, and were turning in good average speeds in the trade winds. Then *Geronimo* pulled off the course headed from Brest. With a combination of aggressive sailing and weak sail construction, they had blown out two of their three gennakers and were forced to make the sail repairs and wait for the next weather pattern to restart. Our chief rival was now the phantom *Orange*, the RTW record holder whose 2002 position we had fallen 600 miles behind after the first five days. We were 'racing' against the daily positions of Bruno Peyron's 2002 RTW record performance. By comparing our progress to that schedule, we tracked how we were doing against that and prior records on a daily basis.

Although we admittedly didn't take the best decision on the start, it was encouraging to see that the crew was sailing the boat very well. After a tactical and sometimes tedious haul south and west to catch the trade winds, by the end of the week, things started to look up. We had two consecutive 450 + nm days that reduced our deficit behind *Orange* 2002 to less than 500 miles.

RTW—WEEK 2

Having recovered from our slow first four days, we were thrilled to gain the lead as a result of our weather fortunes changing. With good boat speed all the way, averaging 15 knots, we made the swiftest crossing of the Doldrums of any of the prior RTW record voyages that we were tracking. The Doldrums is a band usually found just north of the Equator and is the most capricious weather zone of the Atlantic to negotiate. Technically known as the Intertropical Convergence Zone, or ITCZ—it is where the northeast and southeast trade winds converge, which suck up all the wind into the atmosphere and leave large regions of ocean windless, but with thunderstorms in other places. As boats are often becalmed in this area, successfully finding a passage or a gap to transit this zone is an exercise in tactical sailing. It was our swift passage through the Doldrums that enabled us to meet our first objective. We reached the Equator in eight days!

Passing through the trade winds en route to the Equator we encountered the huge abundance of flying fish. Silvery blue and up to ten inches in length, flying fish glide along the top and leap or 'fly' out of the water as a survival mechanism to flee from predators. They can clear the water's surface by 15 ft and fly up to 200 ft horizontally. As impressive as this is, the problem when sailing through waters that are home to copious schools of these fish is that these creatures mistake the boat for a predator. Flying out of the water to flee, many collide with the boat and are instantly killed upon impact. Hitting the boat with such constancy that it seems like it is raining fish, cleaning up their lifeless forms from the decks is a major maintenance job. Although sailors of yore would cook and eat the fish, it is not as common these days. Frankly, they really stink. My crew, as resourceful as they were, found another use for them as we crossed the Equator.

When the Equator was close in reach, crewmembers took the initiative to assemble odious items (which included flying fish) that would be used in the infamous crossing of the line ceremony. A ritual that originated centuries ago and adapted over time, it initiates equatorial newcomers. Sailors who have never crossed the Equator before are sufficiently hazed with the mock intention of supplicating the Grecian god Neptune, ruler of the sea, for a boat's swift and safe journey. Acting on behalf of Neptune, one or two crewmembers, dressed up as the god and his posse, deliver the hazing.

Since the presence of other initiates would buffer the intensity of the experience, my heart went out to Mark Featherstone, the only one of our crewmembers who had not yet crossed the Equator. As the only newbie, all eyes would be on Mark. As we crossed the Equator around midday, King Neptune and Badger Bag summoned Mark from his position in the cockpit and prodded him to the mast with their makeshift tridents. Donning costumes made out of toilet paper, King Neptune and Badger Bag hustled Mark forward onto the trampoline. To the crew's shouts and condemnations, a grisly mixture of food slops and dead flying fish was poured over his head while Badger Bag lashed him with dead fish. A flying fish was shoved down his shorts and a squid drenched with Tabasco in his mouth. Mark took it all in his stride and was the perfect initiate. Afterwards, many of the crew followed Mark's example and took a bucket bath and shave.

As we sailed downwind in the Southern Atlantic, one of the crew noticed a tear in the big gennaker right down the middle of the sail. To repair it, we could not roll it in fully as we normally would because the rip would then be buried in the folds and we would not be able to get to it. Awakening the rest of the sleeping crew, together we wrestled the huge sail to the trampoline and hoisted a smaller gennaker, called the 'blast reacher', in its place. Five of the crew went to work putting Kevlar patches on the blown seam and then stitched up the edges of the patches before successfully re-hoisting it.

We ended our second week in high spirits, in part because the crew was so pleased with the caliber of their mates. Everyone was working hard to earn the respect of their fellow crewmembers. Every crewmember performed superbly, bringing either great experience or special expertise to *Cheyenne*. It was our ability to work together that enabled us to push into the lead. We had moved approximately 116 miles ahead of *Orange* and were very encouraged to be ahead of their record pace at this point in the course. As we started the left turn in the South Atlantic and were eagerly gearing up for the challenges of Southern Ocean sailing, we felt confident facing whatever may come our way. *Cheyenne* was in her best condition ever and our crew was well prepared.

RTW—WEEK 3

By the beginning of week three we were making up for our sluggish trip from the start line down to the Canaries. Riding winds between 25 knots that sped us southeast, our considerable progress was facilitated by a placid sea state as a result of our being relatively close to a high-pressure system. Covering 566 miles in 24 hours at an average speed of 23.6 knots, our lead over the 2002 RTW record track of *Orange* grew to over 430 nm. We were just under 1400 nm from the longitude of the Cape of Good Hope. Maintaining this speed meant that we were poised to make the second fastest Ouessant to Cape of Good Hope passage. *Geronimo* had set the fastest time last year at 16.5 days. With these good winds we were looking at an 18-day trip.

Our 24-hour run on Saturday was by far our best on this record attempt, and was highlighted by a potentially serious on-board electrical problem in the afternoon. Our sailing instrumentation system shorted out due to the high humidity on board that condensed into water that was leaking down the wiring into the circuitry boxes. We had to rely on sailing the old-fashioned way—with a compass and the wind vane atop the mast. Tracing the wiring back to the junction boxes, Adrienne and Nick finally found the source of the shorting and sealed the wet connections. Dave Scully replaced the destroyed power converter by wiring in my little laptop converter. It was a six-hour project. What a relief that the repairs were made and our attempt wasn't jeopardized.

That day, we had a close look at a pair of killer whales as they dived under our bows. Because hitting a whale can harm both the whale and the boat, it is fortunate that our rudders made a continuous loud humming noise that turned into a screech at over 25 knots, warning them of our arrival. In addition to icebergs, boats have been known to collide with cargo containers and whales, resulting in irreparable damage. Despite meticulous preparation, these high performance multihulls cannot be expected to make it round the world without mandatory repairs at sea. On day 16 and with a full day's lead over *Orange's* 2002 record pace, we were hit by the first of three major breakages that would threaten to finish our RTW attempt. The forestay—the 1½-inch diameter cable that holds the 148-ft mast upright from the bow—had become either disconnected or broken. We couldn't even see the forestay as it was inside the roller foils and the furled Solent, but after taking everything apart we found that the fitting at the bow had become disconnected. None of us had experienced this type of failure before.

Fortunately, we were sailing downwind with little back-pressure on the mast when this occurred, otherwise the mast would have fallen over because the angle of support from the port and starboard shrouds provides minimal support. Hope was slim of reconnecting the forestay, as such a job is normally done in a rigging shop with specialized heavy equipment. With this weighing heavily on my mind, I pointed the boat downwind toward Cape Town, anticipating that we would probably have to retire from our record attempt.

To my surprise, my crew, which included qualified riggers plus some very hard-working guys, were able to reconnect the forestay using only hand tools. Such unwavering effort, combined with a wide range of skills, defines the most professional sailors. This crew was capable of fixing things where normal circumstances would have dictated retiring to the nearest port. Adding to this happy surprise, we did not incur a major setback in mileage lost. Even during the 18-hour repair job, we were able to achieve respectable downwind progress along the course to cover 196 nm over 12 hours for an average of 16 knots. 'Not bad,' we thought 'for running repairs.'

The following day brought steady westerlies that powered us past our next milestone: Cape of Good Hope. On the 18th day, we crossed the imaginary line extending due south from the Cape of Good Hope even though there was still 400 miles of water between us and the Cape.

Southeast of the Cape of Good Hope on day 20, we felt the increased wind chill factor. It was becoming extremely cold as we crossed 50 degrees South latitude. In addition to hats and gloves and all the layers of clothes we were wearing, we pulled down balaclavas over our faces. We had crossed the Antarctic Convergence where the cold water of only 40°F (5°C) is at the surface. As if to provide a visual reference for the invisible bitter coldness that we defended our bodies against, we soon passed two icebergs, but fortunately at a safe distance of a couple miles. Evincing that they were game to endure any harsh conditions their Skipper led them into, the crew tried not to reveal the discomfort of sailing duties on deck while they sailed without letting up. The Southern Ocean vaunts the harshest sailing conditions on Earth, as testified by the many lives this region has claimed. Without landmasses to mitigate them, waves reach mountainous heights, as big here as any other place in the world.

I became increasingly concerned as the wind angles for best speed continued to lead us progressively farther south. Meteorologist Ken

Campbell forecasted more of the same and emphasized that the farther south we got, the fewer miles were required to cross a degree of longitude. By the logic of shorter distances and stronger winds, one would just keep working south until close to Antarctica. However, it's a fine balance. Should we continue south indefinitely into progressively icier and inhospitable waters? Should we risk getting trapped by a violent storm there, which would block us from sailing back north except very slowly upwind? I ultimately had to make the decision as to what level of risk I was willing to take and how much cold the crew should be exposed to. In addition, the danger of hitting a 'growler' was a significant risk. I finally decided against sailing any farther south in this part of the ocean. I gave the command to turn due west toward Kerguelen Island at a slightly reduced speed. Although Adrienne and Ken were not very happy about my decision, I had a clear concept in my mind: we were fast enough to get the RTW record without taking extraordinary risk. It was more than important that the boat survive to the finish. The Antarctic Convergence is not at a constant latitude and was especially far north in this region of the western Indian Ocean. Within two days of sailing west, we were positioned north of the Convergence and in fact were able to work our way south as we crossed the Pacific without needing to cross into the cold waters again.

RTW—WEEK 4
In welcome contrast to the previous week, during week four, instead of breaking the boat, we broke records. Making steady and consistent progress, we began the week with 999 miles in the bank over *Orange*'s 2002 position. I was already carefully monitoring what it would take to break the Indian Ocean record. Meanwhile, we learned that we would no longer be alone on the RTW course. Over the weekend, *Geronimo* had restarted, with *Orange II* leaving 12 hours later. Both boats were starting again after having made repairs in port. Within a few days we learned that Bruno Peyron and his crew on the new *Orange II* had suffered a fracture to the underside of the starboard hull and were seeking the shelter off of Fogo, an island in Cape Verde, to try to effect unassisted repairs. After assessing that the damage was not reparable in the water, *Orange II* retired for the year.

Aiming to catch the cooperative wind, we had two reefs and the staysail up in 25 to 30 knots of breeze. Racing ahead of a cold front that was approaching us from behind, we figured the faster we sailed, the longer we'd benefit from those prefrontal conditions of flatter seas and strong winds. We continued to knock out 500-mile days, with one formidable day of 584 nm. When we reached the longitude of Cape Leeuwin at Australia, we had extended our lead over the record to significant 3 days 17 hours.

For us, the week went out on a high note. With continued consecutive 500+-mile day runs, on Saturday, 6 March, we set a new best time for crossing the Indian Ocean. Stretching between the longitudes of the Cape of Good Hope in South Africa and Australia's South East Cape in Tasmania, we had claimed the Indian Ocean Record at 9 days 20 hours 29 minutes against the previous best time by *Club Med* during The Race at 10 days flat. This was subsequently ratified by *The Guinness Book of Records*. With my previous Pacific Ocean Record in 1995 and the TransAtlantic Record in 2001, I became the first Skipper to set the Outright World Record for more than one of the oceans.

RTW—WEEK 5

Week five was marked by transitions and milestones on several fronts. On Sunday, 7 March and 29 days into our voyage, we made the idiosyncratic transition from Sunday to another Sunday as a result of crossing the International Date Line at 180 degrees longitude. It was on this same day that we reached the midway mark of our trip with a lead of over 4 days or 1859 miles against the existing RTW record position.

As much as I love being out on the open seas, before we set sail on the RTW, I didn't know exactly how I would deal with the length of time that it took to complete such an event. It was a big adjustment for me to head off on a two-month sailing race. Before this, I'd never sailed for more than 21 days at one time. Reaching our midway mark, I realized that the duration at sea wouldn't be an issue. It wasn't crowded on board. The comfort level was just fine. I had my own bunk and life on board wasn't too bad. Outside of one Southern Ocean period that was pretty cold and miserable for a few days, the conditions really weren't intolerable. I was now able to appreciate how other sailors can be content to do multi-month passages.

We were enjoying our fifth consecutive 500+-mile day en route to our next waypoint, Cape Horn, which loomed 4500 miles away. Our progress continued unabated with a streak of high-velocity days. While transiting into the Pacific Ocean, we clocked our best day yet at 623 miles—our first in the 600s!—extending our lead to a solid 2042 miles ahead of *Orange*. The end of day 31 saw us posting our 9th consecutive 500+-mile day (557) run and a 5-day or 2222-mile lead over the record holder *Orange*.

Onboard, our collective psychological state was growing in complexity. Our satisfaction with our lead was attended by a growing tension as it became increasingly clear that we must keep the boat on course as fast as possible without breaking anything. Maintaining our record pace would become more challenging, as *Orange* had clocked an outstanding Pacific crossing. We took stock of all the equipment problems that beset us in the first half of our trip, while mentally preparing for the many more problems that would likely need solving en route to the finish line.

Day 32 brought an end to our streak of 500-mile days. Heading northeast, somewhat off course in an effort to avoid a weather system south of us, we held to this strategy for two days. Sailing was necessarily slower, resulting in a sacrifice of nearly a day of our lead. Then, just as the winds began to build, signaling the approach of our first storm front, the spinnaker halyard broke. As the big sail draped over the deck and was being pulled into the water, it took all hands to haul it back on deck and get it stowed below. Lightning-quick action saved the sail from getting tangled in the daggerboards and rudders which would have been a huge mess. Because the seas were too rough to send someone to the top of the mast to retrieve the halyard, we retired the spinnaker for the time being.

Despite 10 ft of freeboard, waves break over the side of *Cheyenne*. The storm created a high and chaotic sea state that took its toll as our first two casualties of the trip. Guillermo Altadill was helming the wheel when he was struck from the side by a large wave, knocking the wind out of him as he was thrust into the back beam. Despite having bruised ribs, Guillermo marshaled his strength to return to his sailing watch. Shortly thereafter, a wave of equal force caught Nick Leggatt off guard and threw him face-first into the binnacle with the compass. He sustained a nasty two-inch gash on his left cheekbone and a smaller cut on the bridge of the nose. Dave Scully, our medic in addition to Watch Captain, dialed up via satellite telephone Dr Dan Carlin at World Clinic who recommended closing the wounds with SteriStrip tapes to be followed up with a course of antibiotics. Nick was taken off the watch schedule for a few days to allow the wound to begin to heal properly even though he'd be left with a considerable scar. To allay the risk of incurring any more injuries, I implemented a temporary speed limit of 25 knots until the turbulent sea state calmed.

By the end of Friday, day 33, conditions had improved enough for us to accrue 508 miles in 24 hours stretching our lead to 2000 miles ahead of *Orange*. However, our confidence was tempered by having learned that we were not the only ones faring well. *Geronimo* was thundering ahead on course to rack up 609 miles for their best day yet during their Southern Atlantic leg.

RTW—WEEK 6

As a result of discovering that two out of three bottles of our cooking fuel bottles had already been used, we entered into our sixth week challenged by a bit of domestic drama. We had stocked our cooking fuel supply based on a 66-day voyage. While the first bottle fell only a little short at 20 days, the second bottle lasted only 15 days. Since all of our meals involved cooking dehydrated food, this posed a real problem. We initially suspected that taking the edge off of the frigid Southern Ocean temperatures with hot chocolate at night and coffee in the morning was the prime cause of this dilemma. Because at this rate we would run out of cooking fuel before reaching the Equator, conservation measures were put into effect: Muesli instead of hot porridge for breakfast, cold instead of hot drinks, and experiments with hydrating rice and mashed potatoes with lukewarm water. Although initially lamenting the loss of hot coffee, we cultivated a taste for frappacinos— milk powder and sachets of coffee mixed with cold water. The possibility of our team retiring from the record attempt due to an inability to cook was nil. As it would turn out, the cooking fuel shortage would be the least of our worries for the week.

With Cape Horn looming only several days away, we turned our attention to getting around this maritime milestone safely. Ken Campbell reported that if we arrived there too soon we would have to contend with east winds. Sailing into a strong wind would make the Horn virtually impassable. The best scenario for us was to cross over the top of a low and ride the northwest winds to the Horn where they would diminish. Although that was a nice plan, the trick was to get around this low without getting trapped in the light winds near its center.

To our dismay, we couldn't make it far enough north in time and we were running out of wind. The trouble with running out of wind was that the boat bobs around, and our huge mainsail flogs in the wind, making powerful snaps from side to side. The impact of the sail flapping delivered a heavy blow to the equipment, breaking the head of the mainsail away from the mast. The mainsail track broke at the first reef point. Running along the length of the 143-ft-high carbon-fiber mast, the track is responsible for holding the mainsail to the mast. Thirteen heavy bolts that secured this section of the mast track had sheared. Although the breakage at the first reef at 120 ft high on the mast did not endanger the mast itself, it severely limited the degree to which the mainsail could be raised, which was now only to the second reef, two levels below Full Mainsail. Because less sail translates as less speed, we estimated that if we couldn't make the repair, the reduced area of mainsail would render us so much slower that even our five-day lead over the record would be lost before reaching the finish line. We were in an all-or-nothing situation. We had to find a way to repair the mast.

Reasoning that slower sailing is better than no sailing, we opted to temporarily hoist the mainsail to the second reef point, which would allow us to continue, albeit at a slower pace, around Cape Horn. Because rules governing the Round the World Record prohibit outside assistance, going to port to seek repairs was not an option.

Since every wave would swing the mast and anyone working at that level would get smashed against the mast repeatedly, working 120 ft up on this piece of equipment necessitated calm seas. Initially we planned to take shelter in the more hospitable waters near the Falkland Islands after rounding Cape Horn, before attempting the repairs that would require at least a day. Calculating that our earliest time of arrival to the Falkland Islands would be 3 or 4 days, the thought of several more days' slow sailing on top of losing even more time while stopping to make the necessary repairs was too much for the crew to abide.

In addition to the real possibility of forfeiting our hard-earned lead over *Orange*'s RTW record pace, the suspense of not knowing if the damage was reparable was far too great. We scrapped this plan and immediately began repairs that Sunday. With a 'Do it now' attitude, the *Cheyenne* crew rallied on Sunday morning to make the necessary repairs. Bowman Justin Slattery headed up the mast in the difficult conditions. Hour after hour he worked with a battery-powered drill to extract the sheared bolts. Damian Foxall and Dave Scully joined him for long hours in this difficult work. New bolts were scavenged from other parts of the mast track and traveler tracks on the deck. Finally, after a day's effort, the mast was fixed. I couldn't believe it! And yet, the penalty for this temporary setback was high. While sailing dead slow to enable the work on the mast, we lost nearly a day of our lead. Even more costly was that we were entirely too late to ride the good winds toward and around Cape Horn. All in all, we lost two days of our lead, a disappointment that was buffered by knowing that a slow transit and stop in the lee of the Falkland Islands would have taken much more time. Thus, this was a huge victory by my proactive crew and, besides, we *still* had a lead.

Two days later, after a night of very slow sailing, Brian Thompson and I looked up to notice the headboard of the mainsail hanging loose at the top of the mast. Blinking twice as if to make certain that I was seeing correctly, I couldn't believe that it had happened again! We were baffled that this had occurred in mild conditions without any significant shock loading or sailing error. Once again our mast climbers headed up the mast—this time to the top. At least, by this time, they had established their method. We stripped bolts from everywhere on the boat we could, including winch bases. I thought that this had better be the last time for mast track breakages because I didn't know where we would find the parts for another repair.

Finally we were going again, but our lead over the record was by only two days and the weather forecast was a mess for the return up the Southern Atlantic. After all we had come through, we still might lose it all. Meanwhile Olivier de Kersauson and crew onboard *Geronimo* were hot on our trail having passed the Cape of Good Hope Sunday night, almost precisely on our same time and they were maintaining a strong run into the Indian Ocean. Our morale lifted somewhat later that day when our speed increased due to consistent northwesterly winds, which drove us 242 nm in 12 hours for an average speed of 20.2 knots.

Thirty-nine days, 16 hours and 16 minutes after our start in France on 7 February, we passed Cape Horn just 5 miles south of the lighthouse. Despite multiple setbacks, we reached this point faster than any prior boat on the RTW course. After the hardships we endured, achieving this milestone filled us with the optimism that we could actually pull the RTW record off. Our spirits were high. We were again entertaining the heartening prospect that if we could just stop having breakages we would have a very good chance at this record.

Entering one of the most tactical periods of our sailing, which would involve crossing an expansive high-pressure ridge, which emerged on our forecasts like a wall of no wind, left no time for us to rest on our laurels. As we went about planning our routing carefully, we considered trading speed for position. We sought to dodge the high-pressure systems coming off the Argentine coast by speeding eastwards past the Falkland Islands, before turning north where another ridge of high pressure awaited us. To avoid becoming becalmed, we settled for the more modest opportunity to keep the boat moving in the direction of north. I felt if we could make contact with the better wind pattern within a day, we would eliminate one more setback that could slow our record pace.

Despite this improvement, by the end of the week our margin over *Orange* had narrowed to 755 nm. Three days of weak and adverse winds, coupled with time lost Sunday and again Tuesday to repair broken mainsail mast tracks, cost us nearly half of our 4½-day lead.

RTW—WEEK 7

Nevertheless, the prevailing mood was one of optimism as we began week seven. We were closing in on the Equator and the South Atlantic and it was getting warmer and warmer by the day. After a month in foul-weather gear, the crew welcomed the chance to peel off the layers of clothing to soak up the sunshine in shorts and T-shirts.

After Friday and Saturday's slow breaching of a high-pressure ridge, we opportunistically sailed Saturday night's cold front to make excellent 28–30-knot progress with the Solent and full Main all day Sunday. Now over 800 miles, our lead over *Orange* 2002 was back on the upswing. Shredding up the miles heading NE along the Brazilian coast on Monday, we put in another excellent day's run of 539 nm stretching our lead over the 2002 Round the World record pace to 1040 miles.

We had 5500 nm minimum distance back to the official RTW start-finish line at Ouessant, France, and were pleased to be sailing 23+ knots straight down the shortest possible course. Taking a more direct route, we had an advantage over *Orange* whose crew had sailed a more classic wide course around and through the South Atlantic High, which added hundreds of miles to their route.

Our main objective for the week was to enter the southern hemispherical trade winds and hopefully, have a spirited run to the Equator, which we intended to reach by the end of the week. Standing in our way was a pocket of low pressure developing off of the coast of Brazil that our forecasters had told us we would encounter midweek. We planned to slide up the inside of the low and to catch the decent winds emanating from the NE or E on the other side of this weather pattern.

Our first attempt on Tuesday to cross the trough north of the low failed. It started typically enough with light winds as we sailed eastbound. We actually got to the East side of the trough but were then becalmed that night as the trough redeveloped in front, of us. On Wednesday morning, we made our second attempt and were able to free ourselves from that weather pattern. Nonetheless, by the end of Wednesday, our lead over *Orange* 2002 had diminished to 893 miles.

Our travails with temperate winds were far from over. Despite extracting ourselves from the torpid conditions of the trough, our pace continued to be slow-going as we tacked upwind between 33 and 31 West longitude over the day in an effort to reach the trades for better speed North to the Doldrums. The ever-variable tropical conditions off the Brazilian coast had us feeling like a donkey chasing after the proverbial carrot. Every time we reached the position our weather routers directed us to be—the coordinates where we expected to find stronger winds—the winds skirted away from us two degrees or so further north or east. The developing lows in the trough lying just west of our position, which we had crossed 30 to 40 hours ago, had weakened the trade winds and kept them moving continuously northeast of our position and out of our reach.

On Friday, 26 March 2004, day 49, we breathed a collective sigh of relief, when we at last made it to the Southern Hemisphere tropical trade winds. Harnessing 15 knots of wind with full mainsail and Solent, we achieved 18–22 knots of boat speed on a northerly course. After the last three days of averaging 250 miles, we were under pressure to pull off a couple of 450–500 nm- days to maintain our record pace. By the end of the day, we made a 516-mile run averaging 21.5 knots to reassert a 3-day lead over the RTW record pace of *Orange*.

A testament of the excellent speeds we had achieved with *Cheyenne* on the RTW was the deteriorating condition of the starboard-side toilet seat, which had started developing stress cracks into our Southern Ocean run. Sitting on a toilet seat whilst the boat launches off of Southern Ocean waves and crashes into troughs is tantamount to riding a bucking bull. The shock load, augmented by a seated body rising and falling according to this dynamic, is tremendous and exceeds the standard specifications by which toilet seats (and possibly human butts) are made.

Relief came in an unexpected package, though not one that could be applied to our toilet seat dilemma. Despite *Geronimo*'s impressive pace, we learned that their time crossing from Cape of Good Hope, South Africa to South East Cape at Tasmania, Australia (approximately 10 days and 19 hours) was nearly one day slower than our new Indian Ocean Record set on 6 March with a time of 9 days 20 hours 29 minutes and 27 seconds. As the shelf life of any record can be brief when formidable competition is present, it was heartening to learn that we would be holding onto our three-week-old record for longer than three weeks.

It was *Geronimo*'s continuous turnout of outstanding daily speeds that had prompted a journalist to ask me if, while driving toward the finish line, I worried that we might break the official RTW record only to have it broken again by *Geronimo* less than three weeks later. My reply was one of perspective: 'That's getting ahead of ourselves,' I told him. 'We haven't finished the Round the World, much less captured the record. But if it happens, it happens—that's sport. Our mission is to set the official Round the World record. It would be icing on the cake to keep the record until at least next year.'

RTW—WEEK 8
We began week eight by crossing the Equator for the second time at 8.13 am on Sunday, 28 March and re-entering the Northern Hemisphere with a flourish to clock a 543-mile run over 24 hours. This advanced our lead to an imposing 3 days or 1645 miles over *Orange*.

We were additionally delighted to have set two new segment bests for our RTW attempt. Our time of 50 days 3 hours 3 minutes from the Ouessant start to the second Equator crossing was 3 days 1 hour faster than the record set by *Orange* in 2002. Our 10 days 10 hours 47 minutes passage from Cape Horn back to the Equator was 3 hours faster than *Club Med*'s record set during The Race 2001. We were surprised to hear about our latter segment record since we had thought ourselves unfortunate over having our speeds reduced significantly by lack of wind. Perhaps the South Atlantic is difficult for all ocean racers.

Later that day, we finally hit the Doldrums and had to deal with the inconsistent winds there. Our momentum slowed considerably to average just 12.75 knots of boat speed, by which we covered 153 nm in 12 hours. The passing through of several squalls kept the standby watches busy with plenty of sail changes. While some of the crew donned full foul-weather gear, others seized the opportunity to take a proper shower. Standing under the mainsail during a downpour is comparable to standing under a waterfall. As if to alleviate our ennui, we were treated to a dolphin show that featured over 50 dolphins jumping and spinning 360-degree somersaults around the boat. This crossing of the Doldrums proved more typical, in contrast to the swifter trip we made on the way south.

Midday on Monday we exited the Doldrums to fully exploit the steady NE trade winds. With 22,000 miles in our wake and just 3200 to go to the finish, we planned on sailing the remainder hard, while concomitantly avoiding the risk of breaking anything, which would threaten our attempt at this critical stage.

Later that afternoon, our RTW attempt came close to ending for good. One of the crew informed me that he had heard a new creaking noise originating from the starboard bow. Immediately, Nick Leggatt and I threw on our harnesses and ran up to the bow to investigate the cause. We were taken aback by what we saw. The half-meter carbon and steel pin that holds the front beam to the boat had broken in the middle and worked halfway out on one side. Another two hours in this upwind sailing and it would have come completely out, the front beam disconnected, then the mast would have fallen over from lack of support. Needless to say, that was a close call.

Going into damage control mode, we slowed *Cheyenne* while the crew went to work trying to pound the pin back into place. Despite their efforts, it only went back in part way. Then the drilling and bolting started. A temporary fix was achieved, with the whole operation completed in four hours. Although likely to hold until the finish, we would have to take it easy on the boat, which was a shame. An excellent wind pattern was present, tempting us to pour it on. Instead we had to sail slower and conservatively.

This marked the third time in our voyage, which underscored the fact that an average-quality crew would not have been able to make the repairs necessary to continue with the record attempt. It was incontrovertibly clear that the creative ability of our crew to make major repairs without stopping would account for our success if we broke this record. On Wednesday, 31 March, boat builder-in-residence, Mike Beasley, created a new pin with carbon and resin, which was then inserted to reinforce the broken pin. The repair was now strong enough for us to sail directly on course under full main and Solent at 24–26 knots. The smoothing of the seas and clearing of the skies seemed to outwardly express the inner relief we felt.

Crossing the Tropic of Cancer heading northbound on Thursday, 1 April, our attention once again turned tactical. Our emerging

North Atlantic routing plan involved riding the leading edge of a low-pressure system, where the sea state was low (i.e. small waves), which meant we could go for maximum speeds while posing minimal risk to the boat.

However, gaining such an auspicious position was tricky. The low comprised a small narrow band of wind, which left little margin for error. If we strayed into the low, looming rainsqualls and variable winds would set our speeds back to preclude the 500-mile days we were counting on to get to the finish line. At this point, we were looking at a target arrival time between noon and 6 pm on Monday, 5 April. If we should fall out of this narrow band, we would still get there but about a day later.

An excellent example of how on-shore weather routing can assist such an endeavor as ours was the tactical advantage we were enjoying. In contrast to all the previous RTW attempts, we were sailing a relatively direct route from the Equator to Ouessant. Normally, the strategy is to sail downwind over the top of the central high-pressure area known as the Azores High. Although this is secure, it is a lengthy route. Thanks to Ken Campbell at Commanders Weather, we had found a very precise and direct route that would take us between a series of smaller lows and highs, allowing us to avoid both light winds and violent conditions. With the forecast for only one light air transition in the Bay of Biscay, it looked like this strategy would pay off.

On Friday and about 638 miles SW of Cape Finisterre at the northwest corner of Spain, we managed to capture a terrific 590-nm day run with 24.6 knots of boat speed, to outdistance *Orange*'s RTW position by 1660 miles. As if to prove that Friday's outstanding run would not be an isolated event, on the following day we powered on to cover a formidable 497 miles. On Saturday, with a six-day lead over *Orange*, we were homing in on the finish line by a mere 700 miles.

The possibility that we might cross the finish line as early as Monday, 5 April had dawned on us midweek. Although our stated goal had been to simply break Bruno Peyron's 64-day 8-hour record, we harbored the secret ambition to crack it in 60 days. The prospect of a 58-day time was all consuming. Before the start, I believed the potential of *Cheyenne* was to sail RTW in just under 60 days, and under outstanding conditions, in 58 days. We were sailing at the estimated potential of the boat.

RTW—WEEK 9: A DREAM COME TRUE

This direct route to the finish line had one requirement which now loomed large: somewhere along the way we would have to cross a weak trough with virtually no wind. Our routing provided by Ken Campbell allowed us to delay the interception of this light air, but finally we had come upon it. The wind speeds plummeted and we feared that we would be becalmed and not be able to move at all. We put up the 'Code 0', which is a big gennaker designed for conditions of minimal wind. Sailing at what seemed like a snail's pace, we were able to keep moving and managed to cover 294 miles during that critical 24-hour period.

When we broke through to the other side of the trough, our speeds started to accelerate. Optimism abounded as we had just overcome our last weather problem. All we had to do was not lose the mast and the record would be ours. As we made our way over to the coast of France, we maintained our pace with just a double-reefed main in 30 knots of chilly wind. With our arrival imminent, a subdued excitement permeated the atmosphere on board. Nobody slept or ate what remained of the freeze-dried food. For those last six hours of the trip, the crew amiably joked and talked amongst themselves.

As we moved closer to the finish, we were taken aback when we experienced a horrendous sea state. The tidal race at this corner of France is severe and, at the time of our finish, the wind was blowing in the opposite direction of the run of the tide-creating, washing-machine conditions with short steep waves. As I steered toward the finish line, my gleeful crew retained their concentration. We would have to reef for these difficult conditions, or risk breaking the boat. I listened carefully to the advice of Jacques Vincent sitting on the beam behind me. At the right moment, I called for the first reef—and the crew quickly took it before returning to our celebration. Then the time came for the second reef, and that was put in quickly. We were all smiles and cheers as we crossed the finish, despite the fact that we were still bashing through the waves. It was Monday, 5 April 2004 and just 58 days 9 hours 32 minutes 45 seconds after we left the official WSSRC start line at Le Stiff lighthouse on the French island of Ouesssant. We had shattered the two-year-old Round the World Sailing record by almost 6 days (5 d 23 h 4 m 39 s exactly).

As we came through the finish, the crew ecstatically jumped around. High-fives and high-tens abounded. Everyone hugged one another, shook hands and took photos of each other in order to capture this once-in-a-lifetime moment. Among all this jubilation, we even remembered to wave at the cameramen taking pictures of us from their position aircraft flying overhead. It was quite a celebration and a wonderful moment. There was a huge sense of relief that we had done it, that we had accomplished what we had set out to do, that, in fact, we had succeeded beyond our wildest expectations. Everyone was just so happy. It was a satisfying moment for us all.

When we arrived at our dock in Plymouth, England later that night, we hadn't expected the reception that awaited us. In the darkness of the night, the floating dock swayed under the load of the many people who stood waving and cheering us home. As we approached, the crew let off handheld flares that lit up the night like fireworks and illuminated familiar faces amid the crowds. When asked if I ever thought I would make it, I honestly replied, 'When we started out, I thought the chance was 50/50 that we would get around. Then I wondered that the boat might not be fast enough.' A battle-weary *Cheyenne*, the boat that had delivered us through 58 days of extreme sailing, was left to rest within the sheltering confines of the harbor.

At our celebratory dinner the next evening, I offered my toast to 'The Team'. I proudly stated, 'We have achieved something of great importance in sailing. It was achieved because every member of this crew performed at the highest level and we also put it together as a unified team. Our success was not primarily attributable to a "boat" but rather to those who sailed it. Your expertise and efforts in solving each equipment problem as it arose differentiated this crew from others who have sailed around the world. We should all be proud of what we have accomplished and that we did it as a Team.'

POST RTW

In retrospect, the weather really did not account for our success. Our luck with the winds was just average. Our winds overall were milder than most passages round the world. We never had 40 knots of wind, which was good because in anything over 35 knots sailors are slowing down in defense against the sea state. We were very fortunate to be able to sail the direct route from the Equator to the Finish, but we had poor winds in the early part of the trip and we were forced to take a long way around the high pressure during our route south from the Equator to the Southern Ocean. With the duration of a global trip, I believe that luck with the winds averages out. We lost about three days due to equipment repairs, which was a lot. But the real success was that the crew was able to make the repairs. If not, we wouldn't have made it to the finish at all.

Although we had set a new RTW record, we were not showered with awards and recognitions, in fact practically none. In a great irony, we were not awarded the Jules Verne Trophy, which was supposed to go to the holder of the official RTW Record. Originally created in the early 1990s by Olivier de Kersauson, Tituouan Lamazou and Florence Arthaud, the Trophee Jules Verne was intended to attract a $1 million prize from a sponsor and possibly to put RTW record attempts into a 'race' format. Hopes of a prize or other financial gain never materialized, but the Jules Verne Trophy became the parlance for the RTW record, even though the official record is ratified by the World Sailing Speed Record Council. An entry fee is now required to be eligible to win the Trophy. The fee was set at 30,000 Euros for a first-time contender like me but 12,000 Euros for someone who had sailed for the Trophy before. Before we started, I told Olivier de Kersauson, who remains firmly in control, that I would pay only the same amount my competitors—he and Bruno Peyron—were paying. Olivier declined my offer of 12,000 Euros and awarded the Jules Verne Trophy to himself after finishing 5 days slower than us!

Because records are made to be broken, I always knew that my record would be beaten, certainly within five years, and more likely within three years. I knew I'd never keep this one forever. Even on our record-breaking attempt, there were two other contenders going after the RTW record. De Kersauson, on his second start, actually finished the course, albeit 5 days slower than us. Bruno Peyron started twice but had to turn back each time due to equipment failure. In this sense, our record survived four attempts after our start. In the early part of 2005 Bruno Peyron bounced back for another RTW attempt in his lighter and more powerful *Orange II*. Just as we had broken his prior record by a huge margin of nearly six days, he broke ours with an eye-popping time of just 50 days 16 hours 20 minutes.

It did bother me a little bit that holding the RTW record was so fleeting, but I am content with having achieved my goal of breaking it. We held the record and that was the priority. We made our mark on the RTW history. I was really pleased that we got the record on this attempt because, if we hadn't, I don't know if I would have been able to muster such an outstanding crew to try again.

Monday, 5 April 2004 was one of the most memorable days of my life. This was the capstone of my sailing career. I had come into this sport just 12 years earlier and had methodically set official world records every year since. I'm sure it surprised the sailing community, especially the French, that a newcomer who was not even a professional sailor would come into the sport and do this. In the end, I had broken more records than anyone in the history of sailing—and that included all the most important records. At last I had achieved my highest goal in sailing: the Round the World record. I had done virtually everything I had hoped to do in the sport. My sailing program was complete.

21. THE FIRST SOLO NONSTOP AIRPLANE FLIGHT ROUND THE WORLD, MARCH 2005

Steve is now quite literally at the mercy of the winds. 'Cause without that tailwind he won't be able to get back.

Paul Moore, Mission Control Project Manager

It was through my friendship with Barron Hilton that I got back into gliding and eventually conceived the idea to circumnavigate the globe nonstop in an airplane.

I had gotten my glider or 'sailplane' license back in 1975; however, because there weren't any great places to glide in or around Chicago, I never did anything with it for a long time. Barron's Flying M Ranch extends over nearly 800,000 acres and covers an area that begins 25 miles south of Yerington, Nevada, and stretches as far as the shores of Mono Lake in California. The gliding conditions in the high desert east of the Sierra Nevada, where Barron's ranch is situated, are among the best in the world. During the day, the hot, dry air coming off the Earth's surface creates extraordinary thermals that carry a glider skyward. Once winter gives way to spring, it is a custom of Barron's to invite his friends who, like himself, are aviation enthusiasts to his ranch for long weekends of airplane flying, soaring and ballooning. It was while experiencing the camaraderie and the mutual passion of gliding at the Flying M Ranch that I got excited about the sport again.

In 1981, Barron Hilton, along with Helmut Reichmann, started the Barron Hilton Cup, an international soaring competition. They decided that the pilot making the best distance flights from six geographical regions of the world, plus the world champions for each class of glider over the previous two-year period, would win the Barron Hilton Cup. Barron invites these winners together with distinguished aviators for a fabulous week of flying and fellowship at his Flying M Ranch. In 2004 I was the winner of the Barron Hilton Cup for the region encompassing western United States and South America.

Soaring is the most beautiful and graceful form of aviation. Not to be confused with hang gliding, gliders are actual airplanes without engines. Most commonly they are flown in thermals, which are rising columns of air that the pilot seeks out then circles tightly in the lift to gain altitude, then glides on course, finding the next thermal where he can recover the altitude lost during the glide. Climbing in the thermal is done at a low speed such as 55 knots, but faster speeds such as 90 knots during a glide where there is little or no rising air. Therefore, the speed to fly is slow in lift and fast in undesirable sink.

In addition to thermals, soaring can also be done in a 'mountain wave'. A wave is triggered when relatively strong wind is blowing close to perpendicular to the crest of a mountain range. A wave of rising air forms which reaches to higher altitude than thermals. These waves can be strong, enabling fast distance flights along the wave, or very high flights by concentrating on climbing in the strongest part of the wave. Today's high-performance gliders are built solely from lightweight composite materials. Fiberglass or carbon fiber is embedded in resin offer an efficient strength-to-weight ratio. The flight characteristics of modern high-performance gliders are equally impressive. Glide ratios of 50 to 1 or better are available on some glider models and 60 to 1 is found on the very best. That means it is possible to glide over a mile with the loss of only 100 feet of altitude in still air without the advantage of any lift from thermals or wave.

My interest in gliding inevitably began to gravitate toward record-breaking. Sitting around the table after lunch at the Flying M Ranch, the Barron Hilton Cup Competition Director, Hannes

Linke, mentioned that there was an interesting project developing which involved flying for the gliding altitude record in 'space suits'. Immediately fascinated by this idea, I asked to be introduced to the pilot who was working on this project. The following week, I was on the phone with Einar Enevoldson, a recently retired NASA test pilot who was also a life-long glider pilot. During our conversation, Einar shared with me his vision of attempting to fly a sailplane into the stratosphere. He explained that it was possible to fly a sailplane as high as 100,000 ft and literally double the current altitude world record, which was set by Bob Harris at 49,009 ft in 1986.

Einar invited me to meet with him at NASA's Dryden Center located at Edwards Air Force Base in the Mojave desert north of Los Angeles, where meteorologists had been studying high altitude wave and its importance to flying and developing aircraft for high-altitude flight. There, I was shown a computer simulator of a glider of Einar's design developed by the aeronautical engineers, and was invited to fly this simulator to 105,000 ft to get the feel of flying a glider in such thin air. I was immediately convinced that this was important science that had real potential of resulting in a fantastic glider altitude record. The demands of gliding at these high-altitude attempts actually required two pilots and I wanted to be one of them. With characteristic modesty Einar agreed that we could pursue the project together and that I could even be the first-named pilot, or 'pilot in command'.

Since the task of designing a totally new glider capable of flying to 100,000 ft would have to wait until a later date, I bought a high-performance German-built glider, a DG-500, whose airfoils would reasonably support flight to 62,000 ft. Einar secured the loan of full-pressure suits from NASA. These are effectively space suits, which use pure oxygen to provide a breathing altitude of 8000 ft and oxygen pressure on the body equal to about 35,000 ft even if the outside pressure is near zero as in space. Hence the parlance of calling them 'space suits' even though the model we were using was the same as used in the SR-71 and the U-2 high-altitude spy planes where they protect the pilot in case of cabin depressurization or bailout. In return for the loan of the pressure suits, we would collect data in support of NASA's meteorological studies.

We started the long process of modifying the glider to accommodate the full-pressure suit systems and converted the flying instruments to operate at extreme altitude and cold. We needed liquid oxygen dewars, or tanks, to run the full-pressure suits and batteries to operate face-plate and foot-heaters as well as the increased instrumentation. We used military lithium batteries because lithium batteries still put out power when at cold temperatures. The DG-500 was a motorglider, which had a small 50-horsepower motor and stowable propeller behind the pilots. Motorgliders can take off from the ground rather than requiring a tow plane. We removed and sold the motor so we could use the engine bay for the oxygen dewars and the batteries.

The weather phenomenon we needed for reaching such extreme high altitude is the Polar Vortex. Around the 1980s, scientists became aware of this very high-speed band of wind that circles the North and South Poles during winter for about four months, ending in early spring. The ceiling on normal mountain wave is the tropopause—the boundary between the troposphere at low altitude and the stratosphere, which starts above the tropopause. A wave will not propagate though this boundary layer where the air no longer gets colder with increasing altitude and the windspeeds typically drop. Typically, the tropopause is in the region of 35,000 ft but previous altitude records have been flown as a cold front approaches which has the effect of briefly pushing the tropopause to as high as 55,000 ft. The benefit of having a Polar Vortex overhead is that it dissolves the tropopause 'boundary', allowing the mountain wave to subsequently extend to extraordinary altitudes sometimes as high as 300,000 ft.

Although we conducted our testing in California in the Sierra Nevada wave, to reach the edges of the Polar Vortex necessitated going to Norway or Sweden near the Arctic Circle, or far south in the South Island of New Zealand or Patagonia in Argentina or Chile. We chose New Zealand because of the ease of logistics and the support of local glider pilots.

My project to break the altitude record for gliding, the Perlan Project, has been going on for five years now. During this time, we have been able to ascertain that the glider and pressure systems are sorted out and working reliably. We have made three test flights in California over 40,000 ft, with the highest altitude being 43,000 ft. Having made three attempts over three seasons in New Zealand, and four attempts in our first season in southern Argentina, we have yet to succeed in getting into the Polar Vortex. However, our enthusiasm has not waned. The Perlan Project is just too important and too exciting to give up on. Currently, we are making plans for another season of attempts in Argentina.

A collateral benefit of the Perlan Project was that I happened to meet and then partner with Terry Delore. During our first Perlan season in Omarama, New Zealand, Terry and other excellent glider pilots were flying support for Einar and me by looking for the best wave lift. One of the pilots suggested I discuss with Terry the possibility of making world record attempts together. I was surprised when Terry, who has left a significant mark on this sport, enthusiastically responded to this idea. At age 17, Terry Delore became the World Champion in hang gliders. Subsequently he has flown over 6000 hours in sailplanes and set a number of world records. We all knew he was good—I would soon learn that he is as good as anyone in the world at speed and distance flying.

After returning to New Zealand the next month to make some record attempts, just two weeks later I got to be pilot with Terry for my first glider world record. Although we both would be listed as pilots for any record that we set together, we would take turns as to who would be listed as the first pilot or pilot-in-command. The flip of a coin determined that I got to be first listed on our first world record, then Terry on the second, etc. 15 November 2002 brought us a good wave day. Taking to the air, we waited for the wave to line up. We made a couple of trial starts then I just flew around for two hours while Terry caught up on his sleep. Finally all the essential elements came together and we got it right: we blasted around a 500-km (310-mile) Triangle course in a mere 2 hours 44 minutes to set a new world record speed of 187.14 km/h (116.28 mph). We superseded the prior world record by 16 km/h (10 mph), which was held by the most prolific glider record-setter, Hans Werner Grosse of Germany. Our records program was off and running.

In December, I came back to New Zealand and we pocketed the 1000-km (621-mile) Out and Return record. By this time, Terry and I had established our method of operation. We would each fly approximately half the time. When it came to the most difficult flying problems, like finding a thermal in weak conditions, Terry with his extraordinary flying ability would take the controls to solve the problem.

The sport of gliding is seemingly boundless for the obsessive record-breaker. With all the various classes of gliders and records for each class, gliding provides many records to break. In the unlimited Open Class, which is 'open' to any type of glider, there are 21 world records. We want them all!

The greatest arena for speed and distance records now seems to be the Andes Mountains of Argentina. German pilot Klaus Oh-lmann had in the last couple of years been breaking records then breaking them again with gay abandon. Wanting to see this for myself, on 1 January I flew my Citation down to San Martin de Los Andes, Argentina to meet Klaus. He took me along on a two-day flight where he was trying to set up a distance record attempt, but unfortunately we could not get far enough south to stage the attempt. Indicative of great sportsmanship, Klaus showed the terrain and logistics to me as a new competitor. I learned a lot about the Argentine wave and how to fly it enough to determine that this is where I wanted to fly. So inspired was I that I returned to the States and promptly bought the best-performance glider I could find. In summer 2003, Terry, with our expert team member Tim Harrison, came to Nevada to prepare my glider. Confirming that my investment was a sound one, on our fifth attempt, Terry and I secured the 750-km (466-mile) Triangle world record. A few weeks later we exceeded the 1250-km (776-mile) Triangle record by a miniscule .01 km/h. Because the requirement for a world record is to break the prior record by a margin of 2 km/h (just over 1 mile), I could only file it as a US National Record. Funny how the US National Record is now faster than the world record!

The next two wave seasons in Argentina proved hugely successful for us there. We flew the first 2000-km (1242-mile) Out and Return glider flight. However this record was short-lived. After only 11 days, French pilot Jean-Marie Clement broke our record. Then, as if to underscore that the most magnificent glider record competition of all time was going on in Argentina, Klaus Ohlmann broke Jean-Marie's record 8 days later. We were not deterred. We had our sights on completing the longest Triangle. No one had flown a long triangle in Argentina because it required leaving the strong Andean wave to make the downwind corner of the triangle. On 13 December 2003, we sent a shock wave through the glider community by achieving this goal, flying the longest Triangle at 1508.42 km (937 miles). Terry says this is technically the most difficult gliding task that has ever been flown. As can be expected, Klaus Ohlmann lusts for our record and has made several attempts, but so far to no avail. During our 2004 season, although Terry and I captured only one record in Argentina, it was a great one: the Free Distance Record.

We would start from El Calafate, a town far south in the Patagonian region of Argentina. Since gliders are not authorized for night flight in Argentina, we would take off at the first minute of legal daylight: 4.36 am. After crossing the start line we tracked north past the glaciers, lakes with icebergs, the spectacular spires of

Fitzroy and Torre Egger. Even though we were initially flying low at only 9000 ft, the frigid temperatures had caused my toes to go numb. They seemed on the verge of freezing solid and if they did I would have to call for a landing to save me from serious frostbite. Soon the temperatures warmed and I settled in for a long day. It was forecast to be a good day for wave flying, but not with the extraordinary conditions that are associated with world records. We would struggle for hours at low altitude but at least were able to fly slowly north without stopping to make climbing turns.

As conditions improved and we had covered two-thirds of the planned distance, we reached a towering wave cloud near the popular glider center of Chos Malal. This was the place to climb as high as possible, perhaps up to 35,000 ft, to reduce the need for stopping for climbs further north. As we climbed through 20,000 ft at our outstanding climb rate, we switched our oxygen supply from the hospital-style nose canulas to oxygen masks more suitable for high altitude. Soon we were at 25,000 ft and climbing and I didn't feel like I was getting the proper amount of oxygen. But I was right in the middle of preparing a plastic bag for peeing, then I would look into the problem with the oxygen. I was soon out cold.

As Terry continued the climb through 30,000 ft he felt a jarring as my leg twitched and heard a gurgle. He looked back to me in the back seat and my face was blue and I was completely unconscious. Terry's first thought was that I had died of a heart attack, but in any case an emergency descent was in order. Jet pilots are trained so they know the emergency descent procedure by rote—Terry knew what to do from his vast experience of flying gliders. He pulled out the spoilers for drag, nosed the glider over into a maximum speed descent then flew to the other side of the wave, where the air was descending as fast as it was going up when we were climbing. In less than three harrowing minutes, Terry had us below 15,000 ft. At that altitude, I regained consciousness and asked, 'What's with the dive?' 'Geez, Steve, I thought you were dead—we better get you to a hospital.'

After some animated discussion, I realized the oxygen failure was due to the plastic tube disconnecting from the mask, as the two kinds of plastic had different contraction rates as the temperatures got colder during the climb. I had just survived a near-death experience. 'Terry, I'm fine now—we might as well continue the record attempt.' Soon we were in the climb back to 30,000 ft beside the same, stacked wave cloud. In case you were wondering: there was no pee in the plastic bag, and I didn't need to go any more!

We continued on along the crest of the highest part of the Andes and flew to the last minutes of legal daylight, then landed at the hot, mosquito-invested San Juan Airport. We had achieved a new Free Distance Record in gliders at 2192.7 km (1362 miles) from southern Argentina to the northern provinces. This record stands as proof there is no better glider pilot in the world than Terry Delore. And just for good measure, he saved my life too. In our gliding records program so far, Terry and I have broken 10 of the 21 Open Class records and we are still looking forward to doing more of this!

'What is the most important flight remaining to be done in aviation?' This was the question we were discussing after a day of flying at Barron Hilton's Flying M Ranch in the summer of 1999. Among those present at dinner that evening was Dick Rutan, who made the historic *Voyager* non-stop, non-refueled circumnavigation flight with Jeana Yeager in 1986. That night, Dick said that it was now conceivable to make a solo nonstop circumnavigation flight. Since 1986, technology had developed so that a lighter, more fuel-efficient airplane could be built. Aviation pioneer Wiley Post was the first to grab hold of this dream and run with it when he made the first solo round the world trip in 1933, taking 7 days 19 hours and stopping eleven times for fuel. In his day, Post shared the fame of early aviators such as Charles Lindbergh and Amelia Earheart. The possibility of becoming a part of this aviation legacy was alluring. Expressing my interest in this project to Dick Rutan later that evening, he offered to introduce me to his brother Burt Rutan, the innovative aircraft designer and engineer famous for having built the *Voyager*.

In August, I went out to Oshkosh, Wisconsin to the annual Experimental Aircraft Association 'AirVenture,' the largest aviation meeting in the country. Twelve thousand planes come in for this huge event and the daily attendance throughout the six days approaches a million people. This is where I first met Burt Rutan. He had two visionary projects for me to consider. The first was a private spaceship to fly to an altitude of 100-km (62-mile) and win the X-Prize. The second was a solo nonstop round the world airplane flight. At an estimated $7 million, the spaceship project seemed a bit excessive for me, and the risk of experimental rockets scared me. With an estimate of $2.5 million, the solo airplane seemed much more feasible for me and ultimately satisfied my original interest for which I sought the meeting. Subsequently Paul Allen took the space project, spent extra money to do it right and make it safe, then proceeded to win the X-Prize with the famously successful *SpaceShip One*. Looking back, I should have taken both projects!

Before Burt and I got too far into the planning stages, it became evident that business at Scaled Composites, the aviation design company that Burt Rutan headed up, was going though some rocky times. The company that owned Scaled wanted to sell it. This posed a risk that, if I went ahead and invested the necessary funds to get this project rolling, Burt might be unhappy with the new owner and take his loyal engineers 'across the street' to form a new company. My solo airplane contract would be left in the hands of the old company, which wouldn't be able to perform. Eventually Burt organized a management buy-out of Scaled Composites. At the last minute, one of the buy-out investors backed out and Burt called me in England to offer me this share. I accepted on the spot. Now I am pleased to be the 13% shareholder of a fascinating and very successful company. Once I was assured that business at Scaled was on solid ground, we proceeded to the preliminary design stage.

I did not doubt the capability of Scaled to design and build a lightweight carbon composite airplane, even though there were two essential components that must be procured before proceeding: the engine and an autopilot. It had not been decided yet whether the power plant should be propeller or jet engine. Propeller engines are more fuel-efficient than jet engines but less reliable. Therefore, for flying over the oceans, two propeller engines would be required for safety. Concluding that it would be a reasonable risk to trust a single jet engine to make it around the world, I opted for this engine type.

Burt told his friend Dr Sam Williams about the First Solo project. Blind since youth, Dr Williams hasn't allowed his limitation to stand in the way of his becoming one of the most distinguished engineers in aviation history. In 1978, he was awarded the highest award in American aviation, the Collier Trophy, for his work in developing small fanjet engines. His company, Williams International, is the major producer of engines for small private jets as well as for cruise missiles. Quick to recognize that my First Solo would attract attention to the reliability and fuel-efficiency of his jet engines, Dr Williams offered to loan us a production engine together with all maintenance support.

Because the circumnavigation flight time would theoretically take up to 80 hours, during which I would need to nap for short intervals, an equally critical piece of equipment that the success of this project depended on was an advanced autopilot system. Instead of the commonly used analogue autopilots, I needed a digital one that was readily programmable for this mission-specific application. After investigating autopilots made by different companies, the day after Christmas 2002, I flew to Springdale, Arkansas to Tru Trak Flight Systems, Inc., a miniscule company, which had started making digital autopilots for home-built airplanes. There, Scaled's flight test director, Doug Shane, and I reviewed their autopilot and determined that it would work for my solo airplane. At that turning point, I gave the go ahead to design and build the airplane. The project would remain top secret for a long time and went by the code name 'Capricorn', which referred to the requirement for a qualifying Round the World flight. A pilot must fly the distance of the Tropic of Capricorn or the Tropic of Cancer. Since 'Cancer' did not seem to be an auspicious name for a new airplane, *Capricorn* was the obvious code-name choice.

While the plane was being built, I stayed heavily involved in my speed sailing program. While the final design of *Capricorn* was still being worked out in March 2003, I went to St Martin to sail *PlayStation* in the Heinecken Regatta. Aware that Richard Branson's private island, Necker Island, was not very far away, I invited him to sail with us, an invitation he promptly accepted. Richard was fully engaged in sailing with my crew and we managed to be First to Finish and also set the speed record for sailing around the island of St Martin.

Later that day, back at the rented house we were staying in, I pulled out the drawings of the *Capricorn* and shared with Richard my plans to make the First Solo. He was immediately intrigued. He asked me numerous questions about the plane and its design, which by that time I had been working on with Scaled Composites for over a year.

By the time Richard got back to England, he still had the First Solo project on his mind—enough so to consult with Will Whitehorn, his closest advisor. He explained to Will that he really liked and believed in the project and wanted to get involved. I imagine that I could've shown this project to a hundred major corporations and been greeted with yawns, but Richard uniquely was able to envision the public attraction for such an adventure. Beyond coinciding with his idea of good publicity for his airline, Virgin Atlantic Airways, Richard believed that it would help further advance aviation technology. Like all of Scaled's designs, the *Capricorn* was made of composite carbon-fiber materials that offered the lightest and strongest construction possible, helping make it one of the most fuel-efficient airplanes ever built. This airplane and my flight would heighten awareness of the possibility of developing more fuel-efficient commercial aircraft and reducing the consumption of fossil fuels—a good image for Virgin Atlantic to be associated with.

It took us a long time to work out a contract. Then on 23 October 2003, at a press conference held at London's Science Museum, Richard announced Virgin Atlantic Airways' sponsorship of what would now be called the *Virgin Atlantic GlobalFlyer*. Virgin came in as a major financial sponsor and would assist in the public relations department. Since I had no publicity department nor time to attend to that aspect of the project, I welcomed Richard's support and felt extremely fortunate to have as project 'patron' my friend and former ballooning partner.

Naturally a nonstop, non-refueled circumnavigation flight is all about fuel-efficiency. The *GlobalFlyer* was built to carry more than four times its own weight in fuel. We estimated that at takeoff, the plane, with maximum fuel capacity, would weigh 22,000 lbs. On making it back to Salina, it would burn most of its 18,000 lbs of fuel to land near its dry weight of 3700 lbs. Since every bit of weight decreases the plane's performance, to keep the flight as fuel efficient as possible, the aircraft was designed with only the bare essentials in mind. The *GlobalFlyer* would have no anti-icing ability, no lightning strike protection, no weather radar, no air conditioning and only a very rudimentary heating system inside the cabin.

Our determination to economize on weight posed a problem. Opting to forsake the sophistication of fuel heaters, we would have to protect against fuel freezing in some other way. At my flight altitudes, temperatures would range from $-45\,^{\circ}$C to $-75\,^{\circ}$C and on a long flight, the aircraft would become cold soaked where the fuel in the wings slowly proceeds to cool toward the outside temperature. The problem is that kerosene types of jet fuel commonly used will gel or start to freeze between $-44\,^{\circ}$C and $-48\,^{\circ}$C. That is why long-range airliners that fly 15 hours typically have fuel heaters to prevent fuel freezing. We had a different solution: we decided to use a military fuel, designated JP-4, which has a much lower freezing point. Scaled tested samples of JP-4 down to $-85\,^{\circ}$C and it did not freeze. I hoped that test was accurate. If the fuel were to freeze over a continental landmass, causing my single jet engine to stop, I could glide to an airport. The *GlobalFlyer*, with its 114-ft wingspan and sleek design, has a glide ratio without the engine of about

32 to 1. That's equal to the glide ratio of a standard sport glider. From cruise altitude of 45,000 ft, I could glide 272 miles and easily find an airport for a safe landing. But over the ocean I could be over 1000 miles from an airport. Even with a raft, ditching would be a great risk to my life, not to mention the loss of a beautiful airplane.

After several years, our combined efforts and singular vision took tangible form. At a press conference on 8 January 2004, along with Sir Richard Branson and Burt Rutan, I unveiled the *Virgin Atlantic GlobalFlyer* in Mojave, California. After the *GlobalFlyer* dramatically emerged from behind a curtain of white ice mist and colorful strobe lights, I reiterated to the press my aim to become the first pilot to fly solo, nonstop around the world later that year. Turning to look at this amazing, state-of-the-art airplane, I was momentarily transfixed, truly impressed, almost beyond words. Burt Rutan's team at Scaled had turned a dream into engineering reality.

Friday, 5 March 2004, was another huge step forward for the *GlobalFlyer* project. While I was en route to breaking the RTW sailing record with my crew onboard *Cheyenne* and enjoying a four-day lead over the current record holder, *Orange* 2002, I received a call from Scaled Composites. That day, Scaled's Project Engineer and Test Pilot, Jon Karkow, parlayed theory into reality— he flew the *Virgin Atlantic GlobalFlyer* for the very first time. The successful first test flight lasted 1 hour 30 minutes. Jon admitted that prior to takeoff he was a little nervous about flying a type of plane that had never been flown before. After landing, Jon reported that the airplane had 'excellent flying qualities' and that all the aircraft systems operated well and that there were no maintenance complaints to speak of. I was more than pleased with the results of this first test flight, which were beyond our highest expectations. It looked like we had built an excellent airplane.

Although the *GlobalFlyer* was my airplane, when it came time for me to begin test-flying the aircraft, some of the people at Scaled Composites were protective of their role in making the test flights. They also weren't sure if I could handle the plane. Most of the test pilots at Scaled had test-flown military and all sorts of experimental aircraft and they weren't used to a customer starting to fly a new aircraft as part of the flight-test program. Because of the differing handling characteristics from when it's very heavy at takeoff to when it's light at landing, the *GlobalFlyer* was considered a tricky airplane to fly. Because there is only one seat in the *GlobalFlyer*, no instructor can aid or protect a pilot during their first flight.

Actually, my qualifications to fly the *GlobalFlyer* were pretty good. I had gone through training programs in the course of earning Type ratings—special training in various 'types' of plane—to be a captain in four different categories of private jets. Learning the systems and instrumentation of the *GlobalFlyer* was not that dissimilar to my prior training experiences. My experience as a glider pilot was also very relevant. Since the *GlobalFlyer* performs close to a glider in terms of handling, I understood the feel of the high Lift-over-Drag and the kind of landing to execute with this kind of aircraft.

The final step before my first test flight was to fly in a 2-place airplane with Mike Melvill, the Chief Test Pilot of Scaled. Mike had recently achieved his place in aviation history by piloting *SpaceShip One* on the first private flight into space, but he had his start at Scaled by constructing his own home-built Long-EZ. He still flies it and we went up together in his Long-EZ to practice the pattern speeds and landing angles expected in the *GlobalFlyer*. As we strapped in he basically said, 'Look, Steve, show me how you do it.'

After flying the Long-EZ with Mike for $1\frac{3}{4}$ hours, he shared his assessment with the Scaled team after we landed.

'This guy is a sharp cookie. He's got the capabilities and the skill to handle the *GlobalFlyer*. Steve is able to take in information and sort the wheat from the chaff, and decide if what you're giving him is bullshit. He sifts everything through his own experience, then diffuses it, and then applies it the way he sees fit. He will not have any problems.'

After I got the stamp of approval from their best test pilot, Jon Karkow prepped me for my first *GlobalFlyer* flight. He also printed a Test Card, which is a list of tests to be performed on this flight—just like a test pilot. My first flight, on 13 October 2004, lasted a little over two hours and came off without a hitch. Jon Karkow proclaimed, 'Steve did a bloody excellent job.' The next week, the examiner from the Federal Aviation Administration came out to observe my flying and then issued a 'Letter of Authorization'. I was now officially qualified as a pilot for the *GlobalFlyer*.

With Virgin's Kevin Stass, I researched the extremely critical matter of which airport I should choose to take off from on my First Solo attempt. Since we had never test-flown the *GlobalFlyer* at full fuel capacity due to the risk posed to the test pilot that there might be structural failure or that the airplane would fail to lift off at the calculated ground roll distance, I would be the ultimate test pilot at the time I started the actual circumnavigation attempt in a prototype plane laden with 18,000 lbs of fuel. Burt Rutan's vote on the subject went to the nearby Edwards Air Force Base because this was the longest runway in the USA, and also has a good overrun. I rejected the recommendation of Edwards AFB in California in favor of central United States after carefully weighing the other major safety factor, which was that I would be pushing the limits of range. If I ran out of fuel toward the end of my circumnavigation, I wanted to be over land where I could glide to an airport, rather than over the Pacific Ocean with only a chance of making it to California. Kevin and I became convinced that Salina, Kansas was the best place for takeoff. The runway at Salina Municipal Airport, although not as long as Edwards, was still very long at 12,300 ft. We further reckoned that the colder temperatures and lower elevation at Salina would enable the *GlobalFlyer* to lift off in a shorter distance. After conveying our interest in using their runway, Salina pulled all the stops to be the base for this flight. They expressed their willingness to provide a hangar, facilities for Mission Control, plus there was a great resource of volunteers from the Aviation School of Kansas State University. I chose Salina.

By late 2004, I believed the *GlobalFlyer* airplane was working well enough to make it around the world, but Scaled proposed more testing. Although acting in the interest of safety, additional testing would mean that we would sacrifice the best jetstreams (which are in January and February) to make this flight. We would miss the season altogether. I came back early from my glider record program in Argentina with a mission: to get control of the *GlobalFlyer* so the schedule would not slip another year. I took delivery of the finished airplane on 15 December 2004 and immediately made plans to fly it to Salina. Although Scaled would still be in charge of maintenance of the aircraft and I would rely on Jon Karkow for all form of advice, I was enormously relieved that at last I had the final say on testing and schedule for the global flight.

Now the owner of the *GlobalFlyer*, I would not hear of postponing the attempt another year. After completing a couple more days of test flights, I made the transition flight from Mojave to Salina, Kansas on 6 January 2005. This was the *GlobalFlyer*'s first cross-country flight during which I expanded the envelope by climbing to 47,000 ft where the previous high-test flight, was 45,000 ft. Then the trouble started. The cabin pressure altitude climbed from its normal 8000 ft indicating that I was losing pressurization. There was a leak somewhere. Responding to this, I put on my emergency oxygen mask and prepared for emergency descent procedures in case the depressurization worsened. An airplane's cabin pressurization is maintained by bleeding air from the engine into the cabin. Plenty of air is pushed in and the excess is pushed out of the aircraft through an Outflow Valve, which operates at a specified pressure to maintain the desired equivalent altitude in the cabin. In this case, not enough air was coming in to offset the leak. Although I wanted to get down to a breathable altitude of 20,000 ft or below, I also did not want to go into emergency descent procedures, such as deploying the drag chutes, unless I had to. The *GlobalFlyer* is so aerodynamic that my maximum descent rate is only 700 ft per minute with the engine in idle. Now I needed to gingerly give the minimum amount of power necessary to maintain a cabin pressurization equal to 12,000 ft or lower. However, this would allow me only an average of 300 ft per minute descent. It took a long time to get down for landing, but once on the ground in Salina I was relieved to have gotten through this teething problem of the airplane and more determined to discover what caused it.

Scaled maintenance crew chief Philip Grassa quickly found the leak. A seam had split open in the Bleed Air Cooler so the air was whistling into the atmosphere instead of into the cabin. It turns out that seam had failed before, re-welded, and failed in the same place. It was a used part! Reconditioned or used parts are the bane of aircraft maintenance. The standard procedure in aviation is when a part fails, it is exchanged for a reconditioned part. Reconditioned parts are bench tested and certified for airworthiness before they are resold. The truth is that bench testing often does not discover the problem, or the repair fails soon after reinstallation in an airplane. This time I firmly specified to Scaled that I must have only new parts for the critical systems of the *GlobalFlyer*.

The end of January found us constantly monitoring meteorological data for the right combination of cold, dense air and calm wind conditions for a safe takeoff that would allow me to initially climb to a 45,000-ft cruising altitude. For the meteorologist for the First Solo attempt, I chose David Dehenauw, who had served as the assistant to Luc Trullemans for my 2002 balloon circumnavigation, which was so brilliantly routed. Even though he is a television weatherman in Belgium, David is primarily a research meteorologist, precisely the type of person I needed to figure out the jetstream and bad weather locations long in advance. I was required by FAI rules to declare my route well in advance of the flight starting and then stick to that route. Unlike ballooning or sailing, I could not change the route to chase better winds once this flight was launched. David was exactly the right person to bring together this long-range forecasting so the proper decisions on takeoff time and routing could be made.

The weather at the end of January and the beginning of February led to further delays. A tentative plan to take off on Wednesday, 26 January was scratched when the jetstream, which is essential for the aircraft to make the 23,000-mile flight, was too far north. If I were to have followed that jetstream where it had been located, the route would have been too short for me to meet the minimum distance requirements for setting an official circumnavigation record. Then, during the first weeks of February, the jetstream was directly over Kansas, and had I taken to the sky, the resulting turbulence would have been too high. The *GlobalFlyer* was engineered to withstand only 2 Gs of load when full of fuel early in the flight. This meant that I must avoid turbulence during the early stages of the attempt or risk structural failure such as a wing breaking off. Although my strategy was straightforward enough—takeoff in calm air, climb on course to the initial cruising altitude of 39,000 ft where the turbulence is much less than the middle altitudes, then enter the jetstream—I patiently awaited the right weather conditions in order to do this.

It turned out to be a bit of a long wait before launching the circumnavigation flight. The winds were uncooperative. Although I don't like delays, in all my records projects I've had to learn to relax and wait until the weather is right. When we passed the midpoint of February, I started to become anxious. In cold weather, jet engines develop more thrust and so they only need a short runway; however, after February, it would become increasingly difficult to get cold enough conditions for a short enough takeoff roll on the runway—and the jetstream speeds on average would be waning. If March came and went without a 'Code Green', we'd have to wait for the next favorable weather season, which wouldn't be until next December, nine long months away. So I was determined to be ready for the very first acceptable weather pattern.

By the end of February, both the weather and airplane preparations had come together. I was pleased and relieved when a favorable weather window finally opened. On Saturday, 26 February, I issued a 'Code Green' for a takeoff on Monday the 28th. 'Green' means that we believed that the takeoff would happen on that day.

On Sunday, the 27th, Richard Branson and the British press arrived in Salina for the event. Soon after a Virgin Atlantic Airways

747 landed at the Salina Municipal Airport, everyone onboard was transported to the *Virgin Atlantic GlobalFlyer* hangar for a quick reception and press conference. The atmosphere was charged with anticipation. In attendance was Kansas Lt. Gov. John Moore, who said how pleased he was to have the *Virgin Atlantic GlobalFlyer* project stationed in Salina, exclaiming that it was a 'compliment to Salina, the airport authority, Kansas State University and the Chamber of Commerce'. In a gesture of welcoming, Salina Mayor Monte Shadwick gave me the keys to the city. As a sign of faith in our project, Richard Branson gave me his Breitling wristwatch complete with an emergency locator transmitter to wear during my flight. He challenged me to bring myself and his slick watch 'back in one piece'. Although Burt Rutan couldn't make it to Salina, Scaled's Project Engineer, Jon Karkow, was on hand to work in Mission Control throughout the flight.

As I awoke on Monday morning, 28 February 2005, I paused to think about how all the years of preparation—building the plane, test-flying it, months of flight planning, and weeks of waiting for good weather conditions—were finally reaching a denouement as this great aviation adventure was about to get underway. Depending on the weather conditions that day, we estimated that my takeoff time would be between 2.00 and 6.00 pm. As it turned out, the wind would have some say in this. When the wind started to kick up to 25 knots, creating turbulence that could cause the wings to flap during takeoff and possibly break the main spar of the wing, we just went on hold. I was simply not willing to risk the potential of structural damage due to turbulence, a risk that was highest when the airplane was at its heaviest during takeoff. If something were to happen that close to the ground, there'd be no recovery. There wouldn't be any opportunity to bail out.

While Mission Control personnel carefully monitored conditions, waiting for the potentially dangerous crosswinds to dissipate, Peggy and I went over to Mission Control. There, I spent an hour going over the weather data and saying a few words to the press. I met up with my friends Barron Hilton and Bob Hoover who had flown in to see me off. Tim Cole, John Kugler, and Bert Padelt, the core members of my round the world balloon team, had also come to Salina to offer their support, which I greatly appreciated. One person who I was disappointed couldn't make it was my good friend Stan Nelson who had been designated as the official observer for record certification purposes. He was in hospital with a relapse of his leukemia and had sent Dick Ionata as his replacement. I got

Stan's telephone number in the hospital so I could call him en route to tell him how the flight was going.

As the sun inched closer to the horizon late that afternoon, the wind persisted throwing us into a race against time. Burt Rutan had repeatedly told me that it was extremely important for me to take off in daylight. In normal airplanes, night takeoffs are just as easy, but in the *GlobalFlyer* if things started to go wrong during takeoff or climbout, I would need all the visual references available to keep this airplane under control. We had been briefed that the normal weather pattern at Salina was that the thermally induced winds subside at sunset. Sure enough, just as the sun started to go down, the wind socks lining the tarmac began to sag, indicating a reduction in the wind speed and optimal takeoff conditions. All systems were suddenly 'go'.

The ground crew, in their matching orange jumpsuits, rushed to get in the last little bit of fuel that the wings could accommodate. The press hurriedly assembled behind a cordon. I maneuvered myself sideways through the door of the *GlobalFlyer* and settled into the tiny cockpit. As the encroaching nighttime sky diminished what was left of the daylight, the crew and support vehicles began to back away and Richard wished me a safe and successful journey. After extracting a promise from me that I would make it back okay, Peggy leaned in and kissed me good luck. Once we said our goodbyes, I installed the plug hatch, which was the door to the cockpit. Sunset gave way to twilight as I started the engine up from my position at the end of Runway 35.

Sitting alone on the runway facing north, from my vantage point, I could see on my right the hundreds of well-wishers from Salina who made a quarter-mile ribbon along the tarmac in patient anticipation of the *Virgin Atlantic GlobalFlyer* takeoff. Along the freeway at the end of the runway, hundreds of cars had parked, their drivers waiting to observe the same event. I was touched by their show of enthusiasm and was reminded of the outpouring of hospitality that the townspeople of Salina, the airport staff, and students at Kansas State University of Salina had shown us since we arrived there. We couldn't have asked for more. Everything we needed and wanted was offered to us. Reflecting appreciatively on all the time, energy, talent and funding so many people had contributed to this circumnavigation attempt, I did not feel alone, nor that I was departing on this adventure solely for myself.

I called the Tower, '*Virgin Atlantic GlobalFlyer* November 2-7-7-Sierra Foxtrot requests clearance Round the World to Salina.'

Waiting for the tower to give me the clearance, I consciously took deep breaths to soothe my nerves and focus my attention. Although I was certain that we had done all our homework to get the plane off the ground, like ballooning, the most dangerous time was the takeoff. In this case, it was more so since the *GlobalFlyer* had never flown at full fuel capacity before. There was no guarantee how it would perform under this enormous load. With this weighing heavily on my mind, I concentrated on achieving my first objective, which was to gain the necessary speed to get this fuel-laden plane off the ground. If the *GlobalFlyer* were not able to reach liftoff speed by the end of the runway, the decision to abort would have to be made at the halfway point down the runway. The abort procedure would be dramatic: cut off the engine, deploy both drag chutes, and apply the brakes. The reason it takes the remaining half of the runway to stop is because the *GlobalFlyer* has very light-duty brakes in order to save weight during the circumnavigation attempt, and the brakes would 'fade', losing their effectiveness trying to stop this heavy airplane. If I tried to stop too late, I would careen off the end of the runway and crash into the ILS antenna structure making a very dramatic fireball. I would be relying on Clint Nichols, our performance engineer from Scaled, who was in the tower calling out the required speeds at specified points as I accelerated down the runway. If I were behind the required speeds, I would have to make my decision whether to abort. This scenario was running through my mind when the Tower answered my request. '*Virgin GlobalFlyer* cleared around the world as filed'.

A few moments later I was ready for takeoff on Runway 35.

Releasing the brakes and bringing up the throttle, I started down the runway. The computer limiting maximum power for normal takeoffs had been disabled. The engineers from Williams had calculated the maximum power that I could manually set without damaging the engine. I set the power at the precise maximum permitted. At Clint's first speed callout at the intersection of the first taxiway, I was slightly behind the required speed, which forced me to think about the abort procedure, as it might be necessary. By the time of Clint's second callout, the acceleration had improved and I was relieved that I was ahead of the minimum speed required. I was confident my speed was going to be sufficient for liftoff. My attention turned to picking the proper moment to pull the stick back and rotate for liftoff. At 8000 ft, the exact roll distance calculated by Clint Nichols, the *GlobalFlyer* wings arched upward and the plane surged into the air at 6.47 pm, the very end of official daylight. For that moment, I held my breath. If the wing spar were going to break, it would've been then. Exhaling, I felt this huge sense of relief as one of the greatest risks ever to my life passed.

Moments after taking off and still within a close proximity to the runway, I put the nose over to level the plane out in order to increase my speed before I ascended into the evening sky. Onlookers on the ground gasped in fear, as it appeared that I was suddenly losing altitude and that I might dive toward the ground and crash. It was really an illusion of perspective. Flying away from the onlookers, my level off appeared to be a dive. No one moved until I re-established a climb and I soared away from Salina. I later learned that Peggy, who was standing at the end of the runway with Richard, didn't appreciate that little level-out maneuver.

My next objective was getting through any turbulence and reaching my first cruising altitude of 39,000 ft. Air Traffic Control gave me all the climb clearances, which got me up to altitude without delay. After ascending to my targeted altitude, I leveled off the plane and settled in for the long haul.

Although small, the cockpit was generally well organized. Although some of the instrumentation was common to other jet aircraft, much of it was unique. On the left were the gauges and fuel transfer switches. In the center was the Chelton Flight Management System and to the right were the autopilots and flight recorders. My seat was big enough to shift around in and could recline if I desired. However, because I wanted to have immediate access to all the information and controls, I never reclined the seat.

For the first leg of my flight, I headed north to catch the best jetstream going over the Atlantic. As I neared the Canadian border, only eight hundred miles into my circumnavigation attempt, my GPS (Global Positioning System) went out. My instrumentation readings said I was getting error messages I'd never seen before such as LOI and LON. Relaying these cryptic acronyms to Mission Control, I was not consoled to learn that they stood for 'loss of integrity' and 'loss of navigation'. I had lost my primary navigational system and surely would not be able to find my mandatory waypoints that I must cross over in order for this to qualify as an official RTW flight. I couldn't believe such a setback was happening so early into the flight! Determined to rectify this glitch, I received navigational instructions from Mission Control while we tried to figure out what was going wrong.

Since the NASA STARS system and the GPS are on a very similar frequency, it was initially thought that the GPS failure could be connected to the experimental STARS video link. However, when I switched the video-streaming equipment on and off, that didn't help. Then I tried switching autopilots but that didn't help. I altered the speed of the engine, but that didn't fix the problem. We then thought that the engine igniter might be the source of the problem only to find out that it wasn't. After exhausting all the potential causes of the GPS failure, feelings of resignation started to well up within me. Although the GPS failure wasn't life-threatening, the success of the mission was jeopardized.

With a huge effort using secondary navigational sources like VORs and a lot of help from Mission Control, perhaps it would have been possible to make it around the world without the GPS system. However, it would not be possible to cross over the 49 pre-declared waypoints. To be eligible for an official FAI Round the World record there were a number of rules I had to adhere to. I had to fly a distance that was equivalent to the distance of the Tropic of Cancer. These required waypoints exceeded the minimum distance. Although I could deviate from course between those waypoints, I would have to travel over them. Without the GPS functioning, making it to the waypoints—the whole point of the mission—would be impossible.

Onboard the chase plane nearby, Richard Branson encouraged me to go ahead and continue the flight, even if I couldn't fly over the waypoints and get the official record. At least I'd still be the first to fly solo, nonstop around the world in the eyes of the public. I retorted even doing that would be risky and it would be impractical to comply with the instructions of Air Traffic Control. I decided that unless the GPS reception was fixed, I should fly out into the Atlantic overnight and then come back to return to Salina, Kansas. At least then I would be left with a chance of mounting another attempt that season.

Just as my disappointment was reaching a saturation point, all of a sudden the GPS kicked back in and started working fine. I relayed the good news to Mission Control and, after some investigation, they figured out that the problem was related to the transition from United States to Canada. We eventually learned that my GPS was programmed to work only on the new Wide Area Augmentation System ('WAAS'), which was only available in the United States. Fortunately, after about an hour, my GPS found the international standard GPS reception and automatically switched to that.

Coming into my first morning, I discovered that the risk factor of my attempt had just multiplied when I looked down and noticed that the Emergency Oxygen switch had been tripped accidentally. The control panel of my oxygen system had unguarded switches which were located at the entry of the aircraft. I must have bumped the switch while climbing in or moving equipment around in the cockpit. Moreover, I realized that it must have happened a while ago—my entire oxygen supply was gone. There was no oxygen left in the bottle. In a blink of an eye, the stakes had really gone up for me. In jets, we practice emergency descents—put on the oxygen mask and pull out the speed brakes and dive to a safe altitude. The GlobalFlyer didn't have speed brakes and it was so slick that it would take a very long time to sideslip down to a survivable altitude like 25,000 ft. My only source of pressurization was the single jet engine. If the engine failed, I'd have no oxygen and not enough time to descend to an altitude where there was some. I didn't want to tell Mission Control about this because they probably would have insisted that I land because of this increased danger. I decided to take the risk that this engine wouldn't quit and have faith that the integrity of the pressurized cabin would remain intact.

Later that day, I reached North Africa and then flew northeastward through Morocco and onto Casablanca where the chase plane, which was carrying Virgin's Will Whitehorn, still photographer Thierry Boccon-Gibod, and a Discovery Channel cameraman, planned to intercept me. In addition to the media purposes of photography and interviews, it was a relief to have a chase plane. If I had to land anywhere along the route, the chase plane would land and the three pilots—Alex Tai, Adam Letts and Mark Marshall—would immediately swing into action helping me secure the GlobalFlyer and figure out what to do next.

Because I was flying Eastbound in order to get a tailwind and therefore in the opposite direction that the sun rises and sets, I only had about six hours of daylight each day. Therefore, the chase plane carefully timed its fuel stops so that it could do its intercepts during daylight. Another issue that had to be considered and addressed was our difference in speeds. Although my Citation X could catch up with and fly as high as the GlobalFlyer, it can't fly as slow. After getting permission from Air Traffic Control, the Citation pilots would set their autopilot with an altitude typically 500 ft different from what I was flying, for example 44,500 ft if I were cruising at 45,000 ft. They would put out flaps and leading-edge slats to reduce the stall speed of their wings and then fly by me higher, lower or to the side, to get the photographs and film footage. I'll admit it was an eerie feeling to see this big airplane come cruising by at close quarters with a speed that was only 50 mph faster than the *GlobalFlyer*. Then they would circle back to make additional passes until they were satisfied with the shots they got.

After a few passes at the Casablanca intercept, Alex Tai decided to try one at 300 ft overhead. The wingtip vortices descended to the *GlobalFlyer*, disturbing the airflow and killing the lift on the left wing. The wing dropped abruptly as if I were in a 15-degree turn. There was nothing I could do until the dynamic stopped, at which point I angrily blurted out that the chase plane was never to fly that close overhead. I was trying to baby this *GlobalFlyer* with shallow turns and turbulence avoidance for fear of structural failure, and here my own chase plane was creating the biggest in-flight risk of all! This little drama and verbal exchange was captured on film. Needless to say, they were especially careful on all the subsequent intercepts.

In addition to the encouragement I received from the chase planes in the air, I was fortunate to have a wonderful support team back at Mission Control, who did everything in their power to make me feel as if I were not alone. Despite a heavy workload and the resultant lack of sleep many of the Mission Control personnel experienced themselves, throughout my flight, they tried to make me feel optimistic and confident at every opportunity. Every hour Chief Engineer Jon Karkow would call me from Mission Control on the satellite telephone to collect data on fuel tank levels, fuel temperature and engine parameters. This would allow him and Performance Engineer Clint Nichols to calculate fuel consumption and determine whether I was on track to make it around the world. Intent to put a long-distance smile on my face, Jon was always cheerful when he greeted me. He'd jokingly call me 'captain' or refer to himself as the 'information pest', which acknowledged the tedium of our hourly task. Jon also felt the hourly telephone reports would help keep me alert in what he presumed was an exceedingly boring flight. Actually I was never bored. I would constantly scan my instruments, calling up different pages of data on the screens. I would compare that to my abbreviated Flight Manual for normal operation. I would also pull out my charts and pay close attention to the navigation as reported to me on the Chelton Flight Management system.

After I made a swing north to the coast of the Mediterranean in order to stay on standard airways, I dove southeast through Algeria and Libya. Upon reaching central Libya I hooked up with the powerful Subtropical Jetstream, which would power me across the

Middle East, Asia and most of the way across the Pacific. I was really moving, with over 100 knots of tailwind over the Persian Gulf, when I got the fateful call from Jon Karkow. I could immediately tell a difference in his mood. His jovial demeanor was absent and had been replaced with a gravity that I had not observed in him thus far into the flight. Based solely on the tone of his voice, my stomach muscles tightened as I braced myself for bad news. Jon told me that there was a discrepancy in the amount of fuel I had left. My heart sank as he informed me that it didn't look like I'd have enough fuel to make it back to Salina.

'This has to be a mistake!' was my first thought. I didn't want to believe it was true.

There are essentially two—and only two—means of determining how much fuel the *GlobalFlyer* had. The first is by the fuel burn, which is 'totalized' by our instrumentation system, and the second is by a series of probes located in the aircraft's fuel tanks. During testing, we had determined that the probes were notoriously inaccurate and we had decided that the Totalizer readings were what we would rely on. So I had not been concerned with the discrepancy that I could see between fuel levels given by the Totalizer system and by the Probe system. Jon and Clint had been tracking the discrepancy since the beginning and had now concluded it was not inaccurate probes, but rather I had lost fuel. Jon said I had lost over 2000 lbs of fuel and it seemed to have occurred early in the flight. In addition, he was not sure if the leak had stopped completely or if it would resume in full force at some later time.

Jon did not have to tell me the implications of this calculation. I already knew. Even if the leak had stopped, this fuel deficiency was still a huge problem since the *GlobalFlyer* was designed to carry enough fuel to make it around the world with a minimal reserve of 1000 lbs. The odds had been reshuffled; they were no longer in my favor. I was no longer the house, but the player. Unlike the malfunctioning of a piece of equipment, such as the GPS, that could be fixed, the fuel loss meant exactly that—loss—something that could not be remedied. I was not going to be able to complete the First Solo Nonstop RTW. At first I was crushed with disappointment, but I am no stranger to failures. Of course, all of us have major disappointments in our lives, but I immediately thought of the one that was most similar to this one. It was in 1998 when my balloon went down in the thunderstorm into the Coral Sea. In that case, I felt I had lost my chance to win a place in aviation history by making the first Round the World balloon flight. But then, I was lucky to be alive and in fact was able to make a comeback four years later with the First Solo RTW Balloon Flight.

It was only minutes later that my thoughts moved away from my disappointment and on to solving the next problem, one that was going to be a big mess. I would have to land in some distant place, secure, repair and still fly the *GlobalFlyer* back to Salina that year so I could make another attempt the following year. Should I land immediately at Dubai, which was just ahead? Should I continue on to Hong Kong where my chase team could land and prepare everything for me? Or might I even be able to make it to Honolulu? I decided to keep going to see how the information concerning the fuel loss from Jon and Clint might change.

Back in Salina, the time of the late-night Press Briefing at Mission Control was coming up. This is when the press would convene in the Mission Control headquarters and receive an update from the personnel there on how my circumnavigation attempt was going. It was during such press conferences that visual images of me in-flight would be broadcast on a huge video monitor, while Mission Control personnel briefly interviewed me on a speakerphone for the audience to hear. The visual imagery was provided by NASA. A by-product of the experiment I was carrying for NASA was that there was a continuous video stream from the *GlobalFlyer* to satellite and back to Mission Control. The test package was called STARS and it was a new telemetry system, which NASA plans to use as a 'mission termination system'. Since space rocketry began in the United States, instructions to terminate or blow up an out-of-control rocket have been sent by radio signal from a ground station to the rocket. With STARS, the stream of telemetry will go from rocket to communications satellite to Johnson Space Center and instructions, like self-destruct, will come back to the rocket by the same path. Instead of telemetry, we substituted video, which was just fine with the NASA scientists. They didn't care whether data or video was being sent from *GlobalFlyer* through the STARS system, their objective was to work on the communication links and tune the quality of the transmission. *GlobalFlyer* was the perfect test bed because is provided about three continuous days of testing for NASA. For Mission Control, the STARS video link meant that a live interview of me could be done while in-flight in conjunction with using the satellite telephone.

Before the Press Briefing that night, Paul Moore, the press officer for Virgin Atlantic, called me on the satellite telephone. He had heard about the fuel problem but did not want to announce it until the morning Press Briefing. This would give him time to be sure of the problem and plan his media strategy for largest publicity impact.

'Paul, what am I supposed to say when, during the interview, they ask me how the flight is going?' I responded.

He suggested I just say that the flight is going fine.

'You mean I'm supposed to say that everything is hunky-dory when I just found out the whole flight is busted? I won't do it; you're on your own.' I did not participate in the Press Briefing that night.

Throughout the night at Mission Control, Jon and Clint ground through the data to get a more accurate assessment of the implications of the fuel loss. There was still hope. Actually, the fuel loss early in the flight was greater than previously calculated at 3100 lbs and probably was through the fuel vents as air expanded during the three hours of climb to the initial flight altitude of 39,000 ft. The exact reason why fuel was dumped out the fuel vents would not be known until post-flight analysis. The good news was that the tailwinds had been far better than required by the design of the aircraft. During preliminary design, I agreed with Scaled that the airplane should be capable of carrying enough fuel to make it Round the World with an average tailwind of 50 knots. We were doing better than that so far. Still, for a person like me who had built a career on making informed decisions based on well-researched facts and figures, it was unnerving that there were still many blanks to fill in. Since I was flying at a different weight level, we didn't know how accurate the performance calculations were. This was the airplane's 29th flight and the performance was still not known as well as we'd like. Up until this flight, I'd never really flown at these altitudes on a sustained basis.

Knowing that the forecast tailwind for the Pacific was going to be sensational, even then, as I was just entering China, I believed I had a good chance of getting back to Salina. I might make it! I called my friend Stan Nelson at the hospital to check in and see how he was doing and tell him the encouraging news on my fuel situation. Stan was excited to hear from me and to learn this bit of news before anyone else. I hope it cheered him up. That moment was priceless. Stan died shortly after my flight. That was the last time I spoke with him.

Taking a proactive stance in the situation, Clint calculated the most efficient speed to fly at each fuel weight, which would be as slow as possible to save fuel, but not so slow that the angle of attack of the airplane would create too much drag. My assignment was to fly the *GlobalFlyer* as precisely as I could at the speeds Clint assigned.

China distracted me enough to take my mind off the fuel problem. The Chinese air traffic controllers made me work. In every other country, we had successfully made the arrangement for Mission Control to give all position reports to air traffic control. China wouldn't hear of it. I would have to be on the radio constantly, making position reports. This was complicated by the fact I had only entered the essential waypoints in the Chelton before the flight. Now I had to scramble to re-enter every waypoint so I could estimate the time that I would cross. This was a good demonstration of why most jets require two pilots. It seems that it takes one of the pilots to talk to and meet all the requirements of the air traffic controllers. I was relieved when, five hours after entering Chinese airspace, I flew over Shanghai and left China.

As I crossed over Japan, I went through a brief review with my team to be sure we all agreed that I had enough fuel to make the next landmass, which was Hawaii. There was clearly enough fuel for that. We agreed there would be another review before I got beyond Hawaii to assure that I could make it to the California coast.

As I flew out into the Pacific, the word came through that I had exceeded the previous jet airplane distance record. This was held by a B-52 bomber flying from Okinawa to Madrid, Spain in 1962—a record that had stood for 43 years at 12,532.28 miles (20,168.78 km). It is interesting that the fastest, farthest, and highest jet airplane records date back to the 1960s and 1970s. The altitude record was set in 1977 in a MIG-25 Foxbat at 123,524 ft (37,650 m) and the speed record by the SR-71 Blackbird in 1976 at 2193.16 mph (3,529.22 km/h). It seems that most of the development of aircraft in recent decades had been directed at greater economic efficiency rather than improved performance.

The jetstreams over the Pacific lived up to the forecast. By the time I crossed north of Hawaii, I was convinced that I had enough fuel to complete the flight. After a brief review with my team to ensure we were on reasonable footing for me to complete the flight, I concluded, 'Let's go for it.' The nonstop circumnavigation record was firmly within my reach. The media team was enjoying the drama surrounding my fuel shortage and the worldwide attention it was attracting, so they didn't want to be so quick to pronounce that the fuel was now sufficient. Meanwhile, my attention shifted away from the fuel problem to taking care of the airplane and myself. Sleep is the biggest health problem confronting me on such a long solo flight. The public was surely curious how I would make a nonstop three-day flight. Even Charles Lindbergh, who prided himself on being able to stay awake for extended periods of time, started hallucinating and nodding off during his 33-hour first solo TransAtlantic flight. While the autopilot is key to being able to get any sleep, an extensive alarm system was required to wake me up. Alarms were set up for any divergence from normal engine parameters, departure from set altitude or course, loss of cabin pressurization, countdown timer, and change in airspeed. It was change in airspeed, which was the most sensitive and problematical. We felt we needed to control the *GlobalFlyer* airspeed within three percent, so the sensitivity of the airspeed alarm was three knots plus or minus from the speed when the alarm is turned on. It proved very difficult to stabilize the airspeed so closely. Before planning to sleep, I would try to set the throttle to a stable setting near my targeted airspeed, then turn on the airspeed alarm.

I was wearing race car earphones, which were left over from my days of competing in the 24 Hours of LeMans and the Daytona 24-Hour car races. These are custom-molded hearing aid style earphones which race car drivers wear inside of the helmet. Just the right thing—in addition to protecting against hearing damage due to the jet engine mounted just over my head, I was able to hear the alarms and radio communications perfectly. Realizing that my life depended on hearing the alarms, I would not take the earphones out even once during the flight. I would optimistically set the countdown timer to 20 minutes, since I would never want to sleep more than 20 minutes at one time. That was wishful thinking, because some alarm, usually the airspeed alarm, would sound within five minutes. I would reset the throttle and countdown timer and try for another nap. My naps ranged from one minute to five minutes. On the first and last night of the four-night flight, I deliberately did not sleep at all and the total amount of sleep for the other two nights was a little less than one hour. The naps were refreshing and effective in getting me through this endurance flight, but I knew that I would have to catch up on much of the lost sleep after landing.

Taking care of the airplane involved a lot of attention to shifting and balancing the fuel load. The Fuel Fraction of *GlobalFlyer* is 83%—a percentage that is unprecedented in aviation. This means that 83% of the takeoff weight is fuel—the other 17% is the airplane and me. Throughout the flight, I had to pay careful attention to the distribution of the fuel amongst the 13 fuel tanks to reduce stress on the airframe and assure proper trim for efficient flight. The largest tanks were the two huge booms, which were divided into fore and aft tanks. When out of balance due to automatic fuel transfer, Jon Karkow would contact me to transfer fuel selectively, using the fuel pumps. This was not an option with the outer wing tanks that just used gravity flow. The only control I had over the outer wing tanks was to open the valves. The fuel from the outer wing and wingtip tanks would be used last so that the airplane could benefit from the improved efficiency of added wing loading as long as possible. In the back of my mind was a potential problem: if the valves for these tanks did not open properly or the gravity flow did not work because the fuel had gelled due to cold soaking, I would not be able to use that fuel and once again there would be a shortfall in the fuel required to make it back to Salina. Just past Hawaii, I opened the valves and was enormously relieved when I could see from the probe gauges that the fuel was shifting. My last fuel concern had passed.

I crossed the US coastline near Los Angeles at around 7.30 am on Thursday morning, 3 March. As I entered the United States, the sun began to rise, and so did my energy level in response to making it to this milestone. Apparently, public interest in my record-breaking attempt also peaked. I was informed that the *GlobalFlyer* website (www.virginatlanticglobalflyer.com) had experienced such a huge increase in traffic since the launch of the mission that the site managers had to considerably upgrade its capacity to meet the unexpected demand. A week before the launch date, the site was getting about 250,000 hits a day which I thought was pretty good. Then in the first 24 hours since I lifted off, another 8 million hits were logged. The interest soared as the flight progressed, and by the end there would be an incredible 130 million hits over the three flight days. Astounded by these numbers, *GlobalFlyer* media manager Paul Moore commented that the Internet traffic levels may have set a new Guinness World Record and was 'an example of how this project has really captured people's imagination'.

Four hundred miles out over Alamosa, Colorado I pulled the power to idle for the glide to Salina. I was back to handling my own communications with Air Traffic Control, and numerous airline pilots were asking the controller for my position so they could point out this historic flight to their passengers. Bob Scherer, a friend of the project, launched his Beech Starship, a high-performance twin pusher aircraft, from Salina with Richard Branson on board. He wanted to be first to congratulate me. As I got closer, the celebrating in the air began. One after another in rapid succession, airline pilots were calling in, 'Congratulations, Steve, from America West 238', 'Congratulations from United 732' and so on from about 20 other airliners. Near the end one was 'Fossett, you're a stud'. Normally protective of essential communications on their frequencies, the air traffic controllers silently tolerated this outpouring of support. I couldn't answer because I needed to stay focused on my preparations for landing, but I was nonetheless moved. Here were the professionals of aviation, the airline pilots, showing their excitement for a major flying achievement and their respect for me as a fellow pilot.

But I wasn't on the ground yet and I knew there was another risk: 'Could I get the gear down?' This was the big question running through my mind. On test flights, the nose landing gear had been slow to extend when the oil in it had been cold and thick. At 10,000 ft in my descent, I held the switches down to lower the main landing gear. It was slow, but worked and two green lights indicated the main gear was locked down. Next, I released the nose gear—nothing happened. I flew away from Salina to give me time to solve this problem. What a shame it would be, to land without nose gear. I had visions of scraping to a stop on the runway with the bottom of the nose ground away. In anticipation of problems, Jon Karkow had flown up next to the *GlobalFlyer* to assure that the gear deployed properly before I came in for landing. Jon's recommendation was fly slow to get the nose gear door open. I slowed to just above stall speed, and I could hear the wind noise as the gear doors opened. Next Jon told me to fly fast so the nose gear would be pulled down by the wind flow. I sped up to maximum speed and after a minute the nose gear locked down with a clunk. I triumphantly announced '3 greens' and turned toward the Salina airfield.

On my final approach to landing, I crossed a waypoint one mile from the end of the runway, which we named 'Wildcat One', referring to the Wildcats of Kansas State University whose School of Aviation supported my flight and provided 11 students as team members. Wildcat One was the point I crossed at takeoff and now represented the official point of having successfully circumnavigated the globe. I deployed one drag chute to slow to touchdown speed. When this featherweight airplane touched the runway there was not a hint of a bounce. On Thursday, 3 March 2005, at 1.37 pm local time, the *Virgin Atlantic GlobalFlyer* returned to Salina Municipal Airport and I had just made the First Solo Nonstop Airplane Flight Round the World. My flight time for the 22,936-mile (36,912-km) journey was 67 hours 1 minute 10 seconds. Despite all the potential setbacks en route, I had made it back to Salina. The reality of my achievement didn't really sink in until I taxied the plane, turned it around and saw all the spectators that lined the runway who were there cheering me home. I was touched that so many people were interested in the project.

As I taxied the plane toward the hangar, Richard Branson and Jon Karkow motioned to me with two larger than life black-and-white checkered flags to the place where the *Virgin Atlantic GlobalFlyer* would come to a stop. Bringing the plane to a halt, I turned off the engine, opened the door and climbed out of the plane. My legs were a bit wobbly from not having stood on them for nearly three days and I was grateful that Crew Chief Philip Grassa steadied me as I climbed out onto a short ladder. After nearly three days in the sky, during which I survived only on 'power naps' and diet milkshakes, I was happy to put my feet on the ground again. As I stepped onto the tarmac, the first person to greet me was Peggy, followed by Richard who had brought with him a magnum of champagne. Immediately after I took a ceremonial sip from the bottle, Richard grabbed it away from me, gave it a quick shake, and mercilessly sprayed me with the champagne. After I had said a few words to the press, I was taken in a convertible along the flight line to receive the handshakes and applause of the crowd. As much as I needed to sleep, I knew it was going to be hard to actually get any. That night, there was a victory party planned, where Kansas Governor Kathleen Sebelius, my team and many supporters would turn out to toast the success of our mission. At 5 am the next morning, there would be interviews with the morning television shows followed by a press conference. Proper sleep would have to wait until the following night.

At the press conference the next day, I returned Richard's Breitling emergency locator watch.

'Why didn't you have more faith in me, Richard? I wasn't going to need a rescue,' I said jokingly as I handed it back to him. He subsequently auctioned the watch off on eBay for $20,000, which was contributed to Orbis, one of his favorite charities. In attendance was David Hawksett of Guinness World Records, who presented me with a certificate for my First Solo. Accepting the plaque, I said how this was the culmination of a five-year ambition and how delighted I was that it turned out on the first try, which was usually not the case with my adventures. Circumnavigating the globe in the *Virgin Atlantic GlobalFlyer* was one of my proudest achievements. In the days and weeks that followed, I received many warm and wonderful letters and e-mails of congratulations from people all over the world. One that is particularly special to me is from Dick Rutan. His letter symbolizes a circle of completion of the circumnavigation aviation dream that was first initiated by Wiley Post, was refined by Dick Rutan and Jeana Yeager in the *Voyager* 1986 nonstop crewed circumnavigation flight, and was perfected by the record-breaking *Virgin Atlantic GlobalFlyer* solo nonstop circumnavigation flight of 2005.

LETTER FROM DICK RUTAN

My hat's off to Steve Fossett for a picture-perfect landing in Kansas after his grueling and record setting nonstop world flight.

I've said many times that I hoped *Voyager*'s records would be broken in my lifetime, and I congratulate Steve for shattering the world record in nonstop time around the world by more than half.

The risks, the concerns about sweating fuel, the challenges and the sleeplessness certainly brought back some memories of my 1986 nonstop world flight in the *Voyager*. But I believed then, as I do now, that without risk, there is no progress, and without progress, there is no America.

I also need to congratulate my brother, Burt Rutan, for yet another incredible, beautiful, and uniquely successful design.

The team behind Fossett's grand adventure—Jon Karkow, who oversaw construction and flight test, Mission Control, and the Weather team must be commended as well. These journeys cannot be successful without the talent behind the scenes; truly the wind beneath the wings of projects and successes such as *GlobalFlyer*.

Like Lindbergh in 1927, who opened a new era in commercial air travel, Fossett's 2005 flight will open a new era in transglobal air racing. Perhaps racing planes similar to the *Virgin Atlantic GlobalFlyer* could become as common as NASCAR ground vehicles.

But back to today, for a man who flew over sparse bodies of ocean fearing he didn't have the fuel to complete the flight, and certainly knew he 'wasn't in Kansas anymore,' Steve has got to be thrilled to be back. I'm sure he's exhausted, and plans a nice, restful nap. Sweet dreams of your sweet success, Steve!

Dick Rutan
Voyager Commander
1st Nonstop and Un-refueled World Flight, 1986

EPILOGUE

F lying the *GlobalFlyer* to the Smithsonian was a special moment for
me. For this final flight I flew from our base in Salina, Kansas to
Washington, DC. I made a low pass over the main runway at Dulles
International Airport, circled to land, then taxied up to the door of
Udvar-Hazy Center of the Smithsonian's National Air & Space
Museum. There I turned the *GlobalFlyer* over to the Director, General
Jack Dailey. The project was complete. The success was greater than
we imagined when we started. The original goal was to fly the First
Solo Nonstop Round the World. Once that was completed in March
2005, I made two other flights in February and March 2006, which
broke the Absolute Distance Record and the Absolute Closed Circuit
Distance Record. The remarkable achievement of the *GlobalFlyer*
program was 3 of the 7 Absolute World Records of Airplanes. Three
of the other 4 are held by the SR-71 'Blackbird' and the fourth was
altitude record by the MIG-25 'Foxbat'.

I continue to reflect on what I have done and how it fits into my
life and what I represent. Before the records projects, I sought to be
a 'participant' in the goals and events which are part of the tapestry
of our culture, like swimming the English Channel, running the
Boston Marathon, climbing the Matterhorn, and completing the

Iditarod. These are projects that I imagined many people would like to do, but haven't. I relished doing them, even if the only recognition would be having a good story to tell friends at a cocktail party. The theme changed when I set my first official world record in 1993, which was the sailing speed record Round Ireland. This was a revelation to me: that with the best equipment and a superior team, I could do something faster than anyone has ever done. As the successes continued, I expanded my horizons into more fields where I found that, with the effort, organization and support team, I could attack the most important records. As I write this, I count 115 official world records set in five different fields: balloons, airplanes, sailboats, gliders, and airships. I do not know if anyone has set more total records but surely no one has set the outright, open or absolute records in 5 sports. In the case of sailing, my total of 31 world and race records, including the most important, has never been done in the sport's history.

People often express surprise that I seem to be just a regular guy. They're right, mostly. My appearance is strictly average, my athletic ability is mediocre, and there is nothing dramatic about my speech or demeanor. I will admit to one strength: the ambition to succeed. I am bemused when people are surprised that I am such a low-key person because it adds to their curiosity: 'How could Steve do that?', I understand part of the answer: I think about what is the most interesting thing I could do, then investigate, then plan and organize a good team. Then I methodically pursue the goal. I have a lot of self- confidence, and while I believed that I could do many things, I also have been surprised that I could take on some of the grandest records and succeed. Sometimes I cannot recognize the possibilities until I get involved in the sport, then it seems that the opportunities pop out of the woodwork.

'Aren't these projects risky?', I'm often asked. They sure are! People often presume that I'm a thrill-seeker, but I am not. I do not enjoy roller coasters and you won't find me bungie-jumping–an activity whose appeal seems to be based on experiencing the fear and thrill of falling without control. It is a disadvantage that my pursuits are inherently dangerous. A large part of my effort is to reduce the risk.

'Is it worth the risk?' For all the preparation and attention to good procedures, I have been confronted with dangerous situations surprisingly often. The worst was my fall from 29,000 feet in a ruptured balloon, but I've had life-threatening situations in gliders and sailboats. After that fall in the balloon, I had to do some serious self-examination. With the broad public following my balloon RTW attempts, it was becoming increasingly apparent that I was conveying a message. For many it was the romance of round the world flight in a graceful balloon. Others I have met or receive letters from were inspired that I would take on such difficult projects and they decided they would now go out and pursue some adventure of their own. These were the most complimentary congratulatory letters I have received because the writers had been motivated to some sort of action as a result of what I had done. They got the message. It is not important to pursue the same sports or endeavors that I have because those were chosen by me to fit what interested me most and, besides, my pursuits have generally been very expensive, which suited me after a successful business career. Everyone should consider what interests them most, set a goal, then pursue it. I was also fully aware there would be another message if and when I succeeded in the First Solo RTW: With persistence, remarkable goals can be achieved. The realization that I would earn a place in aviation history and that I would motivate other people is part of the reason I took the necessary risks.

If I got to lead my life over again, would I do it differently? Actually, I'm very pleased with my life so far, but I could do much better. In high school, I joined the cross-country running team. But there was no future in distance running for me because I am the wrong physical build with short legs and a heavy frame. I should have pursued football. Since I was attracted to the individual events in track, I should have taken up hammer throw, even though it would have required special arrangements since it wasn't offered in high school. There are so many sports to choose from and I should have made a thoughtful analysis and choice so I would have a chance to experience success. It is important to have a successful career, but I wasted so many years. Coming out of university, I knew I wanted to be in financial trading but then lost five years because I chose computer systems. I should have sought from the beginning a job with direct exposure to the financial trading business, like a clerk on the exchange floor, even if the starting pay was poor. Once in trading, I lost years in the roller coaster of making and losing money. With what I now know about risk management, I could have been more successful in business, and earlier.

I have few regrets about what I have done. I only regret what I have not done. In my early 30s and involved in driving race cars, I had the ambition of driving in the Indianapolis 500, but never got my program together. At age 51, I had a plan to break a pure athletic record: the 24-Hour Road Cycling Record. I would have started high on Fremont Pass in the Colorado Rockies to get the advantage of riding downhill, then ridden out into the plains past Dodge City, Kansas for a one-day distance of around 540 miles. The best day for tailwinds would be chosen by my meteorologist, and a support team would assure that I lost no time en route. I didn't make the attempt and now, aged 62, an extreme endurance record would probably not work.

One of the greatest satisfactions in life is being who you want to be. When asked who is my hero or my mentor, I'm stumped. I have read much history of exploration and adventure and am especially fascinated with the expeditions to reach the North and South Poles. Perhaps the most admirable of all explorers was Fridtjof Nansen, the Norwegian who got nearest the North Pole in 1895 in the remarkable expedition of the Fram. Throughout the danger and hardship of all of his expeditions, he never lost a man, which demonstrated superior organization skills. After his explorations he led the League of Nations' refugee resettlement efforts during the Russian Revolution, for which he was awarded the Nobel Peace Prize in 1922. But I have never sought to be like someone else, and I do not advocate that anyone try to do the same things that I do. My life has become a collage of what I perceive to be the most exciting, meaningful, or interesting adventures. There is pattern: each endeavor has been the pursuit of a personal achievement, which reaches back to my youth working my way up the ranks to Eagle Scout and, later, climbing mountains. Over time I have constructed an identity that is uniquely me.

I am often asked if I'm about done with adventure projects. Somehow people think I'll go on the lecture circuit and relate all my past achievements. In fact, I do enjoy telling about my past projects. Yes, my grand round the world projects in balloons, sailboats and airplanes are complete. My solo balloon capsule and the solo airplane are in the Smithsonian, and my sailboat is retired from speed sailing. But my attention is focused on the future because I love the adventure and the sense of achievement if I succeed. Great ideas abound. There are places yet to be explored and important records to be broken. These may be in completely different fields than my past records, but I have the self- confidence to know that I can prepare for and organize these new endeavors. Once again, I hope in the future to have a new story to tell of an achievement which was thought to be too difficult, or doable only by a professional in the field.

STEVE FOSSETT RECORDS

AIRPLANE

First Solo Non-Stop Airplane Flight RTW, Absolute Non-Stop RTW Speed Record, 67 hrs 1 min 10 secs, 342.2 mph (550.7 kph), 22,936 miles (36,912.68 km), Feb 28–Mar 3, 2005

Longest Distance Aircraft Flight, Absolute Non-Stop Distance Record, 76 hrs 42 mins 55 secs, 25,766 miles (41,467 km), Feb 8–11, 2006

Closed Circuit Distance, Absolute Closed Circuit Distance Record, 25,294 miles (40,707 km), Mar 14–17, 2006

U.S. Transcontinental Records: West to East (non-supersonic), 2 hrs 56 mins 20 secs, 726.83 mph (1169.73 km/h) Feb 5, 2003

East to West (non-supersonic), 3 hrs 29 mins 35 secs, 591.96 mph (952.67 km/h) Sept 17, 2000

Turboprop (Unlimited), with Joe Ritchie, 3 hrs 51 mins 52 secs, 549.18 mph (880.01 km/h) Feb 5, 2003

Perth–Hobart, Australia (Unlimited), Fastest world record by non-supersonic airplane, 742.02 mph (1194.17km/h), July 30, 2001

Perth–Brisbane, Australia (Unlimited), Australia Transcontinental Record, 705.06 mph (1134.69 km/h), July 28, 2001

Goose Bay–Berlin (Unlimited), TransAtlantic Record/non-supersonic airplanes, 649.93 mph (1,045.97 km/h), October 8, 2000

5000 km Speed Record (H-Class), 572.29 mph (921.02 km/h), July 14, 2000

2000 km Speed Record (H-Class), 598.26 mph (962.81 km/h), Nov 26, 1999

Los Angeles–Honolulu (Unlimited), 4 hrs, 11 mins, 5 secs, 609.84 mph (981.44 km/h), Mar 23, 2000

Round The World Records (medium airplanes – H-Class), Eastbound, 559.89 mph (901.07 km/h), Feb 16, 2000; Westbound, 500.56 mph (805.59 km/h), Nov 24, 2000

BALLOONING
First Solo Balloon Flight RTW, Absolute RTW Speed Record, 13 days 8 hrs 33 mins (14 days
    19 hrs 50 mins to landing), 20,626.48 miles (33,195.10 km), June 19–July 4, 2002
24 Hour Record, 3,186.80 miles (5,128.65 km), June 30–July 1, 2002
Second Solo RTW attempt, Absolute World Distance Record,* 10,360.61 miles; Absolute
    World Duration Record,* 6 days 2 hrs 44 mins Jan 13–20, 1997
First Solo Flight Across Pacific, Absolute World Distance Record,* 5,435.82 miles, Feb 17–21,
    1995

GLIDERS (with Terry Delore)
Distance (Free) World Record, 2192.9 km, Dec 4, 2004
Triangle Distance (Free) World Record, 1508.42 km, Dec 13, 2003
Out-and-Return Distance (Free) World Record,* 2002.44 km, Nov 14, 2003
1500 Kilometer Triangle World Record, 119.11 km/h (74.02 mph), July 30, 2003
750 Kilometer Triangle World Record, 171.29 km/h (106.44 mph), July 29, 2003
500 Kilometer Triangle* World Record, 187.13 km/h (116.27 mph), Nov 15, 2002
1000 km Out-and-Return World Record,* 166.46 km/h (103.44 mph), Dec 12, 2002
1500 km Out-and-Return World Record,* 156.61 km/h (97.30 mph), Nov 14, 2003
Triangle Distance (Declared) World Record, 1502.55 km, Dec 13, 2003
Out-and-Return Distance (Declared) World Record,* 1804.7 km, Nov 14, 2003

AIRSHIPS
Absolute World Speed Record, 71.5 mph (115.0 km/h), Oct 27, 2004

SAILING
Round the World,* 58 days 9 hrs 32 mins 45 secs, Feb 7–April 5, 2004
TransAtlantic,* 25.78 knots (47.75 km/h), 4 days 17 hrs 28 mins 6 secs, Oct 5–10, 2001
Indian Ocean,* 9 days 20 hrs 29 mins 45 secs, Feb 25–March 6, 2004
TransAtlantic East–West, 9 days 13 hrs 30 mins, 16.92 knots, Feb 15–24, 2003
Round Britain & Ireland, 4 days 16 hrs 9 mins, 15.93 knots, Oct 20–25, 2002
Trans Mediterranean,* 18 hrs 46 min, 24.38 knots, May 23–24, 2002
Plymouth–LaRochelle, 16 hrs 41 mins, 21.28 knots, April 9, 2002
Round Isle of Wight, 2 hrs 33 mins 55 secs, 19.53 knots, Nov 9, 2001
Miami to New York, 53 hrs 54 mins, 17.57 knots May 20–22, 2001
Fastnet Course, 35 hrs 17 mins, 17.14 knots, March 15–17, 2002
Newport to Bermuda, 38 hrs 35 mins, 16.45 knots Jan 12–14, 2000
Round Ireland, 44 hrs 42 mins, 15.84 knots, Sep 8–9, 1993
Hawaii–Japan, 13 days 20 hrs 9 mins, July 22–Aug 4, 1995
Pacific Ocean East–West,* 19 days 15 hrs 18 mins 9 secs, 9.51 knots, May 3–23, 1996

SINGLE-HANDED RECORDS
Pacific Ocean World Record, 20 days 9 hrs 52 mins, Aug 5–24, 1996
Newport–Bermuda World Record, 40 hrs 51 mins 54 secs, June 1999
Transpac, 7 days 22 hrs 38 mins, June 27–July 5, 1999

RACE RECORDS
Newport–Ensenada, 6 hrs 46 mins 40 secs, 18.45 knots (34.17 km/h), April 24, 1998
Chicago–Mackinac, 18 hrs 50 mins 32 secs, 15.55 knots, July 18–19, 1998
Transpac,* 6 days 16 hrs 7 mins, July 4–11, 1995
Singlehanded Transpac, 7 days 22 hrs 38 mins, June 27–July 5, 1998
Miami–Montego Bay,* 2 days 20 hrs 38 mins, Feb 4–7, 1999
Swiftsure, 14 hrs 35 mins 29 secs, May 24–25, 1997
San Diego–Puerto Vallarta, 62 hrs 20 mins, 15.9 knots, Feb 8–10, 1998
Long Beach–Cabo San Lucas, 3 days 2 hrs 59 mins, Nov 4–7, 1995
Windjammers, 4 hrs 41 mins 2 secs, Aug 29, 1997
*record superceded

INDEX

Abruzzo, Richard 102, 106, 118, 164
Adkins, Darrin 155, 158
aircraft:
    Absolute Nonstop Distance Record for
      xviii–xix, 229–53
    Australian Transcontinental Record 81,
      167
    Citation X xvi, 81–2, 154–6, 156, 158, 160,
      165, 167, 168, 242
    Collier Trophy 154, 229
    East to West US Transcontinental
      Record 81, 160
    Falcon 10 121, 154
    5000-km (3107-mile) Closed Circuit
      Out and Return record 154, 158
    Los Angeles to Honolulu record 156
    Perth to Hobart, Tasmania record 168
    Round the World record xiv, 81, 154–6
    Round the World westbound record
      160–1
    Round Trip Transcontinental Record
      160

    2000-km (1242-mile) Out and Return
      record 154
    Virgin Atlantic GlobalFlyer ix–xix,
      229–53
Alcatraz 15, 19–20
Alcock, John 91, 164
Allen, Paul 228–9
Altadill, Guillermo 198, 208
America 92–3
America's Cup 92–3, 129, 199
Anderson, Maxie 106, 164
Anheuser-Busch 122, 179
Antarctica 50–3
Arbor, Pat 41, 56–7
Argentina 225–7
Arthur Anderson 37
Arvidson, Professor Ray 123
Atlantic 152
Australia 165–8, 180–1, 195

Baek, Jeun Heum 99
ballooning 78–9

Absolute Distance Without Landing Record xv, xvii–xviii, 98, 102, 104, 120
Absolute Duration World Record 118, 120
Round the World Flight 140–8, 162–4
Round the World Solo Flights
  1st xiv, 84–5, 102–3, 104–8
  2nd 114–20
  3rd 121–8
  4th 131–9
  5th 164–71, 178
  6th 178–96
TransAtlantic flights 83–91, 92, 98, 118, 178, 191
TransPacific solo flight xiv, xvii, xviii, 92, 98–102, 103, 104, 105, 115
Banner, Kitty 48
Barr, Charlie 152
Barron Hilton Cup 222–3
Bass, Dick 50, 53
Beale Air Force Base, California 187
Beasley, Mike 198, 215
Beaver Creek, Colorado 56, 59, 69, 74, 78, 81, 99, 100, 108, 156, 158, 167, 174, 175, 179, 186–7
Bedford, Chris 130, 154–5
Beech Starship 250
Belarus 114–15
Billones, Lou 101, 116, 124–5
Birch, Mike 75
Black-Scholes Model 38
Blair, Tony 145
Boccon-Gibod, Thierry 242
Bourgnon, Laurent 150
Boy Scouts 8–14, 26
Bradley, Troy 118
Branson, Richard xiii, xiv, xvi, 123–4, 139, 140–1, 142, 143, 145, 146, 147, 155, 157, 188, 230, 231, 232, 236, 237, 238, 241, 250, 251
Breitling Orbiter 3 162–3, 164
Brown, Arthur Whitten 91, 164
Brown, Dennis 80, 85, 123, 165, 180
Brown, Fraser 198
Bud Light Spirit of Freedom 179, 182, 190, 191, 195
Budweiser Cup 122, 140, 162, 163
Busch III, August 121–2, 178–9
Busch Stadium 115, 122

Byron, Lord 20, 21

Cahalan, Adrienne 198, 200, 204, 206
Cameron Balloons 79, 84, 87, 88, 92, 99, 104, 120, 141, 164, 166
Cameron, Donald 79, 88–9, 92, 105, 125
Campbell, Ken 173, 199, 205–6, 209, 216, 217
Capricorn 230
Carlin, Dr Dan 208
cars, racing 34–5
Carstensz, Jan 53
Cessna 27, 158
Chelton Flight Management System xi, xii, 240, 243, 247
Cheyenne 197, 199, 203, 208, 210, 213, 215, 216, 218, 232 see also PlayStation
Chicago Board of Trade 37, 38, 40
Chicago Board Options Exchange (CBOE) 38, 39, 40, 41, 42, 48, 175
Chicago Research and Trading 38
China xiv, 118, 126, 144–5, 146
Chrysler Race 84
Citation X xvi, 81–2, 154–6, 156, 158, 160, 165, 167, 168, 242 see also aircraft
Clement, Jean-Marie 226
climbing:
  Carstensz Pyramid 53–5
  Eiger 22–3
  Kilimanjaro 56–7
  Matterhorn 21, 23–4
  McKinley 47–50, 55
  Mont Blanc 23, 47
  Mt Elbrus 55–6
  Mt Everest 53, 57–9, 73–4, 144
  Mt Lassen 13–14
  Mt Olympus 22
  Seven Summits 47–59
  Vinson Massif 50–3
Clinton, Bill 69–70, 145
Clinton, Hillary 69
Club Med 176, 199, 207, 214
Cohen, Chris 44
Cole, Tim 80, 83–5, 86, 87, 88, 89, 122–3, 124, 125, 126, 164, 165, 166, 167, 170, 178, 180, 181, 189, 191, 194, 237
Commanders Weather 173, 199, 216
Comstock Autopilot 84, 85, 92, 99, 100, 115, 124

Comstock, Bruce 80, 84, 85, 92, 99, 100, 104, 115, 124
Conner, Dennis 77, 129
Cookson Boats 150
Cork Dry Gin Trophy 78
Coville, Thomas 200
Cruikshank, Bob 174–5
cycling 43

D'Avenas, Pierre 160
Dailey, General Jack 195
Dalton, Grant 176
Deering, Chris 150
Dehenauw, David x–xi, 179, 183, 189, 235, 236
Delore, Terry 224–5, 226, 227, 228
Dickinson, Leo 144
Dirks, William 158
Discovery Channel 242
Drexel Burnham 36–7, 40
Drogin, Steve 50

Earhart, Amelia 228
Eckert, Pierre 163
Edwards Air Force Base (AFB) 234
Elson, Andy 104, 105, 144, 164, 166
Enevoldson, Einar 223, 225
EPIRB (Emergency Position Indicating Radio Beacon) 107, 136, 137
Experimental Aircraft Association 'Air Venture' 228
Explorer 172

FAA (Federal Aviation Administration) 233
Falcon 10 121, 154
Fastnet Race 77
Featherstone, Mark 198, 203
Finite Element Analysis (FEA) 150
Flying M Ranch 221–3, 228
Foale, Mike ix
Ford, Betty 69
Ford, Gerald 3, 69
Formula Atlantic 35
Formula B 35
Formula Ford 35
Fossett III, Richard (brother) 4–5, 6, 7, 8, 10
Fossett Jr, Richard L. (father) 3–11, 13, 81–2, 105, 108–9

Fossett, Charalee (mother) 3–5, 9, 81, 82, 108, 109
Fossett, Linda (sister) 6, 7, 9, 10, 81, 82, 109
Fossett, Peggy (wife) 26–34, 39, 40, 44, 56, 59, 69, 74, 78, 90, 95, 141, 237, 238, 240, 251
Foxall, Damian 198, 210
Fraenckel, Alan 114
Fram 13
Francis I. DuPont 31
Fujicolor 75

Gamov, Professor Igor 187
Geronimo 199, 200, 201, 204, 206, 209, 211, 213–14
Gide, André 114
Gillan, Sean 172
Glacier National Park 10
gliding 221–8
    Free Distance Record 228
    1000-km (621-mile) Out and Return Record 225
    1250-km (7760-mile) US National Record 226
    Perlan Project 224–5
    750-km (466-mile) Triangle world record 226
    2000-km (1242-mile) Out and Return Record 226
Gordon Bennett International Balloon Race 114
GPS (Global Positioning System) 89, 101, 240–1, 244
Grand Canyon 10
Grassa, Philip x, 235, 251
Grosse, Hans Werner 225
Groupe Pierre Premiere 75
Guinness Book of Records, The 207

Habeler, Peter 50
Halliburton, Richard 20, 21
Harrer, Heinrich 23
Harris, Bob 223
Harrison, Tim 226
Hawksett, David 251
Head, Ray 195
Hempleman-Adams, David 179
Henriot, Jim 47
Hernreich, Bob 69

Hero 20–1
Hilton Earthwinds 78, 85, 102–3
Hilton, Barron 102, 103, 148, 179, 221, 222,
    228, 237
Hogg, Peter 111
Holland, Buddy 154
Homasuik, Mikhail 127
Honey, Stan 159, 174, 177, 200
Hoover, Bob 237
Hornbein, Dr Tom 186
Hudson, Cliff 48
Hunt, Bunker 36
Hunt, Herbert 36

IBM 28, 30–1
Iditarod Trail Sled Dog Race, The 60–70,
    74
Immarsat C 87, 95
India xiii–xiv
Ionata, Dick 237
Ireland xv–xvi
Irens, Nigel 150
Isle of Wight 92

Japan xiv, 146
Jet Services V 152, 176, 177
John Muir Trail 13
Johnson, Bruce 60–1, 62, 63
Jones, Brian xvii, 162–3, 164, 179
Jules Verne Trophy 198, 219

Karkow, Jon xii, xvi, 232, 234, 237, 243,
    244, 246, 249, 250, 251, 252
Kemper, Bo 45–6, 104
Kersauson, Olivier de 199, 201, 211, 219
Kevlar 141, 203
Kirkland, Bob 59
Kittinger, Joe 164
Klikunas, Len 17
Knox-Johnson, Robin 177
Krieling, Randall 36–7
Kugler, John 79–80, 83, 123, 165, 181, 237
Kurtis, Bill 108

Lakota 75–6, 77, 92, 94, 97, 111, 112, 113, 130,
    159
Leadville 100 59
Leander 20–1, 22
Leggatt, Nick 198, 204, 208, 215
Letts, Adam 242

Lewis, Cam 172, 173
Libya xii, 117, 125, 143, 243–4
Lindbergh, Charles 78, 91, 122, 164, 195–6,
    228, 248, 252
Lindstrand, Per xiv, 139, 140, 141, 142, 143,
    147, 157
Loyola University 104, 115
Lucic, Albert 11

MacAleavy, Cathy 78
MacMillan, Harold 129
Madden, Mike 62
Madec, Serge 152, 177
Marshall Field's 32–4, 37
Marshall, Mark 242
Mattus, Tom 173
Melvill, Mike 233
Melvin, Pete 149, 150
Merrill Lynch 35–6
Methodist Youth Fellowship (MYF) 11
Meyer, Russ 81
Milk, Andy 166
Milleret, Nancy xv
Mizell, Archie (uncle) 5
Moore, Bill 17–18
Moore, Paul 221, 245–6, 249
Morrelli, Gino 150, 153
Morrow, Baiba 53, 54–5
Morrow, Pat 50, 51, 53, 54–5, 56
mountaineering *see* climbing
Mountain Man Triathlon 56
Muir, John 9, 13, 92
Murphy, Con 78
Mylar 105, 106, 119–20, 141

Nansen, Fridtjof 13
NASA:
    Dryden Center 223–4
    Jet Propulsion Laboratory (JPL) 123
    Kennedy Space Center ix–x
National Air & Space Museum,
    Smithsonian xiv, xviii, 120, 195–6
National Association for the Protection
    of Man Apes (NAPMA) 17
National Geographic 106, 120
National Oceanic and Atmosphere
    Administration (NOAA) 85, 87, 89,
    183
National Science Foundation (NSF) 50
Necker Island 230

Nelson, Stan 237, 238, 246
Newman, Larry 102, 103, 107, 164
Nichols, Clint xv, xvi, 239–40, 243, 244,
    245, 246–7
9/11 174–5
Noble, Alan 92

Oeleric, Kate 108
Ohlmann, Klaus 225–6
Orange 198, 201, 202, 203, 204, 206, 208,
    209, 210, 212, 213, 214, 216, 232
Orange II 199, 200, 206, 219
Orbis 251
Orteig Prize 122

Pablo, Mike 155, 156
Padelt, Bert 123, 165, 178, 180, 237
Peyron, Bruno 172, 173, 198, 199, 201, 216,
    219
Philmont Scout Ranch 11–13
Piccard, Bertrand xvii, 162–3, 164, 179
Piper, Laurie 138
PlayStation 149, 150–4, 156–8, 159–60, 172,
    173, 174, 176–7, 178, 197, 200, 230
    see also Cheyenne
Post, Wiley 228, 252
Pyewacket 200

Qaddafi, Colonel 117, 143

Reed, Jim x, xi
Regan, Shaun 167
Reichmann, Helmut 222
Rice, Bob 85–6, 87, 89, 111, 132, 133, 143,
    144, 146, 159, 160, 164–5, 166, 167,
    169–70, 179
Rinearson, Pat xv
Ritchie, Joe 37–8, 73, 108, 120, 127, 162, 170,
    179, 181–2, 186, 189
Ritchie, Molly 120
Robertson, Cliff 195
Robson, Paul 165, 180, 195
Rosenlaui Mountain Climbing School 22
Royal Road to Romance (Halliburton) 21
Rozière balloon 79, 84, 87, 106
Russia 126–8
Rutan, Burt 228, 229, 232, 234, 237, 238,
    252
Rutan, Dick xvii, ix, 78, 228, 252–3
Ryan, Shorty 165, 194

sailing 74–8, 110–11
    America's Cup 92–3
    Chicago-Mackinac 129
    East to West TransPacific record 111
    Fastnet Course World Record 200
    Indian Ocean Record 214
    Miami-New York World Sailing Speed
        Record 172–3
    Newport-Bermuda Outright (crewed)
        record 130, 155
    Newport-Ensenada 129
    Pacific Ocean Singlehanded World
        Record 112, 207
    Round Britain & Ireland 93
    Round the World Record 149, 150, 152,
        155, 197–220
    Route Du Rhum 93–7, 98, 149
    San-Diego-Puerto Vallarta 129
    Singlehanded Transpac 129–30
    Singlehanded Trans-Pac Race 113
    TransAtlantic Record 149, 152–3, 156–8,
        172, 173–4, 175–7, 207
    24-Hour Record 149, 150–1, 175–6
    Two Handed Round Britain & Ireland
        76, 77
    West to East Pacific Ocean Record
        111–12
    World Sailing Speed Record Council
        (WSSRC) 198, 201, 217, 219
Sagon, Ed 78
San Francisco Chronicle 16, 17, 19
Sartore, Joel 106
Saum, Nick 80, 99, 100, 104
Scaled Composites 229, 230–1, 232, 233,
    237, 239
Scherer, Robert xi, 249–50
Schiff Scout Reservation 12
Schoen, Dr Brownie 186
Scully, Dave 75, 76, 158, 175, 176, 198, 204,
    208, 210
Sebago 200
Sebelius, Kathleen 251
Sequoia National Park 9
Shackleton, Ernest 13
Shane, Doug 230
Sheese, Red 166
Sierra Club 9
skiing 42–3, 156
Slattery, Justin 198, 210
Smith, Dick 165

Snowbird Everest Expedition 58
Sony 150, 178
SpaceShip One 229, 233
Stanford 15–19, 21, 24–5, 26
Stars & Stripes 129, 130
STARS 240–1, 245
Stass, Kevin xiv, xv, 233–4
Stockment, Dick 45–6, 48, 49, 56
Stokes, Paul 85
Stratobowl, The 105
Stuart-Jervis, John 114
Sturtzenberger, Jack 23–4
swimming:
    Alcatraz 15, 19–20
    Bosporus 22
    Channel 43–7
    Golden Gate Bridge 18–20
    Hellespont 20–2

Tai, Alex 155, 160, 166, 167, 242, 243
TEMA automatic shutoff fitting 132–3
Thompson, Brian 77–8, 111, 130, 158, 198, 211
Touche-Ross 31, 32
Tru Trak Flight Systems, Inc 230
Trullemans, Luc 163, 179, 180, 181, 182, 183, 184, 188, 189, 190, 192, 235

Uhlmann, Fred 36
University of California, Berkeley 15–16, 19

Van Audernaerde Endurance Trophy 47
Van Dyke, Paul 198
Victor Awards 103
Vincent, Jacques 198, 217
Virgin 141, 142, 242
Virgin Atlantic Airlines 155, 230–1, 236–7, 245–6
Virgin Atlantic GlobalFlyer ix–xix, 229–53
Voyager xvii, 228, 252

Ward, Milton 54
Washington University, St Louis 26, 30, 115, 121, 122, 179, 185
Webb, Matthew 44
Webster, William 121
Week on the Concord and Merrimack Rivers, A 110
Wells, Frank 50
Whitehorn, Will 230, 242
'Wildcat One' 250
Williams International 229, 239
Williams, Dr Sam 229
World Loppet League 42–3
Wright Brothers 78
Wright, Ben 150–1, 158, 174

X-Prize 228–9

Yeager, Jeana xvii, 78, 228, 252
Yellowstone National Park 10
Yost, Ed 186